Brother Swaggart, Here Is My Question About The Holy Spirit

Brother Swaggart, Here Is My Question About The Holy Spirit

By Jimmy Swaggart

Jimmy Swaggart Ministries
P.O. Box 262550 • Baton Rouge, Louisiana 70826-2550
Website: www.jsm.org • Email: info@jsm.org
(225) 768-7000

ISBN 978-1-934655-68-9
09-114 • COPYRIGHT © 2011 World Evangelism Press®
11 12 13 14 15 16 17 18 19 20 21 22 23 / CW / 13 12 11 10 9 8 7 6 5 4 3 2 1
All rights reserved. Printed and bound in U.S.A.

TABLE OF CONTENTS

INTRODUCTION

We believe there is one God but manifested in three Persons, *"God the Father, God the Son, and God the Holy Spirit."* Concerning this, D.R. McConnell says that *"the Father's exclusive role is as the 'Source' of Creation (Gen. 1:1; Neh. 9:5-6; Ps. 90:2; Isa. 44:24; Jer. 32:17); the Son's exclusive role is as the 'Agent' of Creation (Jn. 1:3; Col. 1:16; Heb. 1:2); and the role of the Holy Spirit is that of 'Executor' (Gen. 1:2; Job 26:13; 33:4; Ps. 104:30; Isa. 40:12)."*[1]

McConnell went on to say, *"the creation is 'from' the Father, 'through' the Son, and 'by' the Holy Spirit."*

Every work carried out on this Earth by the Godhead, with the exception of the First Advent of Christ, has been done through the Person, Agency, Work, and Office of the Holy Spirit. Even with Christ, the Holy Spirit was involved in every capacity of His Life and Ministry.

The Cross of Christ opened up legally the Means by which the Holy Spirit works to a grand degree, of which we will study more later. We now are privileged to live under the New Covenant, once again, all made possible by the Cross, which gives the Holy Spirit great latitude to work within our hearts and lives, at least if the Cross of Christ is the sole Object of our Faith. Unfortunately, most of the modern church little understands the Means and the Way the Holy Spirit works, which means that such lack of knowledge hinders what He can do. Hopefully, we can provide some truths in this Volume that will help us to understand the Holy Spirit a little better, which can make all the difference in the world in our life and living.

AN ILLUSTRATION

The other day I was reading a statement made by a particular preacher who is Pentecostal, but from the things he said, I feel he little understands the work of the Holy Spirit beyond speaking in Tongues, etc. While speaking with other Tongues is of immense significance, which we will as well address in this

Volume, still, that is only a small part of the Work of the Holy Spirit within our lives. To be sure, the Work of the Holy Spirit is not merely a side issue or something that is optional. The Holy Spirit seeks to be involved, and is supposed to be involved, in every facet of our life and living, irrespective as to what it might be, and I speak of that which is Righteous.

Some time back, I was reading part of a book written by a Pentecostal educator, and he made the statement that modern man is facing things which are not addressed in the Bible. His contention was, and I suppose still is, that modern man needs both humanistic psychology and the Bible in order to live a wholesome, productive life. If the statement weren't so patently ridiculous, it would be close to blasphemy. The very idea that the Holy Spirit, Who is God, and Who is the Author of the Word of God, doesn't understand modern man, portrays a tremendous ignorance as to Who the Holy Spirit is, and what He can do. Peter said, and I quote from THE EXPOSITOR'S STUDY BIBLE:

> "Simon Peter, a servant and an Apostle of Jesus Christ *(the position of 'servant' is placed first; if one cannot be a true servant for the Lord, then one cannot be an Apostle; the Lord guides the Church by the Office of the Apostle through the particular Message given to the individual, which will always coincide directly with the Word of God; Apostles aren't elected, they are called of God)*, to them who have obtained like Precious Faith with us *(proclaims the Faith that Gentiles can now be Saved exactly as Jews, in fact, all coming the same way)* through the Righteousness of God and our Saviour Jesus Christ *(this Righteousness is obtained by the Believer exhibiting Faith in Christ and what He did at the Cross)*:
> "Grace and Peace be multiplied unto you through the knowledge of God, and of Jesus our Lord *(this is both Sanctifying Grace and Sanctifying Peace, all made available by the Cross)*,"

ALL THINGS THAT PERTAIN UNTO LIFE AND GODLINESS

"**According as His Divine Power has given unto us all things** *(the Lord with large-handed generosity has given us all things)* **that *pertain* unto life and Godliness** *(pertains to the fact that the Lord Jesus has given us everything we need regarding life and living)*, **through the knowledge of Him Who has called us to Glory and Virtue** *(the 'knowledge' addressed here speaks of what Christ did at the Cross, which alone can provide 'Glory and Virtue')*:"

EXCEEDING GREAT AND PRECIOUS PROMISES

"**Whereby are given unto us exceeding great and Precious Promises** *(pertains to the Word of God, which alone holds the answer to every life problem)*: **that by these** *(Promises)* **you might be partakers of the Divine Nature** *(the Divine Nature implanted in the inner being of the believing sinner becomes the source of our new life and actions; it comes to everyone at the moment of being 'Born-Again')*, **having escaped the corruption that is in the world through lust.** *(This presents the Salvation experience of the sinner, and the Sanctification experience of the Saint.)*"

GROWING IN GRACE

"**And beside this** *(Salvation)*, **giving all diligence** *(refers to the responsibility we as Believers must show regarding the Christian life)*, **add to your Faith Virtue** *(this is Faith in the Cross, which will bring 'Virtue'; the type of 'Virtue' mentioned here is 'energy' and 'power')*; **and to Virtue knowledge** *(this is the type of knowledge which keeps expanding)*;

"**And to knowledge temperance** *(self-control)*; **and to temperance patience** *(our conduct must honor God at* all times, even in the midst of trials and testing*)*; **and to patience Godliness** *(being like God)***;**

"**And to Godliness brotherly kindness** *(carries the idea of treating everyone as if they were our own flesh and blood 'brother' or 'sister')***; and to brotherly kindness charity** *(love).*"

FRUITFUL

"**For if these things be in you, and abound** *(continue to expand)***, they make *you that you shall* neither *be* barren nor unfruitful in the knowledge of our Lord Jesus Christ.** *(Once again, this 'knowledge' refers to what Christ did at the Cross, all on our behalf.)*

"**But he who lacks these things is blind, and cannot see afar off** *(the reason one may lack these things is he is spiritually blind; in other words, such a one has made something other than the Cross the Object of His Faith)* **and has forgotten that he was purged from his old sins.** *(Such a Believer is once again being ruled by the 'sin nature' exactly as he was before conversion, which is always the end result of ignoring the Cross.)*"

DILIGENCE

"**Wherefore the rather, Brethren, give diligence to make your Calling and Election sure** *(this is what Jesus was speaking of when He told us to deny ourselves and take up the Cross daily and follow Him [Lk. 9:23]; every day, the Believer must make certain his Faith is anchored in the Cross and the Cross alone; only then can we realize the tremendous benefits afforded by the Sacrifice of Christ)***: for if you do these things, you shall never fall** *(presents the key to Eternal Security, but with the Promise being conditional)***:**

"**For so an entrance shall be ministered unto you**

abundantly into the Everlasting Kingdom of our Lord and Saviour Jesus Christ. *(The entrance into the Kingdom is solely on the basis of Faith evidenced in Christ and the Cross [Eph. 2:13-18; Jn. 3:16])*" **(II Pet. 1:1-11).**

THE REVELATION

In 1997 the Lord gave me a Revelation of the Cross of Christ, which has so revolutionized my life and my Ministry, that I would like to think I'm not the same person that I was before the Revelation was given. And yet, what He gave me was not new in the least, but rather, that which He had already given to the Apostle Paul. Actually, the Revelation was given in three parts over a period of several weeks. It consisted of the following:

• The sin nature: the Lord took me to the Sixth Chapter of Romans and showed me what the sin nature is, and how that ignorance as to how this works, causes failure, even abject failure, in the hearts and lives of Believers. In other words, it's imperative that we know and understand this great Truth given to us by the Apostle Paul, even as the Lord gave it to him.

• The Cross of Christ: in showing me the Truth of the sin nature the Holy Spirit, however, did not then show me the solution to the problem, that coming some days later. Very simply put, while in prayer, the Lord told me the following. He said:

1. The answer for which you seek is found in the Cross of Christ.

2. The solution for which you seek is found in the Cross of Christ.

3. The answer for which you seek is found only in the Cross of Christ.

It was that simple, that to the point. The Lord was showing me that the Cross of Christ pertained not only to our Salvation but, as well, to our Sanctification, in other words, how we live for the Lord on a daily basis. He took me to Romans 6:3-5; I Corinthians 1:17, 18, 23; 2:2; Galatians, Chapter 5; 6:14; Ephesians 2:13-18; Colossians 2:14-15.

Some weeks later, the Lord showed me the part played by the Holy Spirit in all of this. To explain that great Truth to me, and in no uncertain terms, He took me to Romans 8:1-2. In fact, the great Truth that He gave me, from that which was given to us by the Apostle Paul, is little known in the modern church, if at all. In fact, I personally believe that this simple explanation given to me by the Lord as it regards how the Holy Spirit works, this Truth, although first given to the Apostle Paul, has little been understood since, if at all. In other words, that which the Lord gave me that morning may very well be the first time it was given to anyone other than to the Apostle Paul. Of course, that statement is speculative at best; however, I do know that the closer we get to the end of the Church Age, more Truth, I believe, will be revealed and, in fact, is being revealed.

The Holy Spirit works exclusively by and through the Means of the Cross of Christ. In other words, it is what Jesus did at the Cross that gives the Holy Spirit the legal Means, and one might say the legal right, to do all that He does. In fact, this is so ironclad that He Himself calls it a *"Law."* He said through Paul, *"For the Law of the Spirit of Life in Christ Jesus has made me free from the Law of Sin and Death"* (Rom. 8:2). In fact, we will have much more to say about this later on in this Volume.

SALVATION

I gave my heart to Christ when I was eight years old. Strangely enough, I was Saved on a Saturday afternoon while standing in front of a moving picture theater. I was in line with a group of other kids waiting to buy a ticket, at least when the ticket window opened, to go to the movie.

As I stood in that line, the Lord spoke to my heart saying to me, *"Do not go into this place, give Me your heart, for you are a chosen vessel to be used exclusively in My Service."*

Now, someone may ask as to how an eight-year-old boy can hear such and know that it's the Lord? Better yet, the question may be asked as to how the Lord actually spoke to me?

The only thing I can answer to that is that I knew beyond the shadow of a doubt it was the Lord, and the Way and Means in which He spoke to me was to my heart. I would hope that all would realize that the Lord is capable of doing whatever it is He desires to do. To be sure, He knows perfectly as to how to make Himself known to an eight-year-old child, or anyone else for that matter.

I was startled when the Lord spoke to me but did nothing, not really knowing what it all meant.

A few moments later the Lord said the same thing to me again, *"Do not go in this place, give your heart to Me, for you are a chosen vessel to be used exclusively in My Service."*

By that time the ticket window had opened and I had moved up in the line until it was my turn to purchase the ticket. I laid my quarter on the counter, and the lady dispensing the tickets reached up on the old fashioned spool to pull it down and give me a ticket. The spool jammed and she began to work with it.

I will always believe that the Lord had that spool to jam to give me a few more moments. That was all I needed. I picked up my quarter and left.

I remember walking down to the end of the street and going into Vogt's Drugstore and buying an ice-cream cone. I walked back out, stood on the street corner, and all of a sudden it happened.

It was like someone had lifted fifty pounds from my frail shoulders. I've often wondered how a person feels, who has been in deep sin and then gives his heart and life to the Lord, if I felt as good as I did that Saturday afternoon when Jesus Saved my soul.

Not going to the movie, I got home much earlier than I normally would have.

My Mother quizzed me immediately as to why I was home so quickly. In a matter of fact way I said to her, *"I got Saved!"* I remember that she started to cry and I really did not know what she was crying about. However, one thing was certain; I knew that I was Saved.

THE BAPTISM WITH THE HOLY SPIRIT

Even though my entire family attended a small Assembly of God Church, still, no one in my family had, as of yet, been baptized with the Holy Spirit; in fact, at that stage they knew very little about the Holy Spirit. But, all of that was to change.

My Grandmother was the first one in our family to be baptized with the Holy Spirit with the evidence of speaking with other Tongues. To be sure, that changed everything.

It seemed to irritate my Mother and Dad. My Grandmother was my Dad's Mother.

It was during the summer months, and I wasn't in school. I arose that particular morning and walked into the living room. Seeing my Mother and Dad standing beside my piano, I stopped for a few moments to listen to what they were saying.

I remember hearing my Dad say, *"Mama has gone crazy over religion."* He went on to say, *"Ever since she's been to that meeting, she speaks in this gibberish that no one can understand."* He added, *"And all she talks about is Jesus."* He then said, *"Now, I love the Lord as well, but I don't think we have to talk about Him all the time."*

My Mother nodded in agreement!

Somehow, even though what my parents were saying was very negative, still, it did not come across to me that way. I knew my Grandmother and loved her dearly. I wanted to know what they were talking about.

I said nothing but hastily went outside, got on my bicycle, and immediately rode up to my Grandmother's house. It was to be a meeting that would change everything.

I walked into the house and immediately said to her, *"Nannie!"* This was the name I had started calling her from the time I began to speak. *"Daddy says that you have something that makes you speak funny. What is he talking about?"*

I can see her face even yet. She laughed and said, *"Jimmy, let me fix this cup of tea, and I'll tell you what has happened to me."*

She prepared her hot tea and came into the room and sat

down, putting the tea on a little table beside the chair. I sat down on the floor, looking up at her, and then my Grandmother began to tell me how the Lord baptized her with the Holy Spirit. She went in to some detail, telling how that she had gone to this meeting up close to Monroe, Louisiana, and had gotten hungry to be baptized with the Holy Spirit. She went on to state how that she had asked the Lord for this experience during the nights that she had attended the meetings, but to no avail. In other words, she had not received.

She told me how that the noon hour came on that particular day, and she told some of the friends that she had met at the meeting that she wasn't going to eat lunch but was, rather, going out to a little cope of trees and there seek the Lord, asking Him to baptize her with the Holy Spirit. She went on to state that several ladies went with her.

She told me how that she began to pray, asking the Lord to baptize her with the Spirit, and, all of a sudden, it happened. When she began to tell me how that the Lord filled her, she began to speak with other Tongues. All of a sudden, the Power of God hit her as she sat before me.

She raised her right hand, continuing to speak with other Tongues, and for the first time in my life I felt the Power of God.

I looked down at my arms, and chill bumps had broken out all over them. To say that I was intrigued would be a gross understatement. In fact, I went back that afternoon, had her tell me the same thing all over again, and once again, the Power fell. This went on for days. It being the summer months and me not in school, I took full advantage of the free time and had her tell me this experience at least twice a day, which went on for several days.

WHY WAS I SO INTERESTED?

I was extremely interested simply because every time she would get to that place in the telling of her story that she was filled with the Spirit, the Power of God would come upon her, and she would begin to speak with other Tongues. Every time it happened, I would feel it as well, and I came to the place very quickly that I wanted to be filled with the Holy Spirit also!

Some weeks later, in a morning prayer meeting in our church, the Lord wondrously and graciously baptized me with the Holy Spirit with the evidence of speaking with other Tongues.

When the Lord filled me, it was as though a pool of light settled around me, actually light that I could see with my eyes. When my Mother and Dad took me home, I was still speaking with other Tongues. In fact, I went for several days and spoke very little English.

During that time, my Mother sent me to the Post Office to get a three-cent stamp (that's what a stamp cost in 1943).

I remember laying the nickel on the counter at the Post Office, opening my mouth and trying to ask for a stamp, but instead, I began to speak with other Tongues. The man behind the counter looked at me very strangely and said, *"Son, I can't understand what you're saying."* I tried it again, and again I began to speak with other Tongues. Even though I was speaking a foreign language, I didn't look foreign, and the man must have been puzzled, even as I was.

I was embarrassed, so I grabbed my nickel and ran out of the Post Office without getting the stamp.

Strangely enough, when I got home, and my Mother asked me where the stamp was, I could speak English. I told her what had happened.

In back of our house was a cope of woods. I found a log, made it into an Altar, and went out every day to pray. In fact, in those days, actually for several years, I was in a prayer meeting several times a week. Some may ask the question as to how in the world an eight-year-old boy, even nine or ten, could be interested in prayer meetings.

At our prayer meetings, which were conducted most of the time at either my Grandmother's or my Aunt's home, the Power of God would at times fall to such a degree as to defy description. I can recall at least one time, and there is a vague recollection of several other times, when I would literally go into a trance and stay that way for several hours as the Spirit of God moved upon me. Even at the tender ages of eight and nine, I knew I was called to preach. All during those formative years, I knew I would be an Evangelist.

THE HOLY SPIRIT AND FRANCES

And yet, what the Holy Spirit would enable us to do in the coming years, as it regards the Work of God being furthered all over the world with untold numbers of people coming to Christ, He gave me Frances to help me get this thing done. Without her, it could not have been accomplished, I think!

Very early in my Ministry I learned what the Anointing was. However, it was not until 1997, when the Revelation was given, that I learned and, thereby, understand how the Holy Spirit works as it regards our everyday life and living. As it pertains to the Anointing of the Holy Spirit upon this Ministry, I have watched the Lord give the same to Frances, Donnie, and Gabriel. In fact, I've seen this same Anointing rest upon all the Ministers who are on our staff, and thereby engaged in this Ministry, enabling us to take the Gospel all over the world. I would be reluctant to name any of them, outside of my immediate family, for fear that I would miss some. But, the truth is, as the Lord gave me this Revelation of the Cross in 1997, He has, in fact, given it to my entire family as well as all of my associates. I even feel that this tremendous responsibility of taking this Message of the Cross to a hurting world and a dying church is upon all who are associated with this Ministry. I speak of all the members of Family Worship Center as well as those who worship with us all over the world by the means of Internet, Radio, and Television.

THERE IS YET VERY MUCH LAND TO BE POSSESSED

About thirty-five hundred years ago the Lord spoke to

Joshua saying:

"Now Joshua was old and stricken in years; and the LORD said unto him, You are old and stricken in years *(Joshua, at this time, was 101 years of age)*, and there remains yet very much land to be possessed" (Josh. 13:1).

The notes in THE EXPOSITOR'S STUDY BIBLE say:

"*The account in this Chapter given to us concerning the possession of the land, or the lack thereof, points to every Believer that which the Lord has prepared for us; however, there are enemies between the Promise and the Possession. God has a Perfect Plan for us, but, regrettably, so few of us press through to that Perfect Plan. We all too often stop short! The words, 'There remains yet very much land to be possessed,' should strike long, hard, and true to the heart of every Believer.*"

The next few Verses of this Thirteenth Chapter of Joshua spell out the land that had not been possessed by the Children of Israel, and of which the Lord reminded Joshua.

In the Thirteenth Verse he said, *"Nevertheless the Children of Israel expelled not the Geshurites, nor the Maachathites: but the Geshurites and the Maachathites dwell among the Israelites until this day."*

Once again, let me quote from the notes of THE EXPOSITOR'S STUDY BIBLE:

"*The word 'nevertheless' proclaims failure among the people of God to possess all that was promised. Such is the sad condition of far too many Believers. While some Victories are won, 'nevertheless' some things remain – things which steal, kill, and destroy. How many enemies remain unsubdued in the hearts of Believers?*

"*There is only one way that Victory can be attained in*

the life of the Christian. Not ten ways, not five ways, not even two ways, only one way.

"All Victory over sin, and in every capacity, and, to be sure, sin is the problem, was purchased and thereby attained at the Cross of Calvary [Eph. 2:13-18; Col. 2:14-15; Gal., Chpt. 5; 6:14]. As a result, the Believer's Faith, and this is so very, very important, must ever have the Cross of Christ as its Object [Rom. 6:3-14]. If the Believer is faithful in anchoring his Faith in the Cross of Christ, and maintaining his Faith in the Cross of Christ, the Holy Spirit, Who works exclusively within the parameters of the Finished Work of Christ, will, without fail, subdue every enemy within our hearts and lives [Rom. 6:14; 8:1-2, 11]. That, and that alone, is God's Prescribed Order of Victory; otherwise, instead of the Believer subduing the enemies of his soul, the enemies of his soul will subdue him."

CHAPTER ONE

What Part Did The Holy Spirit Play In Old Testament Times?

QUESTION:

WHAT PART DID THE HOLY SPIRIT PLAY IN OLD TESTAMENT TIMES?

ANSWER:

Everything that's ever been done by the Godhead on Earth, and for all time, with the exception of the First Advent of the Lord Jesus Christ, has been done by and through the Office, Ministry, and Person of the Holy Spirit. In other words, the Holy Spirit is the Person of the Godhead who executes on Earth that which the Godhead has decided (Gen. 1:2). Even with Christ, as we shall see, the Holy Spirit officiated in the conception of Jesus in Mary, as well as every facet of the Life and Ministry of our Lord. In fact, our Lord did not die on the Cross until the Holy Spirit told Him exactly when to die (Heb. 9:14). Without the Leading and Operation of the Holy Spirit, and that refers to every phase of our life, living, and ministry, nothing is going to be done for the Lord. Anything that is of God must be conceived by the Spirit, birthed by the Spirit, inspired by the Spirit, and carried out by the Spirit. Otherwise, it is a work of man, and no matter how consecrated, can never be accepted by the Lord.

THE DAWN OF TIME

The Bible doesn't teach the young Earth theory, as some claim. In fact, the Bible doesn't tell us how old the Earth actually is, or when God originally created the Universe; it just states that He did. What was the beginning of God's Creation we aren't told. It possibly could have been Angels, which is believed by some scholars. We do know that the Angels existed before Genesis 1:1, for the Bible tells us the following:

"Where were you when I laid the foundations of

the Earth? declare, if you have understanding. *(The Truth that God made all things is obvious according to the Creation. A creation must have a Creator; therefore, the alleged theory of evolution is a farce. Evolution, in fact, cannot even be honestly called a 'theory,' because a theory has to have at least some rudiments of facts to buttress its claims. Evolution has no facts whatsoever.)*

"Who has laid the measures thereof, if you know? or who has stretched the line upon it? *(The idea is that God has planned and created the Universe, down to the most fine detail.)*

"Whereupon are the foundations thereof fastened? or who laid the corner stone thereof *(in fact, the worlds are held up by the Word of God [Heb. 11:3])***;**

"When the morning stars sang together, and all the Sons of God shouted for joy? *(The Lord is speaking here of the completion of the Earth and the Universe, and of the celebration that followed by the Angels of Heaven.*

"Lucifer, before his Fall, was called the 'son of the morning' [Isa. 14:12].

*"There is a possibility that these 'morning stars' who 'sang together' were led in their worship and celebration at that time by Lucifer, the 'son of the morning')***" (Job 38:4-7).**

MOSES

Moses gives his account of the creation of the Universe in the majestic statement, *"In the beginning God created the heavens and the Earth"* (Gen. 1:1). The implication in the Hebrew is that when God finished this creation, it was in a perfect state. In fact, the inspired writers of the New Testament, when alluding to its creation, called it a *"kosmos,"* which refers to *"an ordered system."* In other words, when the Lord originally created this Earth and the Universe, it was not created a formless mass as described in Genesis 1:2. It became that way after a cataclysmic happening. That happening was the revolution of Lucifer against God, which drew away at least one third of the angelic host, and which was the beginning of sin and transgression (Rev. 12:4). This rebellion is what resulted in the Earth being *"without form, and void; and darkness was upon the face of the deep"* (Gen. 1:2).

Incidentally, as an aside, there is no record in the Bible account of dinosaurs, or such like animals, existing on the Earth from the time of Adam. Some claim these beasts lived on the Earth prior to the Flood, with the Flood wiping them out, etc. There is no record of that. In fact, Noah was told by the Lord to take into the Ark, *"every living thing of all flesh, two of every sort shall you bring into the Ark, to keep them alive with you; they shall be male and female"* (Gen. 6:19).

Considering that the Lord said, *"and of every living thing of all flesh,"* and knowing that Noah obeyed Him, if there had been dinosaurs then (before the Flood), there would have been dinosaurs and such like after the Flood. Knowing it is certainly true that those animals actually did exist upon this Earth, for the finding of their bones in certain places proves such, the only time they could have existed is before Adam. As well, there is every indication that God did not originally create any animal to be vicious, but that some of them became that way because of the Fall, which, no doubt, happened as well with the time of Lucifer.

Concerning the animal kingdom in the coming Kingdom Age, those which are now ferocious will be returned to their original docile state, as they were when God originally created them. The Bible states concerning such, and I quote from THE EXPOSITOR'S STUDY BIBLE:

CONDITIONS DURING THE MILLENNIUM

"The wolf also shall dwell with the lamb, and the leopard shall lie down with the kid; and the calf and the young lion and the fatling together; and a little child

shall lead them. *(The character and nature of the planet, including its occupants and even the animal creation, will revert to their posture as before the Fall.)*

"**And the cow and the bear shall feed** *(feed together)***; their young ones shall lie down together: and the lion shall eat straw like the ox.** *(This Passage plainly tells us that the carnivorous nature of the animal kingdom will be totally and eternally changed.)*

"**And the sucking child shall play on the hole of the asp, and the weaned child shall put his hand on the cockatrice's den.** *(Even though some of the curse will remain on the serpent in the Millennium, in that he continues to writhe in the dust, still, the deadly part will be removed [Gen. 3:14])*" **(Isa. 11:6-8).**

Concerning this coming time, the Scripture also says, *"They shall not hurt nor destroy in all My holy mountain: for the Earth shall be full of the Knowledge of the Lord, as the waters cover the sea"* (Isa. 11:9).

Even though the Bible is not a Book which deals with everything about God, confining itself to man's creation, his Fall, and his Redemption, with almost all of it limiting itself to the Redemption of mankind through the Lord Jesus Christ, and what He did for us at the Cross, still, what it does say about other things, such as the angelic host, although very limited, still lends credence to the pre-Adamic creation, etc.

THE SPIRIT OF THE LORD

After Moses told us of the Spirit of the Lord moving upon the face of the waters in bringing this Earth back to a habitable state, the next time the Spirit of God was mentioned, strangely enough, was by one who had no knowledge of God whatsoever, namely Pharaoh. The Scripture says:

"**And Pharaoh said unto his servants, Can we find**

such a one as this is, a man in whom the Spirit of God is?* (The term 'Spirit of God,' as used by Pharaoh, in the Hebrew is 'Ruach Elohim,' and would have been understood by Pharaoh as referring to the sagacity and intelligence of a Deity. Other than that, he would have had no knowledge as to What or Who the Spirit of God actually was)*" (Gen. 41:38).

THE SPIRIT OF WISDOM

The Holy Spirit is next referred to as the *"Spirit of Wisdom,"* and rightly so. The Word says:

"And you shall speak unto all who are wise hearted, whom I have filled with the Spirit of Wisdom *(the Holy Spirit)*, that they may make Aaron's garments to consecrate him, that he may minister unto Me in the Priest's office" (Ex. 28:3).

THE WORKMEN AND THE SPIRIT OF GOD

"When it came time to construct the Tabernacle and all the Sacred Vessels, the Scripture says:
"And the LORD spoke unto Moses, saying,
"See, I have called by name Bezaleel the son of Uri, the son of Hur, of the Tribe of Judah *(it is believed that 'Bezaleel' was the grandson of Hur, who it is believed was the brother-in-law of Moses, having married his sister Miriam; the choice of these principal workmen was that of God, and not Moses)*:
"And I have filled him with the Spirit of God, in wisdom, and in understanding, and in knowledge, and in all manner of workmanship *(before the Cross, the Holy Spirit only came upon individuals who had been called of God for a certain task, even as Bezaleel; now, since the Cross, the Holy Spirit resides in the hearts and lives of all*

Believers [I Cor. 3:16]),
"To devise cunning works . . ." (Ex. 31:1-4).

THE HOLY SPIRIT ON MOSES

"And the LORD said unto Moses, Gather unto Me seventy men of the Elders of Israel, whom you know to be the Elders of the people, and officers over them *(these were chosen by God, and not by Jethro; it is believed that the Sanhedrin, the ruling body of Israel, originated with the Seventy Elders)*; and bring them unto the Tabernacle of the congregation, that they may stand there with you.

"And I will come down and talk with you there: and I will take of the Spirit *(Holy Spirit)* which is upon you, and will put it upon them; and they shall bear the burden of the people with you, that you bear it not yourself alone *(a pitying Grace relieved him of the weight of his charge while upbraiding him; however, Moses was, in truth, no whit less burdened, for the Spiritual Power granted to the Seventy Elders was taken from him)*" (Num. 11:16-17).

THE PROPHECY OF BALAAM

"And when Balaam saw that it pleased the LORD to bless Israel, he went not, as at other times, to seek for enchantments, but he set his face toward the wilderness. *(Concerning this, Williams says, 'This Chapter shows that the Prophet in his 'madness' was willing to listen to the voice of the Devil, though unwilling to listen to the Voice of the Lord. The corruption, depravity, and rebellion of man's will is fearfully and mysteriously illustrated in Balaam. Even at the time of being consciously subject to the Moving of the Holy Spirit, in his thirst for money he sought by enchantments to become inspired of an unclean spirit. So, knowledge of spiritual things is not Spiritual Knowledge.')*

"And Balaam lifted up his eyes, and he saw Israel

abiding in his tents according to their Tribes; and the Spirit of God came upon him *(but it doesn't mean that he had the Spirit of God, for he definitely didn't!)*" **(Num. 24:1-2).**

JOSHUA

"And the LORD said unto Moses, Take thee Joshua the son of Nun, a man in whom is the Spirit, and lay your hand upon him *(it seems that the hand of Moses was laid upon him in view of all of Israel, at least of its representatives; but let it be noted that the Lord chose Joshua, and not Moses; as well, the Lord had told Moses long before that Joshua would take his place, and Moses, no doubt, did his best to prepare him)*" **(Num. 27:18).**

DAVID

We'll give one more as it regards an individual. Concerning David, the Scripture says:

"And Samuel said unto Jesse, Are here all your children? And he said, There remains yet the youngest, and, behold, he keeps the sheep *(a Type of Christ as the good Shepherd)*. And Samuel said unto Jesse, Send and fetch him: for we will not sit down till he comes hither. *(David was the youngest, and apparently his father Jesse thought it would be useless to bring him into the house. Generally, those who are totally rejected by men are the very ones whom God chooses.)*

"And he sent, and brought him in. Now he was ruddy *(red-haired)*, and withal of a beautiful countenance *(the Hebrew says, 'with beautiful eyes')*, and goodly to look to *(to look at, handsome)*. And the LORD said, Arise, anoint him: for this is he. *(It is believed that David was probably about fifteen years of age at this time. It would be years before he would take the throne, but this is the beginning of the glory days of Israel.)*"

THE SPIRIT OF THE LORD CAME UPON DAVID

"**Then Samuel took the horn of oil, and anointed him in the midst of his brethren** *(this was Samuel's last and crowning work; he would train the man who more nearly than any other approached unto the ideal of the theocratic king, and was to Israel the Type of their coming Messiah; it was Samuel's wisdom in teaching his young men music which gave David the skill to be the sweet singer of the Sanctuary; and we may feel sure also that when David arranged the service of the House of God, and gave Priests and Levites their appointed duties [I Chron. 23:26], the model which he set before him was that in which he had so often taken part with Samuel at Ramah, with, of course, the Lord guiding it all – Smith)*: **and the Spirit of the LORD came upon David from that day forward** *(which would be the means by which all things good were accomplished in David's life; David's name would be the very first human name in the New Testament and the very last human name in the New Testament; in fact, the Messiah would be referred to as 'the Son of David,' because He would come through the lineage of David's family [II Sam., Chpt. 7])*" (I Sam. 16:11-13).

EVERY MIRACLE WAS ACCOMPLISHED BY THE POWER OF THE HOLY SPIRIT

The opening of the Red Sea, the opening of Jordan, the tumbling down of the walls of Jericho, David killing Goliath, in fact, every single thing done by the Lord in Old Testament times, and these times as well, all, and without exception, are by the Power, the Office, the Ministry, and the Person of the Holy Spirit.

Bluntly and pointedly, the Lord told the great Prophet Zechariah that everything that was done for the Lord on this

Earth was always done by the Power of the Holy Spirit. He said:

BY MY SPIRIT

"**Then He answered and spoke unto me, saying, This is the Word of the LORD unto Zerubbabel, saying, Not by might, nor by power, but by My Spirit, saith the LORD of Hosts.** *(The Message of the Vision to Zerubbabel and also to all others, at least according to the need, was: not by military might, nor by political power, but by spiritual energy, he would certainly complete the building of the Temple.*

" *'Not by [human] might, nor by [human] power, but by My Spirit,' presents God's Method of accomplishing His Work. Everything that has ever been done on this Earth, as stated, as it regards the Godhead, has been done by the Holy Spirit, with the exception of Christ, His Life, His Ministry, and His Crucifixion; however, the Holy Spirit even superintended all of that, even from the beginning to the end [Lk. 4:18-19].*

" *If it is claimed to be for the Lord, whatever is being done must be done by the Moving, Operation, Power, and Person of the Holy Spirit through Believers. Otherwise, it will not be recognized by God; in fact, it will be constituted as a 'work of the flesh' [Rom. 8:1].*

" *'Says the LORD of Hosts,' presents God's Supreme Personal Power over everything in the material and Spiritual universe. All is organized under His Command. As well, the word 'Hosts,' as used here, is associated with warfare and relates to the word 'armies.' In other words, He is the 'LORD of Armies.')*"

GRACE!

"**Who are you O great mountain? before Zerubbabel you shall become a plain: and he shall bring forth the**

headstone thereof with shoutings, crying, Grace, grace unto it. *(The question, 'Who are you O great mountain?' is meant to refer to Hystapes, king of the mighty Medo-Persian Empire, who made a decree that the work on the Temple must cease [Ezra, Chpt. 4]. Cyrus, who, in fact, was Esther's son, had, some sixteen years earlier, made the decree that the Temple should be rebuilt. This was in 536 B.C. [Ezra 1:1-2]. He reigned for nine years; his son, Cambyses, reigned seven years; and then Hystapes followed him. He is the one who gave the order that no Temple was to be built in Jerusalem, countermanding, in effect, the order given by Cyrus.*

"The question, 'Who are you O great mountain?,' is asked in sarcasm by the Holy Spirit. In other words, the Holy Spirit is saying, 'Who do you think you are, attempting to stop the Work of God?'

"'Before Zerubbabel you shall become a plain,' means that the Lord will shave the face of this empire, with this king being totally removed. In fact, this was fulfilled in totality; this man was executed by Darius I. He was, in fact, removed because of his efforts to hinder the Work of God.)

"'And he [Zerubbabel] shall bring forth the headstone thereof with shoutings, crying, Grace, grace, unto it,' refers to the Ministry of Christ, which would ultimately come, in which all of this played its part [Jn. 1:17])" **(Zech. 4:6-7).**

THE FOUR GOSPELS

Even though the four Gospels, Matthew, Mark, Luke, and John, were not in the Old Testament, as is obvious, but rather the New, still, what was done then, in essence, came under the heading of the Old Covenant. In fact, John the Baptist was the last Prophet under the Old Covenant. He introduced the Lord Jesus Christ. He did it by proclaiming two major factors of our Lord. They are:

• Jesus would take AWAY the sin of the world: the Scripture says:

"**The next day** *(refers to the day after John had been questioned by the emissaries from the Sanhedrin)* **John sees Jesus coming unto him** *(is, no doubt, after the Baptism of Jesus, and the temptation in the wilderness)*, **and said, Behold the Lamb of the God** *(proclaims Jesus as the Sacrifice for sin, in fact, the Sin-Offering, Whom all the multiple millions of offered lambs had represented)*, **which takes away the sin of the world** *(animal blood could only cover sin, it could not take it away; but Jesus offering Himself as the Perfect Sacrifice took away the sin of the world; He not only cleansed acts of sin, but, as well, addressed the root cause [Col. 2:14-15])*" **(Jn. 1:29).**

While theoretically Jesus did take away all sin, still, it remains for the sinner to exercise Faith in Christ to attain that for which Jesus died. If faith is not exercised in Christ, the sin remains (Jn. 3:16).

• Jesus baptizes WITH the Holy Spirit: what Jesus did at the Cross, which was to atone for all sin, at least for those who will believe, makes it possible for the Holy Spirit to come into the heart and the life of each and every Believer, which He does at conversion, and there to abide forever. Concerning this, Jesus told His Disciples:

"**And I will pray the Father, and He shall give you another Comforter** *('Parakletos,' which means 'One called to the side of another to help')*, **that He may abide with you forever** *(before the Cross, the Holy Spirit could only help a few individuals, and then only for a period of time; since the Cross, He lives in the hearts and lives of Believers, and does so forever)*" **(Jn. 14:16).**

John the Baptist said of Jesus:

"**I indeed baptize you with water unto Repentance** *(Water Baptism was an outward act of an inward work already carried out)*: **but He** *(Christ)* **Who comes after me is mightier than I, Whose Shoes I am not worthy to bear: He shall baptize you with the Holy Spirit, and** ***with*** **fire** *(to burn out the sinful dross [Acts 2:2-4])*:

"**Whose fan** *is* **in His Hand** *(the ancient method for winnowing grain)*, **and He will thoroughly purge His Floor** *('purging it, that it may bring forth more fruit' [Jn. 15:2])*, **and gather His Wheat into the garner** *(the end product as developed by the Spirit)*; **but He will burn up the chaff with unquenchable fire** *(the wheat is symbolic of the Work of the Spirit, while the chaff is symbolic of the work of the flesh)*" (**Mat. 3:11-12**).

WITH YOU AND IN YOU

Before the Cross and due to the fact that the blood of bulls and goats could not take away sins, the Holy Spirit could only be with Believers and not actually in Believers, at least permanently. Concerning this, Jesus said:

"***Even*** **the Spirit of Truth** *(the Greek says, 'The Spirit of the Truth,' which refers to the Word of God; actually, He does far more than merely superintend the attribute of Truth, as Christ 'is Truth' [I Jn. 5:6])*; **Whom the world cannot receive** *(the Holy Spirit cannot come into the heart of the unbeliever until that person makes Christ his or her Saviour; then He comes in)*, **because it sees Him not, neither knows Him** *(refers to the fact that only Born-Again Believers can understand the Holy Spirit and know Him)*: **but you know Him** *(would have been better translated, 'But you shall get to know Him')*; **for He dwells with you** *(before the Cross)*, **and shall be in you** *(which would take place on the Day of Pentecost and forward, because the sin debt has been forever paid by Christ on the Cross, changing* *the disposition of everything)*" **(Jn. 14:17).**

As it regards Believers before the Cross and after the Cross, at least as it respects privileges, Jesus said:

"**And as they departed** *(the two disciples of John the Baptist)***, Jesus began to say unto the multitudes concerning John, What went you out into the wilderness to see? A reed shaken with the wind?** *(Despite appearances – John being in prison – Jesus proclaims what John really is.)*

"**But what went you out for to see? A man clothed in soft raiment? behold, they who wear soft *clothing* are in kings' houses** *(if Herod's gold could have bought John, he would not now be in prison).*

"**But what went you out for to see?** *(The third time this question is posed.)* **A Prophet? yes, I say unto you, and more than a Prophet** *(more than all Prophets before him).*

"**For this is *he*, of whom it is written** *(proclaims John as the last of the Old Testament Prophets)***, Behold, I send My messenger before Your face** *(John was that messenger)***, which shall prepare Your way before You** *(John prepared the way for Christ).*

"**Verily I say unto you, Among them who are born of women there has not risen a greater than John the Baptist** *(places John at the forefront of the Prophets)***: notwithstanding he who is least in the Kingdom of Heaven is greater than he** *(speaks of the New Covenant [Heb. 8:6])*" **(Mat. 11:7-11).**

HOW ARE THE LEAST IN THE KINGDOM OF HEAVEN GREATER THAN JOHN THE BAPTIST?

Considering that Jesus said that John the Baptist was the greatest Prophet ever, how can *"he who is least in the Kingdom of Heaven be greater than he?"*

Jesus was speaking of greatness as it regards privileges.

Under the New Covenant, due to what Christ did at the Cross, Believers now have far greater privileges than those under the Old Covenant. In fact, the least presently in the New Covenant, whatever that means, has far greater privileges now than did John the Baptist or even the great Prophets such as Isaiah or Jeremiah, etc. Please understand, however, this *"greatness"* is not on our part at all, but altogether on the part of Christ and the great Victory He there won.

THE GREAT VICTORY OF THE ATONEMENT

Actually, it is not possible for anyone to properly annunciate that which Jesus did at the Cross of Calvary in the giving of Himself in Sacrifice. It was so encompassing, so total, and so complete that whatever description would be given would fall far short of what actually happened.

I was studying just this morning, reading after an excellent Bible scholar, however, he was totally wrong in his summation of the Atonement. He, in essence, was claiming that Divine Healing is not in the Atonement. Even though he did not go into detail, I suppose he was meaning that if Divine Healing were in the Atonement, Believers would never get sick. However, he was very quick to express the fact that the cleansing of all sin was in the Atonement, despite the fact that Christians, sadly and regrettably, still sin. Our failure doesn't mean the Atonement has failed. As a Baptist Preacher said, *"While we might fail, the Cross of Christ does not fail."*

The truth is, every single thing that man lost in the Fall, and I mean everything, was addressed in the Atonement. That means that every blessing, including Divine Healing, and everything else that one might think, was included in the great Victory there won. Admittedly, we do not now have everything for which Jesus paid such a price, that awaiting the Resurrection; however, we do now have the *"Firstfruits,"* and to be sure, that is enough for us to live a victorious, overcoming, Christian life. Concerning this, Paul said:

THE FIRSTFRUITS

"**For we know that the whole Creation** *(everything has been affected by Satan's rebellion and Adam's Fall)* **groans and travails in pain together until now** *(refers to the common longing of the elements of the Creation to be brought back to their original perfection).*

"**And not only** *they (the Creation, and all it entails)*, **but ourselves also** *(refers to Believers)*, **which have the Firstfruits of the Spirit** *(even though Jesus addressed every single thing lost in the Fall at the Cross, we only have a part of that possession now, with the balance coming at the Resurrection)*, **even we ourselves groan within ourselves** *(proclaims the obvious fact that all Jesus paid for in the Atonement has not yet been fully realized)*, **waiting for the Adoption** *(should be translated, 'waiting for the fulfillment of the process, which Adoption into the Family of God guarantees')*, *to wit*, **the Redemption of our body** *(the glorifying of our physical body that will take place at the Resurrection)*" (**Rom. 8:22-23**).

THE DEFEAT OF SATAN AS WELL
WAS IN THE ATONEMENT

When I say the defeat of Satan, I am speaking of the time that went all the way back to his revolution against God. Even though we know very little about that, still, Calvary covered it all. Paul said:

"**In Whom** *(in Christ)* **we have Redemption through His Blood** *(the outpoured Blood of the Son of God at the Cross is the price for Redemption)*, **the forgiveness of sins** *(a remission of their penalty)*, **according to the riches of His Grace** *(the riches of that Grace gave us the Cross)*;

"**Wherein He has abounded toward us** *(refers to God's Grace being manifested toward us in superabundance,* *again made possible by the Cross)* **in all wisdom** *(insight)* **and prudence** *(to solve the problems of each moment of time)*;

"**Having made known unto us the mystery of His Will** *(refers to the secret purposes and counsels God intends to carry into effect in His Kingdom)*, **according to His good pleasure** *(extended to Believers)* **which He has purposed in Himself** *(originated in His Own Mind)*:

"**That in the dispensation of the fulness of times** *(concerns itself with a well-ordered plan)* **He might gather together in one all things in Christ** *(the Atonement addressed not only man's Fall, but the revolution of Lucifer as well)*, **both which are in Heaven** *(where the revolution of Lucifer began)*, **and which are on earth** *(the Fall of man)*; **even in Him** *(made possible by what Christ did at the Cross)*" **(Eph. 1:7-10).**

THE CROSS OF CHRIST, A TRIUMPH OVER ALL DARKNESS

"**And you are complete in Him** *(the satisfaction of every spiritual want is found in Christ, made possible by the Cross)*, **which is the Head of all principality and power** *(His Headship extends not only over the Church, which voluntarily serves Him, but over all forces that are opposed to Him as well [Phil. 2:10-11])*:

"**In Whom also you are circumcised with the Circumcision made without hands** *(that which is brought about by the Cross [Rom. 6:3-5])*, **in putting off the body of the sins of the flesh by the Circumcision of Christ** *(refers to the old carnal nature that is defeated by the Believer placing his Faith totally in the Cross, which gives the Holy Spirit latitude to work)*:"

WITH CHRIST

"**Buried with Him in Baptism** *(does not refer to Water*

Baptism, but rather to the Believer baptized into the Death of Christ, which refers to the Crucifixion and Christ as our Substitute [Rom. 6:3-4]), **wherein also you are risen with** *Him* **through the Faith of the operation of God, Who has raised Him from the dead.** *(This does not refer to our future physical Resurrection, but to that Spiritual Resurrection from a sinful state into Divine Life. We died with Him, we are buried with Him, and we rose with Him [Rom. 6:3-5], and herein lies the secret to all Spiritual Victory.)*

"And you, being dead in your sins and the uncircumcision of your flesh *(speaks of spiritual death [i.e., 'separation from God'], which sin does!)*, **has He quickened together with Him** *(refers to being made spiritually alive, which is done through being 'Born-Again')*, **having forgiven you all trespasses** *(the Cross made it possible for all manner of sins to be forgiven and taken away)*;"

THE LAW WAS SATISFIED

"Blotting out the handwriting of Ordinances that was against us *(pertains to the Law of Moses, which was God's Standard of Righteousness that man could not reach)*, **which was contrary to us** *(Law is against us, simply because we are unable to keep its precepts, no matter how hard we try)*, **and took it out of the way** *(refers to the penalty of the Law being removed)*, **nailing it to His Cross** *(the Law with its decrees was abolished in Christ's Death, as if Crucified with Him)*;"

THE SPOILING OF PRINCIPALITIES AND POWERS

"*And* having spoiled principalities and powers *(Satan and all of his henchmen were defeated at the Cross by Christ atoning for all sin; sin was the legal right Satan had to hold man in captivity; with all sin atoned, he has no more legal right to hold anyone in bondage)*, **He** *(Christ)* **made**

a show of them openly *(what Jesus did at the Cross was in the face of the whole universe)*, **triumphing over them in it.** *(The triumph is complete and it was all done for us, meaning we can walk in power and perpetual Victory due to the Cross)*" **(Col. 2:10-15).**

WITH BELIEVERS, IN BELIEVERS

As we have already quoted to you from THE EXPOSITOR'S STUDY BIBLE, Jesus was quick to relate to His Disciples that while the Holy Spirit had been with them, now, at least after the Cross, He would be *"in them,"* and forever (Jn. 14:16-17). The Cross of Christ is what made this possible by the sin debt being addressed and, thereby, settled to the satisfaction of God the Father. That's what John was talking about when he said:

"**And He is the propitiation** *(satisfaction)* **for our sins: and not for ours only, but also for** *the sins of* **the whole world.** *(This pertains to the fact that the satisfaction is as wide as the sin. If men do not experience its benefit, the fault is not in its efficacy, but in man himself)*" **(I Jn. 2:2).**

Even as we have stated that the Holy Spirit came into the hearts and lives of some Believers before the Cross, such as the Prophets, etc., to enable them to carry out a particular task, the evidence is that the Holy Spirit limited Himself to this particular activity, whatever it might have been. There is no record that before the Cross the Holy Spirit helped anyone with their Sanctification, that is, as to how one should live for the Lord. In fact, before the Cross, Sanctification was pretty much merely an outward ceremony. In other words, the people were told to *"sanctify themselves"* (Josh. 3:5). Since the Cross, the Holy Spirit is the sanctifying Agent, of which we will have more to say in another Chapter.

JESUS WAS THE EXCEPTION

Our Lord was not born by natural procreation; therefore, He was not subject to the Fall. In other words, He was not born with a sin nature. Yet, there is no record that the Holy Spirit came into His heart and life until He was to begin His public Ministry. Concerning that time, the Scripture says:

"Now when all the people were baptized *(were being baptized)*, it came to pass, that Jesus also being baptized *(this was to testify of His Death, Burial, and Resurrection, of which Water Baptism is a Type)*, and praying *(as He came up out of the water, He came up praying)*, the Heaven was opened *(Heaven had been closed to man since the Fall; through Jesus it would now open)*,

"And the Holy Spirit descended in a bodily shape like a Dove upon Him *(the Holy Spirit is a Person, the Third Person of the Godhead, separate from the Father and the Son)*, and a Voice came from Heaven, which said *(the Voice of God the Father)*, You are My Beloved Son *(literally, 'as for You,' in contradistinction to all others)*; in You I am well pleased *(God is pleased with us, only as long as we are in Christ)*" (Lk. 3:21-22).

THE HOLY SPIRIT AND
THE MINISTRY OF CHRIST

Every Miracle that Jesus performed, every Healing carried out, all and without exception, were done by the Power of the Holy Spirit. Even though Jesus was Very God, still, He was functioning as Very Man, while never ceasing to be Very God. Functioning as a Man, the Man Christ Jesus, He had to have the Help, the Leading, the Guidance, and the empowerment of the Holy Spirit, which He did have, and in a greater measure than any of us. Actually, it was without measure. John the Baptist said of Him:

HE IS ABOVE ALL

"**He must increase** *(He must ever 'increase,' not men, denominations, religious offices, the Virgin Mary, Apostles, etc.)*, **but I *must* decrease** *(the Ministers of the New Covenant must all take note of Divine Praise and self-depletion, as we prepare the way of the Lord to human hearts; we must hide ourselves behind the greater Glory of our Lord; we are successful, only as we succeed in doing this).*

"**He who comes from above is above all** *(refers to the fact that Christ was a Man, but above all that He was more than man, in fact, God)*: **he who is of the Earth is earthly, and speaks of the Earth** *(refers to all men, even the great Prophets, which are of necessity limited)*: **He Who comes from Heaven is above all** *(places Christ in a category above all men, even as He ever shall be!).*

"**And what He has seen and heard, that He testifies** *(refers to that which Jesus received from the Father, which testified of Him and He of it)*; **and no man receives His Testimony** *(means that no man contributed to His Testimony, but that it was all from God).*"

WITHOUT MEASURE

"**He who has received His Testimony** *(refers to all who have believed on His Name and accepted Him as Lord and Saviour)* **has set to His Seal that God is true** *(has to do with man receiving the witness of the Son as the Giver of Eternal Life; as the witness of Jesus is true in every respect, such portrays that God is true to His Word).*

"**For He Whom God has sent speaks the Words of God** *(refers to Christ Who always spoke the Mind of God and, thereby, the Word of God)*: **for God gives not the Spirit by measure *unto Him*** *(refers to the fact that all others, whomever they may have been, and even the very greatest, while having the Holy Spirit, did so by 'measure,' which* *was not so with Jesus; He had the Spirit in totality, hence, the constant healings and miracles)*" **(Jn. 3:30-34)**.

JESUS, ANOINTED BY THE HOLY SPIRIT

Peter said of our Lord:

"How God anointed Jesus of Nazareth with the Holy Spirit and with Power *(as a Man, Christ needed the Holy Spirit, as we certainly do as well! in fact, everything He did was by the Power of the Spirit)***:** **Who went about doing good** *(everything He did was good)***, and healing all who were oppressed of the Devil** *(only Christ could do this, and Believers can do such only as Christ empowers them by the Spirit)***; for God was with Him** *(God is with us only as we are 'with Him')*" **(Acts 10:38)**.

THE BOOK OF ISAIAH

The account we are about to give took place at the very beginning of the Ministry of Christ. The Scripture says:

"And He taught in their Synagogues, being glorified of all *(this was the beginning; it would soon change)*.

"And He came to Nazareth, where He had been brought up *(makes vivid the fact that Jesus was Very Man, even as He was Very God)***:** **and, as His custom was** *(in our language presently He was faithful to Church)***, He went into the Synagogue on the Sabbath Day, and stood up for to read** *(it was common to ask visitors to expound on the Word)*.

"And there was delivered unto Him the Book *(Scroll)* **of the Prophet Isaiah. And when He had opened the Book, He found the place where it was written** *(Isa. 61:1)*,"

THE SPIRIT OF THE LORD

"The Spirit of the Lord *is* **upon Me** *(we learn here of* *the absolute necessity of the Person and Work of the Holy Spirit within our lives)*, **because He has anointed Me** *(Jesus is the ultimate Anointed One; consequently, the Anointing of the Holy Spirit actually belongs to Christ, and the Anointing we have actually comes by His Authority [Jn. 16:14])* **to preach the Gospel to the poor** *(the poor in spirit)*; **He has sent Me to heal the brokenhearted** *(sin breaks the heart, or else is responsible for it being broken; only Jesus can heal this malady)*, **to preach Deliverance to the captives** *(if it is to be noticed, He didn't say to 'deliver the captives,' but rather, 'preach Deliverance,' which refers to the Cross [Jn. 8:32])*, **and recovering of sight to the blind** *(the Gospel opens the eyes of those who are Spiritually blind)*, **to set at liberty them who are bruised** *(the vicissitudes of life at times place a person in a mental or Spiritual prison; the Lord Alone, and through what He did at the Cross, can open this prison door)*,

"**To preach the acceptable Year of the Lord** *(it is believed that the day on which Jesus delivered this Message was the first day of the year of Jubilee)*.

"**And He closed the Book, and He gave** *it* **again to the Minister, and sat down** *(portrays the custom of that time)*. **And the eyes of all them who were in the Synagogue were fastened on Him** *(even though most there would fail to see it, this represented a moment far exceeding anything these people had ever known)*.

"**And He began to say unto them, This day is this Scripture fulfilled in your ears** *(in effect, He is saying, 'I am the Messiah,' the fulfillment of these Scriptures)*" **(Lk. 4:15-21).**

THE TEACHING OF OUR LORD
ABOUT THE HOLY SPIRIT

Jesus, in teaching His Disciples, had more to say about the Holy Spirit the last few days of His earthly Life than He had the three previous years of His Ministry all put together. Why?

There were two reasons for this. They are:

• Jesus was with them in Person and, thereby, met their every need. Now that He is about to leave, He will tell them that He will send them another Comforter, Who will *"abide with you forever"* (Jn. 14:16). That's the reason that after His Resurrection from the dead and His Ascension back to Glory, His followers did not grieve for Him, and for all the obvious reasons. First of all, they knew that He was alive because they had seen Him after His Resurrection. Secondly, He promised to send them the Holy Spirit, and the Day of Pentecost proves the fact that He most definitely did. In other words, they were not serving a dead Saviour, but rather, a risen Lord!

• He plainly told them:

"I have yet many things to say unto you *(pertained to the entirety of the New Covenant that would be given to the Apostle Paul, and which foundation had already been laid by Christ)*, but you cannot bear them now" (Jn. 16:12).

The Holy Spirit would remedy that situation, which He most definitely did.

The following is some of the teaching that He gave to them:

THE SPIRIT OF TRUTH

He said:

"Howbeit when He, the Spirit of Truth, is come *(which He did on the Day of Pentecost)*, He will guide you into all Truth *(if our Faith is properly placed in Christ and the Cross, the Holy Spirit can then bring forth Truth to us; He doesn't guide into some Truth, but rather 'all Truth')*: for He shall not speak of Himself *(tells us not only What He does, but Whom He represents)*; but whatsoever He shall hear, *that* shall He speak *(doesn't refer to lack of knowledge, for the Holy Spirit is God, but rather He will proclaim*

the Work of Christ only)**: and He will show you things to
come** *(pertains to the New Covenant, which would shortly
be given).*"

HE SHALL RECEIVE OF MINE AND
SHALL SHOW IT UNTO YOU

"**He shall glorify Me** *(will portray Christ and what
Christ did at the Cross for dying humanity)***: for He shall
receive of Mine** *(the benefits of the Cross)***, and shall show
it* **unto you** *(which He did, when He gave these great Truths
to the Apostle Paul [Rom., Chpts. 6-8, etc.]).*

"**All things that the Father has are Mine** *(has always
been the case; however, due to the Cross, all these things
can now be given to the Believer as well)***: therefore said
I, that He shall take of Mine, and shall show** *it* **unto
you** *(the foundation of all the Holy Spirit reveals to the
Church is what Christ did at the Cross [Rom. 6:3-14;
8:1-2, 11; I Cor. 1:17-18, 21, 23; 2:2; Gal., Chpt. 5, etc.])*"
(Jn. 16:13-15).

THE HOLY SPIRIT IN OLD TESTAMENT TIMES

As we have already stated, every single thing done on this
Earth by the Godhead, irrespective of the time, whether before
the Cross or after the Cross, has always been done, and without
exception, through the Power, Office, Agency, and Person of the
Holy Spirit. There has only been one exception to this, and that
is the First Advent of Christ; however, even as we've been stating for the last few pages, the Holy Spirit was extremely active
in everything that Christ did. And yet, with the exception of
the Lord Jesus Christ, the Holy Spirit was limited as to what
He could do before the Cross.

The reason had to do with the fact that the sin debt, which
was owed by every human being because of Adam's Fall, could
not be removed by the blood of bulls and goats (Heb. 10:4).

The fact that the sin debt remained, as stated, greatly hindered the Holy Spirit.

When Jesus died on the Cross, paying the price by the shedding of His Precious Blood, the sin debt was forever lifted, and in totality, at least for all who will believe (Jn. 3:16). Now, under the New Covenant, the Holy Spirit is able to function in a brand new dimension.

"Jesus, Your Life is mine,
"Dwell evermore in me;
"And let me see,
"That nothing can untwine,
"Your Life from mine."

"Your Life in me be shown,
"Lord, I would henceforth seek,
"To think and speak,
"Your Thoughts, Your Words alone,
"No more my own."

"Your Love, Your Joy, Your Peace,
"Continuously impart,
"Unto my heart,
"Fresh springs that never cease,
"But still increase."

"The Blessed reality,
"Of Resurrection Power,
"Your Church's dower,
"Life more abundantly,
"Lord, give to me."

"Your fullest Gift, O Lord,
"Now at Your Word I claim,
"Through Your dear Name,
"And touch the rapturous chord,

"Of praise forth-toward."

"Jesus, my life is Thine,
"And evermore shall be,
"Hidden in Thee,
"For nothing can untwine,
"Your Life from mine."

CHAPTER TWO

How Does The Cross Make The Work Of The Holy Spirit Possible?

QUESTION:

HOW DOES THE CROSS MAKE THE WORK OF THE HOLY SPIRIT POSSIBLE?

ANSWER:

Everything the Holy Spirit has ever done on this Earth, with the exception of the time of Creation (Gen. 1:2), has been made possible by the Cross of Christ. Of course, before Jesus came, the Sacrificial System served as a stopgap measure, so to speak. But, inasmuch as the blood of bulls and goats was woefully insufficient to take away sins (Heb. 10:4), this limited the Holy Spirit as to what He could do for humanity. However, to be sure, He did all that was possible for Him to do at the time.

THE SACRIFICIAL SYSTEM

As we have previously stated, the Lord introduced the Sacrificial System immediately after the Fall of Adam and Eve, which caused them to be driven out of the Garden. He did so for many reasons, but the primary reason at the time was that they could have forgiveness of sins and fellowship with Him. However, it had to be through the Sacrificial System, which consisted of a lamb being offered as a whole Burnt Offering. The Fourth Chapter of Genesis sets the stage for the conflict between God's Way, which is the Cross of Christ, and man's way, which is that of his own concoctions. It has held true from then until now.

AN ILLUSTRATION

Sometime back a couple gave an EXPOSITOR'S STUDY BIBLE to their pastor. The pastor was involved in a particular denomination that did not like Jimmy Swaggart at all.

At any rate, the next Sunday morning following the Bible being given to him, he made the statement from behind the pulpit that, *"Jesus didn't pay it all at Calvary's Cross."* Now, that's an interesting statement!

My Grandson Gabriel was talking with the couple and they were asking him, *"Should we leave this church and find another one?"* *"Unequivocally yes,"* Gabriel quickly answered! In fact, as it regards most churches presently, the people would do better if they did not attend. One cannot sit under false doctrine and not be influenced by such, and in a very negative way. Untold millions are in Hell right now because of that very thing, and sadly, untold millions of others, in fact, the majority of the world's present population, are on their way to that place of darkness.

There is nothing in the world worse than a false way of Salvation. Regrettably, if the Church omits the Cross, it has omitted God's Way, and to be sure, there is no other way. To be blunt, it's the Cross of Christ or it is Hellfire. That's the reason the great Apostle wrote to the Church at Corinth saying, *"Christ sent me not to baptize, but to preach the Gospel: not with wisdom of words, lest the Cross of Christ should be made of none effect"* (I Cor. 1:17). Paul wasn't knocking Water Baptism; he was merely stating, and unequivocally so, that the emphasis must always be on the Cross of Christ and never other things, as worthwhile as those things may be in their own right. We should not forget that!

Please remember, we aren't speaking here of mundane matters, but rather, the destination of the eternal soul of man. To be sure, nothing is more important than that. Paul said a long time ago, and it holds true presently:

"**Am I therefore become your enemy, because I tell you the truth?** *(A real friend is one who will tell his friend the truth, even though it hurts.)*

"**They zealously affect you** *(speaks of the Judaizers attempting to subvert the Galatians in order to win them over to themselves)*, *but* **not well** *(not for your good)*; **yes, they would exclude you** *(they would shut the Galatians out from the benefits of the Gospel of Grace)*, **that you might**

affect them *(means to be drawn to their side).*

"But *it is* **good to be zealously affected always in** *a* **good thing** *(Paul wanted the Galatians to be as zealous over Christ and the Cross as it seems they were tending to be over false doctrine),* **and not only when I am present with you.** *(Their zeal for the right thing should be present at all times.)*"

UNTIL CHRIST BE FORMED IN YOU

"My little children *(presents the language of deep affection and emotion),* **of whom I travail in birth again** *(deliver to you again the rudiments of the great Message of Christ and Him Crucified, as though you had never heard it to begin with)* **until Christ be formed in you** *(presents the work only the Holy Spirit can do, and does so exclusively within the parameters of the Sacrifice of Christ, which must always be the Object of our Faith),*

"I desire to be present with you now *(as a loving parent wants to be at the side of a sick child),* **and to change my voice** *(refers to the fact that his true love for them would more profitably come through were he only standing before them in person);* **for I stand in doubt of you.** *(The Apostle was perplexed as to how the Galatians could have forsaken the Holy Spirit, substituting in His Place the cold issues of dead Law. Any Christian who presently has as his object of Faith anything but the Cross is following the same course as the Galatians of old)*" **(Gal. 4:16-20).**

If the preacher is trying to please everybody, above all, he most definitely is not pleasing God. Concerning that, Paul also said:

ANOTHER GOSPEL

The Apostle in speaking to the same Churches in Galatia said:

"I marvel that you are so soon removed from Him

(the Holy Spirit) **Who called you into the Grace of Christ** *(made possible by the Cross)* **unto another gospel** *(anything which doesn't have the Cross as its Object of Faith)***:**

"Which is not another *(presents the fact that Satan's aim is not so much to deny the Gospel, which he can little do, as to corrupt it)***; but there be some who trouble you, and would pervert the Gospel of Christ** *(once again, to make the object of Faith something other than the Cross)***."**

ACCURSED

"But though we *(Paul and his associates)***, or an Angel from Heaven, preach any other gospel unto you than that which we have preached unto you** *(Jesus Christ and Him Crucified)***, let him be accursed** *(eternally condemned; the Holy Spirit speaks this through Paul, making this very serious)***.**

"As we said before, so say I now again *(at some time past, he had said the same thing to them, making their defection even more serious)***, If any** *man* **preach any other gospel unto you** *(anything other than the Cross)* **than that you have received** *(which Saved your souls)***, let him be accursed** *('eternally condemned,' which means the loss of the soul)***.**

"For do I now persuade men, or God? *(In essence, Paul is saying, 'Do I preach man's doctrine, or God's?')* **or do I seek to please men?** *(This is what false apostles do.)* **for if I yet pleased men, I should not be the Servant of Christ** *(one cannot please both men and God at the same time)***"** **(Gal. 1:6-10).**

WHAT TYPE OF OTHER GOSPEL?

The type of gospel of which Paul spoke was anything other than *"Christ and Him Crucified."* Please note the following carefully:

• **The Source of all blessings that we receive from God is** the Lord Jesus Christ (Jn. 14:6; Col. 2:10-15).

• The Cross of Christ, and the Cross of Christ alone, is the Means by which these things are given to us (Rom. 6:3-5; I Cor. 1:17, 18, 23; 2:2; Gal. 6:14).

• The Cross of Christ as the Object of our Faith, and the Cross of Christ alone as the Object of our Faith, is the way and, in fact, the only way that we can receive these things given to us, which Source is Christ and which Means is the Cross (Rom. 5:1-2; 6:1-14; Gal., Chpt. 5; Eph. 2:13-18).

• The Holy Spirit Alone is the arbiter as it regards our Faith and, in fact, everything we do (Rom. 8:1-2, 11; Eph. 2:13-18).

Getting back to the pattern laid down at the very dawn of time, it quickly becomes apparent as to the difficulties faced by the Child of God. Living for the Lord is not a simple thing. The first three Chapters of Genesis give us the re-creation of this planet plus the creation of man and his ignominious Fall. Beginning with the Fourth Chapter of Genesis to the end of Revelation 22:21, instructions are given as to how to live for God. Considering the voluminous amount of information, it should give us an idea as to the complexity of this situation. As we've stated, and say it again, it's not simple! As we have also stated, God has a way and man has a way. They are forever at juxtaposition with each other. Let's see what this Fourth Chapter tells us:

A MAN FROM THE LORD

"**And Adam knew Eve his wife** *(is the Biblical connotation of the union of husband and wife in respect to the sex act)*; **and she conceived, and bore Cain** *(the first child born to this union, and would conclude exactly as the Lord said it would, with 'sorrow')*, **and said, I have gotten a man from the LORD** *(by Eve using the title 'LORD,' which means 'Covenant God,' and which refers to the 'Seed of the woman,' [Gen. 3:15], she thought Cain was the Promised One; she evidently didn't realize that it was impossible for fallen man to bring forth the Promised Redeemer)*.

"**And she again bore his brother Abel** *('Abel' means 'vanity;' Cain being the oldest, this shows that Eve by now had become disillusioned with her firstborn, undoubtedly seeing traits in him which she knew could not be of the Promised Seed; she was losing Faith in God.).* **And Abel was a keeper of sheep, but Cain was a tiller of the ground** *(both were honorable professions).*"

AN OFFERING UNTO THE LORD?

"**And in process of time it came to pass** *(the phrase used here refers to a long indefinite period),* **that Cain brought of the fruit of the ground an offering unto the LORD.** *(This was probably the first offering that he brought, even though the Lord had explained to the First Family the necessity of the Sacrificial System, that is, if they were to have any type of communion with God and forgiveness of sins.*

"*There is evidence that Adam, at least for a while, offered up sacrifices. Cain knew the type of Sacrifice that the Lord would accept, but he rebelled against that admonition, demanding that God accept the labor of his hands, which, in fact, God could not accept. So we have in the persons of Cain and Abel, the first examples of a religious man of the world and a genuine man of Faith.)*"

THE FIRSTLINGS OF THE FLOCK

"**And Abel, he also brought of the firstlings of his flock and of the fat thereof** *(this is what God demanded; it was a blood sacrifice of an innocent victim, a lamb, which proclaimed the fact that Abel recognized his need of a Redeemer, and that One was coming Who would redeem lost humanity; the Offering of Abel was a Type of Christ and the price that He would pay on the Cross of Calvary in order for man to be redeemed).* **And the LORD had**

respect unto Abel and to his offering: *(As stated, this was a Type of Christ and the Cross, the only Offering which God will respect. Abel's Altar is beautiful to God's Eye and repulsive to man's. Cain's altar is beautiful to man's eye and repulsive to God's. These 'altars' exist today; around the one that is Christ and His atoning Work, few are gathered, around the other, many. God accepts the slain lamb and rejects the offered fruit; and the offering being rejected, so of necessity is the offerer.)"*

THE LORD HAD NO RESPECT FOR CAIN'S OFFERING

"But unto Cain and to his offering He had not respect *(let us say it again, God has no respect for any proposed way of Salvation, other than 'Jesus Christ and Him Crucified' [I Cor. 1:23; 2:2]).* **And Cain was very angry, and his countenance fell** *(that which filled Abel with peace filled Cain with wrath; the carnal mind displays its enmity against all this Truth which so gladdens and satisfies the heart of the Believer).*

"And the LORD said unto Cain *(God loves Cain, just as He did Abel, and wishes to bless him also),* **Why are you angry** *(Abel's Altar speaks of Repentance, of Faith, and of the Precious Blood of Christ, the Lamb of God without blemish; Cain's altar tells of pride, unbelief, and self-righteousness, which always illicits anger)?* **and why is your countenance fallen** *(anger, in one form or the other, accompanies self-righteousness, for that is what plagued Cain; God's Righteousness can only come by the Cross, while self-righteousness is by dependence on works)?"*

THE RIGHT SACRIFICE

"If you do well, shall you not be accepted *(if you bring the correct sacrifice, and thereby place your Faith)?* **and if you do not well, sin** *(a Sin-Offering)* **lies at the door**

(a lamb was at the door of the Tabernacle)**. And unto
you shall be his desire, and you shall rule over him** (the
Lord promised Cain dominion over the Earth of that day,
if he would only offer up, and place his trust in, the right
Sacrifice; He promises the same presently to all who trust
Christ [Mat. 5:5])**."**

THE FIRST MURDER WAS CAUSED BY RELIGION

**"And Cain talked with Abel his brother: and it came
to pass, when they were in the field, that Cain rose up
against Abel his brother, and killed him** (the first murder;
Cain's religion was too refined to kill a lamb, but not too
cultured to murder his brother; God's Way of Salvation
fills the heart with love; man's way of salvation inflames it
with hatred; 'Religion' has ever been the greatest cause of
bloodshed)**.**

**"And the LORD said unto Cain, Where is Abel your
brother?** (Adam sins against God and Cain sins against
man. In their united conduct, we have sin in all its forms,
and that on the first page of human history.) **And he said,
I know not: Am I my brother's keeper** (He showed himself a 'liar' in saying, 'I know not'; 'wicked and profane' in
thinking he could hide his sin from God; 'unjust' in denying
himself to be his brother's keeper; 'obstinate and desperate'
in not confessing his sin)**?"**

WHAT HAVE YOU DONE?

"And He (God) **said, What have you done** (this
concerns man's sins, the fruit of his sinful nature)**? The
voice of your brother's blood cries unto Me from the
ground.** (There is some Scriptural evidence that Cain
cut his brother's throat. Thus, with the first shedding of
human blood, that ominous thought sprang up, divinely
bestowed, that the Earth will grant no peace to the one who

has wantonly stained her fair face with the life-stream of man)" (Gen. 4:1-10).

The Sacrificial System would continue until the First Advent of Christ, a time frame of approximately four thousand years. During that time, God raised up a people of which at least some of them among the group would have Faith in God and, thereby, serve Him. To be sure, Israel was raised up from the loins of Abraham and the womb of Sarah, but regrettably, even after they grew into a large nation, most of them did not live for God. In fact, they destroyed themselves by crucifying their Messiah and our Saviour, the Lord Jesus Christ. Irrespective, the price was paid, and the Blood of the Sacred Victim was shed in order that the fallen sons of Adam's lost race could be Saved. The song says:

"Millions have come,
"But there's still room for one,
"There's room at the Cross for you!"

WERE PEOPLE BORN-AGAIN BEFORE THE CROSS?

Yes! People were Born-Again before the Cross, but they did not have nearly the privileges that we presently have since the Cross.

We must remember that while Grace and Truth came by Jesus Christ, still, He operated under the Old Covenant. In other words, the happenings of the four Gospels, Matthew, Mark, Luke, and John, took place under the auspices of the Old Covenant. Admittedly, those times were the doorway to the New Covenant but still were under the Old.

The New Covenant did not come about until the Lord gave its meaning to the Apostle Paul, which, in essence, is the meaning of the Cross. Even though the date is not certain, it is probable that, regarding Paul, this Revelation took place about the year A.D. 44 or 45.

JESUS AND NICODEMUS

Jesus plainly told Nicodemus that for one to enter the Kingdom of God he had to be *"Born-Again,"* and remember, all of this was still functioning under the Old Covenant. The following is the account of this particular meeting between our Lord and Nicodemus:

"There was a man of the Pharisees, named Nicodemus *(said to have been one of the three richest men in Jerusalem)*, a Ruler of the Jews *(a member of the Sanhedrin, the ruling body of Israel)*:

"The same came to Jesus by night *(it is not known exactly as to why he came by night)*, and said unto Him, Rabbi, we know that You are a Teacher come from God *(the pronoun 'we' could indicate that Nicodemus represented several members of the Sanhedrin; Nicodemus addresses Christ here as a man, and not as God; the Cross would change him)*: for no man can do these miracles that You do, except God be with Him *(in this, he is correct!)*."

YOU MUST BE BORN-AGAIN

"Jesus answered and said unto him *(presents an answer totally different from that which he expected)*, Verily, verily, I say unto you, Except a man be born again *(the term, 'Born-Again,' means that man has already had a natural birth, but now must have a Spiritual Birth, which comes by Faith in Christ, and what He has done for us at the Cross, and is available to all)*, he cannot see the Kingdom of God *(actually means that without the New Birth, one cannot understand or comprehend the 'Kingdom of God')*."

THE CONFUSED MIND OF NICODEMUS

"Nicodemus said unto Him, How can a man be born when he is old? *(This proclaims this spiritual leader of*

Israel as having no knowledge at all of what Jesus is say-ing. Had he truly been 'Born-Again,' he would have under-stood these terms.) **can he enter the second time into his mother's womb, and be born?** *(It seems he did not know the language of the Prophets concerning circumcision of the heart [Deut 30:6; Jer. 4:4], and concerning a hard heart and right spirit [Ps. 51:10; Ezek. 36:26-27].)*

    "Jesus answered, Verily, verily, I say unto you, Except a man be born of water and *of* **the Spirit** *(the phrase, 'born of water,' speaks of the natural birth, which Jesus says in the next Verse, and pertains to a baby being born; being 'Born of the Spirit' speaks of a Spiritual Birth, which is brought about by God Alone; and neither does it speak of Water Baptism)*, **he cannot enter into the Kingdom of God."**

BORN OF THE SPIRIT

    "That which is born of the flesh is flesh *(has to do with the natural birth, and is illustrated, as stated, by the phrase, 'born of water')*; **and that which is born of the Spirit is spirit** *(has to do with that which is solely of God; the one [flesh] has no relationship to the other [Spirit] and cannot be joined)*.

    "Marvel not that I said unto you, You must be born again *(evidently addresses itself to the surprise, which must have been registered on the countenance of Nicodemus)*.

    "The wind blows where it lists, and you hear the sound thereof, but cannot tell from where it comes, and whither it goes *(presents the way in which Jesus explains the 'Born-Again' experience; He likens it to the wind which comes and goes, but is impossible to tell exactly how)*: **so is everyone who is born of the Spirit** *(it is a Spiritual Birth, so it cannot be explained intellectually)*."

HOW CAN THESE THINGS BE?

    "Nicodemus answered and said unto Him, How can

these things be? *(Not being 'Born-Again' at this particular time, and despite his vast intelligence in other areas, he has no understanding of this great Truth; he is religious but lost!)*

"Jesus answered and said unto him, Are you a Master of Israel *(was held in very high regard as one of the spiritual leaders of Israel)***, and knowest not these things?** *(As a spiritual leader, he should have known the way of Salvation, but the sad fact was he didn't)***"** **(Jn. 3:1-10).**

In Old Testament Times, which spans all the way back to Adam and Eve, when a person expressed Faith in what the sacrifices represented, they were at that time *"Born-Again."* There has never been but one way of Salvation, and it is the same for all people, and it is by Faith. However, it must be Faith in Christ, and in Old Testament Times, Faith was to be placed in what the sacrifices represented. People were Saved before the Cross by looking forward to that event; people are Saved after the Cross by looking backward to that event. As stated, even though people before the Cross were Born-Again, still, they did not have nearly the privileges that Born-Again Believers had and have after the Cross. Concerning this New Covenant, Paul said:

A BETTER COVENANT

"But now *(since the Cross)* **has He** *(the Lord Jesus)* **obtained a more excellent Ministry** *(the New Covenant in Jesus' Blood is superior, and takes the place of the Old Covenant in animal blood)***, by how much also He is the Mediator of a Better Covenant** *(proclaims the fact that Christ officiates between God and man according to the arrangements of the New Covenant)***, which was established upon better Promises.** *(This presents the New Covenant, explicitly based on the cleansing and forgiveness of all sin, which the Old Covenant could not do)***"** **(Heb. 8:6).**

UNDER THE OLD COVENANT

The following constitutes several things that Believers at that time did not have, which we presently have. They are:

• Under the Old Covenant the Holy Spirit could not come into the hearts and lives of Believers to dwell permanently. It was because the sin debt could not be eradicated by animal blood. It served as an Atonement, but only in a stopgap measure. Now, due to the Cross paying the sin debt, and in totality, the Holy Spirit can come into the heart and life of the Believer, which He does at conversion, and there abide permanently (Jn. 14:16).

• Due to the fact that the Holy Spirit did not function in one's heart and life before the Cross, there was no help in the sanctification process. In other words, there could be no Victory at that time over the sin nature. Presently, due to what Christ has done at the Cross, the Holy Spirit constantly helps us, actually requiring only one thing on our part. The requirement is that our Faith be placed explicitly in the Cross of Christ and no place else. The Holy Spirit, Who works exclusively within the parameters of the Finished Work of Christ, will work mightily on our behalf, which Old Testament Believers did not have.

• Whenever Believers died under the Old Covenant, due to the fact that the sin debt remained, they were not taken to Heaven, but rather, went down into Paradise. They were there comforted, but still, they were captives of Satan. In other words, their being delivered from this place and actually made a captive of Christ, awaited the Cross. Now, since the Cross, when Believers pass away, they are instantly taken by Angels into the portals of Glory, there to be with the Lord Jesus Christ (Phil. 1:23).

• Before the Cross, Believers did not have the Holy Spirit to help them and to intercede on their behalf, which we now have (Rom. 8:26).

This is what Jesus was talking about when He said to His Disciples, *"For He dwells with you, and shall be in you"* (Jn. 14:17).

All of this, even as we've already stated, is why Jesus said that all who were in the New Covenant had greater privileges than John the Baptist, even though he was the greatest Prophet born of woman (Lk. 7:28).

In effect, Jesus will now tell Nicodemus as to how this great Plan of Redemption will be brought about, making the animal sacrifices unnecessary. He said:

THE WORD OF GOD

"Verily, verily, I say unto you, We speak that we do know *(Jesus was speaking of the Triune Godhead, and as well of all the 'Apostles and Prophets'; in essence, He is speaking of the Word of God, and is directing Nicodemus to that Source instead of tradition)*, and testify that we have seen *(means that one can actually 'see' the fruit or benefits of this 'Testimony,' i.e., 'The Word of God')*; and you receive not our witness *(has to do with the Jewish Sanhedrin)*."

HEAVENLY THINGS

"If I have told you earthly things, and you believe not *(refers to the earthly type and events in the Bible, such as the Sacrifices and Feast Days, etc., which Nicodemus no doubt read many times, but was so blind that he did not see nor believe their lessons)*, how shall you believe, if I tell you *of* Heavenly things? *(In effect, this tells us that if we are to know Jesus as God [Heavenly things], we must first know Jesus and the Incarnation [earthly things]. Nicodemus had addressed Jesus as merely a 'Teacher.' So, until he understands God becoming flesh and dwelling among men, he will not understand Heavenly things.)*

"And no man has ascended up to Heaven, but He Who came down from Heaven *(He came down from Heaven and became Man, and approximately three and a half years later will ascend up to Heaven, when His Mission is complete)*, **even the Son of Man which is in Heaven** *(better translated, 'which is from Heaven').***"**

THE SON OF MAN LIFTED UP

"And as Moses lifted up the serpent in the wilderness *(refers to Num. 21:5-9; the 'serpent' represents Satan, who is the originator of sin, who must be defeated, and was defeated at Calvary's Cross)***, even so must the Son of Man be lifted up** *(refers to Christ being lifted up on the Cross, which alone could defeat Satan and sin)***:**

"That whosoever *(destroys the erroneous hyper-Calvinistic explanation of predestination that some are predestined to be Saved, while all others are predestined to be lost; the word 'whosoever' means that none are excluded from being lost, and none are excluded from being Saved)* **believes** **in Him** *(believes in Christ and what He did at the Cross; otherwise, one would perish)* **should not perish, but have Eternal Life** *(the Life of God, the Ever-Living One, Who has life in Himself, and Alone has immortality).***"**

FAITH

"For God so loved the world *(presents the God kind of love)***, that He gave His Only Begotten Son** *(gave Him up to the Cross, for that's what it took to redeem humanity)***, that whosoever believes in Him should not perish, but have Everlasting Life.**

"For God sent not His Son into the world to condemn the world *(means that the object of Christ's Mission was to save, but the issue to those who reject Him must and can only be condemnation)***; but that the world through Him might be saved** *(Jesus Christ is the only Salvation for the world; there is no other! as well, He is Salvation only through the Cross; consequently, the Cross must ever be the Object of our Faith)***" (Jn. 3:11-17).**

THE ROLE OF THE HOLY SPIRIT REGARDING
THE DEATH OF CHRIST

As we have previously stated, the Holy Spirit functioned in Christ to such an extent that Jesus, while on the Cross, did not die until the Holy Spirit told Him to die. Concerning this, the Scripture says:

"**How much more shall the Blood of Christ** *(while the sacrifice of animals could cleanse from ceremonial defilement, only the Blood of Christ could cleanse from actual sin; so that throws out every proposed solution other than the Cross)*, **Who through the Eternal Spirit offered Himself without spot to God** *(in this phrase, we learn Christ did not die until the Holy Spirit told Him to die; in fact, no man took His Life from Him; He laid it down freely [Jn. 10:17-18]; as well, the fact that Jesus 'offered Himself without spot to God' shoots down the unscriptural doctrine that 'Jesus died Spiritually' on the Cross; had He died Spiritually, meaning He became a sinner on the Cross, He could not have offered Himself without spot to God, as should be obvious; God could only accept a Perfect Sacrifice; when He died on the Cross, He took upon Himself the sin penalty of the human race, which was physical death; inasmuch as His Offering of Himself was Perfect, God accepted it as payment in full for all sin – past, present, and future, at least for those who will believe [Jn. 3:16])*, **purge your conscience from dead works to serve the Living God?** *('Dead works' are anything other than simple Faith in the Cross of Christ, i.e., 'the Blood of Christ')*" **(Heb. 9:14).**

When Jesus died on the Cross, He satisfied the demands of a thrice-Holy God, and did so by giving Himself as a perfect Sacrifice, thereby, taking upon Himself the sin penalty of the human race, at least for all who will believe. When He did this, He atoned for all sin, past, present and future, again, for all who will believe (Jn. 3:3, 16).

By atoning for all sin, this made it possible for the Holy Spirit to come into the heart and life of the Believer at conversion, which He definitely does, and there to abide forever (Jn. 14:16-17). In other words, it is the Cross of Christ that made it possible for the Holy Spirit to come to this world in a totally new dimension. That's how important that the Cross of Christ was and is! That's why the Cross of Christ is the Foundation of the Faith. That's why the Cross of Christ must ever be the Object of our Faith, even on a daily basis (Lk. 9:23; 14:27).

"Amazing Grace! how sweet the sound,
"That Saved a wretch like me!
"I once was lost, but now am found,
"Was blind, but now I see."

"'Twas Grace that taught my heart to fear,
"And Grace, my fears relieved;
"How precious did that Grace appear,
"The Hour I first believed!"

"Thro' many dangers, toils and snares,
"I have already come;
"'Tis Grace hath bro't me safe thus far,
"And Grace will lead me home."

"The Lord has promised good to me,
"His Word my hope secures,
"He will my shield and portion be,
"As long as life endures."

"When we've been there ten thousand years,
"Bright shining as the Sun,
"We've no less days to sing God's praise,
"Than when we've first begun."

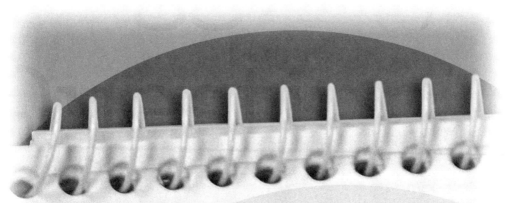

CHAPTER THREE

How Does The Holy Spirit Work?

QUESTION:

HOW DOES THE HOLY SPIRIT WORK?

ANSWER:

Unfortunately, most Believers take the Holy Spirit for grant-ed, if He is given any shift at all. Basically, the non-Pentecostal world, for the most part, ignores Him altogether. Sadder still, the Pentecostal world, which is supposed to be knowledgeable on this subject, limits Him to their prayer language, and I refer to praying with other Tongues. Some things about the Gifts of the Spirit are known as well, but even these things are, sadly and regrettably, falling by the way. Most Pentecostals simply do not know how the Holy Spirit works despite being baptized with the Spirit (Mat. 3:11; Acts 2:4). As a result of this lack of knowledge, this particular Chapter will, without a doubt, be one of, if not the most important Chapter in the entirety of this book. To know how the Holy Spirit works takes one out of the wasteland of quandary into Biblical knowledge that can change one's life. The things we will say in this Chapter, as will become obvious, will be very, very simple but are completely unknown by virtually all of modern Christians. Once we begin to understand the Word of God as we should, it's amazing as to how simple it really is. The problem is that preachers have a tendency to confuse the issue.

WHY DO PAUL'S WRITINGS SEEM TO BE DIFFICULT?

The truth is, Paul's writings are difficult to understand, but only if we don't have the key that unlocks this treasure house of information.

The basic reason has to do with the fact that properly un-derstanding the New Covenant takes us from *"walking after the flesh,"* to *"walking after the Spirit."* To be frank, that's a journey of a lifetime.

Walking after the flesh is that which is indicative to human beings. It refers to our education, motivation, strength, power, talent, intellectualism, etc., in other words, that, as stated, which is indicative to human beings. Functioning after the Spirit instead of the flesh is like a person who is right-handed having to function from a position of being left-handed. It can be done, but it's not simple, quick, or easy. The fact is that most of Christendom functions after the flesh with only brief forays into the world of the Holy Spirit, which is not meant to be the Biblical norm. Instead of us coming into the realm of the Spirit, i.e., *"Holy Spirit,"* we try to bring the Spirit into the realm of the flesh, which will never work. The Holy Spirit, through the Apostle Paul, plainly and bluntly stated:

"So then they that are in the flesh cannot please God" (Rom. 8:8). But then the Apostle stated:

"**But you are not in the flesh** *(in one sense of the word is asking the question, 'Since you are now a Believer and no longer depending on the flesh, why are you resorting to the flesh?'),* **but in the Spirit** *(as a Believer, you now have the privilege of being led and empowered by the Holy Spirit; however, He will do such for us only on the premise of our Faith in the Finished Work of Christ),* **if so be that the Spirit of God dwell in you** *(if you are truly Saved).* **Now if any man have not the Spirit of Christ, he is none of His** *(Paul is saying that the work of the Spirit in our lives is made possible by what Christ did at Calvary, and the Resurrection)*" **(Rom. 8:9).**

WHY IS THE FLESH INSUFFICIENT?

The Apostle readily gives us the answer to why the flesh is insufficient! He said:

"**And if Christ** *be* **in you** *(He is in you through the Power and Person of the Spirit [Gal. 2:20]),* **the body** *is*

dead because of sin *(means that the physical body has been rendered helpless because of the Fall; consequently, the Believer trying to overcome by willpower presents a fruitless task)*; **but the Spirit *is* life because of Righteousness** *(only the Holy Spirit can make us what we ought to be, which means we cannot do it ourselves; once again, He performs all that He does within the confines of the Finished Work of Christ)*" **(Rom. 8:10).**

Even though we addressed it in the notes, which we copied word for word from THE EXPOSITOR'S STUDY BIBLE, still, this is so important that the following needs to be said and emphasized:

The Fall in the Garden of Eden made the physical body, in other words, what we can do as human beings, insufficient as it regards doing and living as we should, as it regards the Lord. So, if we depend upon this particular medium, over and over again the Holy Spirit through the Apostle tells us that we are going to fail.

THE HOLY SPIRIT ALONE CAN MAKE US WHAT WE OUGHT TO BE

This we must understand — that the Holy Spirit alone can make us what we ought to be. That's why this Chapter is so very, very important. If we don't know how the Holy Spirit works, while He most definitely will not leave us under such circumstances, and thank God for that, still, we will fall far short of what He can do, and wants to do, within our lives.

What we are facing in the spirit world, and I speak of the spirit world of darkness, is totally beyond our capacity. This is something the Believer must understand. That's why Paul said the following:

"**Finally, my Brethren, be strong in the Lord** *(be continually strengthened, which one does by constant Faith in* *the Cross)*, **and in the power of His Might.** *(This power is at our disposal. The Source is the Holy Spirit, but the Means is the Cross [I Cor. 1:18].)*

"**Put on the whole Armour of God** *(not just some, but all)*, **that you may be able to stand against the wiles of the Devil.** *(This refers to the 'stratagems' of Satan.)*"

WE WRESTLE NOT AGAINST FLESH AND BLOOD

"**For we wrestle not against flesh and blood** *(our foes are not human; however, Satan constantly uses human beings to carry out his dirty work)*, **but against principalities** *(rulers or beings of the highest rank and order in Satan's kingdom)*, **against powers** *(the rank immediately below the 'Principalities')*, **against the rulers of the darkness of this world** *(those who carry out the instructions of the 'Powers')*, **against spiritual wickedness in high** *places.* *(This refers to demon spirits)*" **(Eph. 6:10-12).**

At this juncture, please allow me to relate a dream which the Lord gave me many, many years ago. I think it will throw some light on the situation.

A PERSONAL ILLUSTRATION

If I remember correctly, the year was 1953. Frances and I were married in 1952, and Donnie was born in 1954. So the occasion must have been the early part of 1953.

At that time, Frances and I lived in a little tiny house trailer. I was just beginning to preach the Gospel.

Frances had already gone to bed. I stayed up, sitting in the front part of the little trailer, studying the Word of God. At a point in time, there seemed to be a most oppressive spirit that came into the room, so powerful, in fact, that I couldn't shake it.

I left out of the little mobile home and started walking up and down the street right beside where we lived, which afforded some privacy, trying to pray. But, it was to no avail; I couldn't seem to pray.

SPIRITUAL OPPRESSION

While Christians cannot be demon possessed (I Cor. 3:16), Christians definitely can be demon oppressed. Oppression comes from without, as demon spirits attack the Child of God, and can do so in many and varied ways. It can take the form of sickness, tremendous nervous disorder, frayed nerves, and emotional instability, and is caused, once again, primarily because the Believer doesn't understand how the Holy Spirit works.

A short time ago while preaching on a Sunday Morning at Family Worship Center and dealing with this very subject, all of a sudden something very important dawned on me. I realized, even while I was addressing the audience, that I had not suffered one moment of demonic oppression since the Lord gave me the Revelation of the Cross in 1997. Being 2006 when I was addressing the audience that Sunday morning, that had been some nine years free of these efforts of Satan.

ALL VICTORY IS IN THE CROSS

Every single thing that the Believer receives from the Lord, and I mean everything, comes from Jesus Christ as the Source and through the Cross as the Means. In other words, it's the Cross of Christ that makes everything possible. It was at the Cross where our Lord satisfied the demands of the broken Law, and did so by giving Himself in Sacrifice, in fact, as a perfect Sacrifice. This being done, this as well satisfied the demands of a thrice-Holy God, at least for all who will believe (Col. 2:14-15; Jn. 3:16). The Believer must understand that! It is the Cross of Christ which has made everything possible. Of course, as I'm sure the reader understands, when we speak of the *"Cross,"* we aren't speaking of a wooden beam, but rather, that which Jesus there did. All of this means that in the Cross is all Salvation, in the Cross is all Victory, in the Cross is all Deliverance, in the Cross is Everything! In fact, the Believer cannot even remotely avail himself of Who Christ is, and What Christ has done, and did it all for us, unless he understands that the Cross of Christ is the Means by which all of this is carried out.

Satan could attack me vehemently before I understood the Cross because I was attempting to throw him off by the means of the flesh. In fact, that's the way that virtually the entirety of the modern church faces the evil one. It's by the flesh, which guarantees failure. That's the reason that Paul also said:

> "For the preaching *(Word)* of the Cross is to them who perish foolishness *(Spiritual things cannot be discerned by unredeemed people, but that doesn't matter; the Cross must be preached just the same, even as we shall see)*; but unto us who are Saved it is the Power of God. *(The Cross is the Power of God simply because it was there that the total sin debt was paid, giving the Holy Spirit, in Whom the Power resides, latitude to work mightily within our lives)*" (I Cor. 1:18).

In other words, the Holy Spirit works exclusively within the parameters of the Finished Work of Christ, i.e., *"the Cross of Christ."*

IN A DREAM I SAW THE SPIRIT OF DARKNESS THAT WAS TRYING TO DESTROY ME

The night in question back in 1953, unable, seemingly, to throw off the powers of darkness, I finally retired to bed. Sometime in the early morning hours before daylight, the Lord gave me the following dream:

In the dream I found myself in the front room of a house with which I was not acquainted. In other words, I did not know where I was or why I was there.

I remember looking around the room of the house where the

dream had placed me, noting that there was absolutely nothing in the room. No furniture, no pictures on the wall, nothing! There was not even a window in the room, only a door that led outside.

My first thoughts were, what am I doing here? Why am I in this place? Somehow, I could sense a foreboding, and my thoughts were, I've got to leave.

I turned to walk toward the door to exit the premises when, all of a sudden, standing in the doorway was the most hideous man/beast that words could ever begin to describe.

It must have stood about six feet tall or taller, and it had the body of a bear and the face of a man. As I looked at its countenance, I've never seen such evil. In fact, from its eyes, which seemed to be pools of evil all directed at me, as it began to descend upon me, it seemed to say, *"I have you now."*

As I looked at this creature, and as it slowly began to lumber toward me, I became so weak that I slumped to the floor. My knees simply would not hold me.

THE WEAPONS OF OUR WARFARE ARE NOT CARNAL

As I lay there on the floor too weak to get up, I began to feel around with my hand, trying to find something with which I could defend myself. There was nothing there! From that I was to learn that *"the weapons of our warfare are not carnal, but mighty through God to the pulling down of strongholds"* (II Cor. 10:4).

This thing was very close to standing over me now, poised to deliver the death blow. Without premeditation and without forethought, I screamed as loud as I could, *"In the Name of Jesus,"* even though my voice was no more than a whisper.

IN THE NAME OF JESUS

When I said that Name, even in my extremely weakened condition, it carried such Power that it was like something had hit this demon spirit in the head with a baseball bat. He clutched his head and began to stagger backwards, screaming all the time.

I learned that the Power of that Name was not predicated on my personal condition, on my personal strength, etc. In other words, it carried a weight, a Power, all its own.

And now I began to gather strength and finally stood to my feet. I said it again, *"In the Name of Jesus!"*

When I said it the second time, my voice was much stronger now, and this man/beast (demon spirit) slumped to the floor, still screaming and clutching its head. In fact, it was writhing on the floor like a snake that had just received the death blow.

Now, instead of it towering over me, I was towering over it.

I opened my mouth and for the third time said, *"In the Name of Jesus!"* Even though I exerted no strength at all, my voice sounded like a veritable Niagara. It was like my voice was connected to a public address system, which made it boom off the walls.

THE SOUND OF THE MIGHTY RUSHING WIND

And then, when I uttered that Name Jesus the third time, I distinctly heard *"a sound from Heaven as of a rushing mighty wind"* (Acts 2:2). I didn't see anything, but I distinctly heard it, and I knew it was the Holy Spirit.

Before my eyes, and mostly to my hearing, this *"Sound"* grew louder and louder as it came into the room. As stated, I saw absolutely nothing, but to be sure, what I heard I knew to be from the Lord.

The Power of that Sound hit that man/beast lying on the floor, and despite its bulk, swept it out the front door like it was a falling leaf in a March wind. I remember in the dream running to the door and looking out, seeing it wafting away on the wind until it was out of sight.

I awakened myself that early morning hour, praising the Lord with other Tongues. I knew that the dream was from the Lord. I knew that He was telling me something; however, at that time, I had no idea as to what it was.

As the years would pass, and the Lord would use us to touch much of this world with the Gospel of Jesus Christ, I came to understand that power of darkness that tried to destroy me. But, above all, I came to understand the Power of the Name of Jesus, which was of far greater magnitude than that of demon spirits. Yet, at the same time, I have learned that the forces arrayed against me and, in fact, every Believer, are so far beyond our capacity, as a mere human being, to oppose. In other words, if we try to oppose the powers of darkness by the means of the flesh, we will be defeated every single time. I had to learn that the hard way, and I greatly suspect that such is the occasion for every Believer as well. In other words, we don't learn these things quickly or easily.

In that dream that night, I learned what the mighty Name of Jesus could do, and I learned the Power of the Holy Spirit. What is impossible for us is nothing for Him. Of course, and as the reader understands, the Holy Spirit is God!

WILLPOWER IS NOT ENOUGH

Regrettably, most Christians are trying to live for God by the means of willpower. If they speak to someone about difficulties, most of the time, they will be told to *"try harder."* The truth is that they can try as hard as they might, but all to no avail!

Many Christians think that when they give their hearts to the Lord, their willpower is greatly strengthened. It isn't! You have the same willpower now that you had before you got Saved. And, if you try to live for God by the means of willpower, which, in effect, is the flesh, you will fail every single time, no matter how hard you try. Paul told us this in the great Seventh Chapter of Romans. This Chapter portrays snapshots out of the Apostle's own life and experience of trying to live for God before he understood the Message of the Cross. To be sure, and regrettably, it was a life of failure.

And yet, when he wrote these words, he full well understood God's Prescribed Order of Victory, but the Lord allowed him to give an example of his own experience that it might be an encouragement to us.

Before understanding the Cross, Paul tried to live for God by his own personal strength, i.e., *"his willpower."* He found to his dismay that it was woefully insufficient. He said:

"For I know that in me (that is, in my flesh,) dwells no good thing *(speaks of man's own ability, or rather the lack thereof, in comparison to the Holy Spirit, at least when it comes to spiritual things)*: for to will is present with me *(Paul is speaking here of his willpower; regrettably, most modern Christians are trying to live for God by means of willpower, thinking falsely that since they have come to Christ, they are now free to say 'no' to sin; that is the wrong way to look at the situation; the Believer cannot live for God by the strength of willpower; while the will is definitely important, it alone is not enough; the Believer must exercise Faith in Christ and the Cross, and do so constantly; then he will have the ability and strength to say 'yes' to Christ, which automatically says 'no' to the things of the world)*; but how to perform that which is good I find not *(outside of the Cross, it is impossible to find a way to do good)*" (Rom. 7:18).

As we stated in the notes, while the will is most definitely important, within itself, it is incapable of carrying out that which we must have. For that to be done, and I speak of Victory over the world, the flesh, and the Devil, the Holy Spirit Alone can carry out such direction of Victory within our lives.

IS THE WORK OF THE HOLY SPIRIT AUTOMATIC?

No! The Work of the Holy Spirit is not automatic.

Stop and think a moment. If the Work of the Holy Spirit within our hearts and lives were automatic, then there would never be another failure on the part of the Child of God. We would never take a wrong direction; we would never fail the

Lord, etc., but, we know that's not the case, don't we? While the Holy Spirit is God and, as such, can do anything, still, He has an agenda within our hearts and lives, and that is that we develop as we should in the Lord, coming from dependence on the flesh to dependence on the Holy Spirit. As we have stated, that is not a quick or uneventful journey. John Newton, who wrote *"Amazing Grace,"* said it well. He wrote:

> *"Thro' many dangers, toils and snares,*
> *"I have already come;*
> *"'Tis Grace hath bro't me safe thus far,*
> *"And Grace will lead me home."*

WHAT IS THE GRACE OF GOD?

The Grace of God is simply the Goodness of God extended to undeserving Saints. In other words, the Lord has many wonderful, good, and beautiful things to give to us, which we could never merit, no matter what we do. However, we limit Him as to what He can do for us and, in fact, desires to do, simply because we don't understand the Way and the Means that Grace operates.

How does it operate?

The Lord doesn't demand very much of us. If He did, most of us, and perhaps all of us, would fall by the wayside, but He does demand one thing, and this is critical to our Living for God, at least living successfully.

He demands that the Cross of Christ ever be the Object of our Faith. We must understand that the Grace of God, i.e., *"the Goodness of God,"* is made available to us strictly by and through the Cross of Christ. In other words, it's the Cross that gives the Lord the legal means to do all that He does for us. As we've stated, while Christ is the Source of all Grace, it is the Cross which is the Means by which this Grace is given to us. This demands that the Cross of Christ ever be the Object of our Faith. That's why Paul also said:

"Christ sent me not to baptize, but to preach the Gospel: not with wisdom of words, lest the Cross of Christ should be made of none effect" (I Cor. 1:17).

Was Paul denigrating Water Baptism? No!

The great Apostle was simply telling us that the emphasis in life and living must always be centered up on the Cross of Christ and never on other things, such as Water Baptism, as good and wonderful and Scriptural as those things might be in their own right.

We must ever understand that whatever it is we need from the Lord, and, in fact, we need everything, such cannot be merited, no matter what we do. We must understand that it's always a free gift, and the way this free gift is received is simply that our Faith be placed in the Means by which it comes to us, which is the Cross of Christ (Rom. 6:1-14; 8:1-2, 11; I Cor. 1:17, 18, 23; 2:2; Gal., Chpt. 5; 6:14; Eph. 2:13-18; Col. 2:14-15).

No, the Holy Spirit doesn't just work automatically within our hearts and lives. As we have stated, He doesn't demand much of us, but He does demand one thing, and that is not debatable. It is that our Faith be exclusively in Christ and what Christ has done for us at the Cross. We are to maintain our Faith in that capacity even on a daily basis (Lk. 9:23; 14:27). With our Faith properly placed, the Lord can and will do mighty things for us.

FAITH IS THE KEY

Faith is the key, but we must always understand, it is Faith in the correct Object, which is the Cross of Christ.

Every human being in this world has faith; however, for the most part, it's not the Faith that God recognizes. In fact, more books have been written on Faith, concerning the Lord, in the last fifty years than all the balance of the Church Age put together. Regrettably, most of the things in those books are not Biblical.

The only Faith that God will recognize is Faith in Christ

and what Christ has done for us at the Cross. That and that alone must ever be the Object of our Faith and must be such on a continuing basis. Concerning this, Paul said:

"What shall we say then that Abraham our father, as pertaining to the flesh, has found? *(Having stated that the Old Testament teaches that God justifies the sinner on the Faith principle as opposed to the merit principle, the Holy Spirit now brings forward Abraham.)*

"For if Abraham were justified by works *(which he wasn't)*, he has *whereof* to glory; but not before God *(the boasting of Salvation by works, which God will not accept).*"

ABRAHAM BELIEVED GOD

"For what says the Scripture? Abraham believed God, and it was counted unto him for Righteousness *(Gen. 15:6 – if one properly understands this Verse, he properly understands the Bible; Abraham gained Righteousness by simple Faith in God, Who would send a Redeemer into the world [Jn. 8:56]).*"

WORKS?

"Now to him who works *(tries to earn Salvation)* is the reward *(Righteousness)* not reckoned of Grace *(the Grace of God)*, but of debt *(claiming that God owes us something, which He doesn't!).*

"But to him who works not *(doesn't trust in works for Salvation)*, but believes on Him Who Justifies the ungodly *(through Christ and the Cross)*, his Faith is counted for Righteousness *(God awards Righteousness only on the basis of Faith in Christ and His Finished Work)*" (Rom. 4:1-5).

JUSTIFICATION BY FAITH

The great Apostle then said:

"**Therefore being Justified by Faith** *(this is the only way one can be justified; refers to Faith in Christ and what He did at the Cross)*, **we have peace with God** *(justifying peace)* **through our Lord Jesus Christ** *(what He did at the Cross)*:

"**By Whom also we have access by Faith into this Grace** *(we have access to the Goodness of God by Faith in Christ)* **wherein we stand** *(wherein alone we can stand)*, **and rejoice in hope** *(a hope that is guaranteed)* **of the Glory of God** *(our Faith in Christ always brings Glory to God; anything else brings glory to self, which God can never accept)*" **(Rom. 5:1-2).**

THE OBJECT OF FAITH

The great Apostle now tells us, as a Child of God, what the Object of our Faith must be. He said:

"**What shall we say then?** *(This is meant to direct attention to Rom. 5:20.)* **Shall we continue in sin, that Grace may abound?** *(Just because Grace is greater than sin doesn't mean that the Believer has a license to sin.)*

"**God forbid** *(presents Paul's answer to the question, 'Away with the thought, let not such a thing occur')*. **How shall we, who are dead to sin** *(dead to the sin nature)*, **live any longer therein?** *(This portrays what the Believer is now in Christ.)*"

THE CROSS OF CHRIST

"**Know you not, that so many of us as were baptized into Jesus Christ** *(plainly says that this Baptism is into Christ and not water [I Cor. 1:17; 12:13; Gal. 3:27; Eph. 4:5; Col. 2:11-13])* **were baptized into His Death?** *(When Christ died on the Cross, in the Mind of God, we died with Him; in other words, He became our Substitute, and our* *identification with Him in His Death gives us all the benefits for which He died; the idea is that He did it all for us!)*

"Therefore we are buried with Him by baptism into death *(not only did we die with Him, but we were buried with Him as well, which means that all the sin and transgression of the past were buried; when they put Him in the Tomb, they put all of our sins into that Tomb as well)***: that like as Christ was raised up from the dead by the Glory of the Father, even so we also should walk in newness of life** *(we died with Him, we were buried with Him, and His Resurrection was our Resurrection to a 'Newness of Life')***."**

RESURRECTION LIFE

Paul continues:

"For if we have been planted together *(with Christ)* **in the likeness of His Death** *(Paul proclaims the Cross as the instrument through which all Blessings come; consequently, the Cross must ever be the Object of our Faith, which gives the Holy Spirit latitude to work within our lives)***, we shall be also** *in the likeness* **of** *His* **Resurrection** *(we can have the 'likeness of His Resurrection,' i.e., 'live this Resurrection Life,' only as long as we understand the 'likeness of His Death,' which refers to the Cross as the means by which all of this is done)***" (Rom. 6:1-5).**

Coming up in a particular Pentecostal Denomination, I often heard preachers mention *"Resurrection Life."* Looking back, I know that most of them were, in a sense, denigrating the Cross of Christ because they would mention that, in essence, they had gone beyond the Cross and were now living the *"Resurrection Life."* Regrettably, that is the thinking of most Christians as it regards Resurrection Living.

The reader must understand, and unequivocally so, that in order to have this *"Resurrection Life,"* which the Lord most definitely wants us to have, and which we can have, we must first realize that it is made possible solely by the Cross of Christ. That means that if the Believer doesn't understand this, he will definitely not enjoy Resurrection Life, and because he will be trying to live this through the flesh.

We must know, first of all, that we have been *"planted together (with Christ) in the likeness of His Death,"* which Paul gives us in Romans 6:3-5, and then, and only then, can we live this Resurrection Life. It is all predicated on the Cross of Christ.

Secondly, we must understand that while the Resurrection of Christ, the Ascension of Christ, and the Exaltation of Christ were all of vast significance, still, they were the result of the Cross of Christ and not the cause. In other words, and we say it again, the Cross of Christ is the *"Means"* by which all things were done, and we mean all things.

So, again we make the statement that the Work of the Holy Spirit in our lives is not an automatic work. For us to have all that He can do, and please believe me, He can do anything, we must ever understand that He does these things on the premise of Christ and what Christ has done at the Cross. That's what gives Him the legal means of all that He does. It only requires of us a small thing, and that is that our Faith be exclusively in Christ and the Cross and nothing else.

WHY IS IT SO DIFFICULT FOR BELIEVERS TO PLACE THEIR FAITH EXCLUSIVELY IN THE CROSS OF CHRIST?

It is difficult for Believers to place their Faith exclusively in the Cross of Christ because it goes against the flesh. In other words, it belittles our human effort, human ability, human strength, etc., which doesn't sit well with most of us.

As well, we as Believers are very proficient at loading up the flesh with Scriptures, which makes us think it's of the Spirit, when it isn't. It's very hard for us to admit to ourselves that what needs to be done, we cannot do. In fact, that's probably the most difficult thing that the Holy Spirit has to do in order for us to understand this great Truth.

For instance, this Sunday morning, preachers will stand before television cameras and tell their audience that if they will take the Lord's Supper every day, or some such time frame, they'll have Victory within their lives and prosperity, etc. Another one tells their listeners that if they will memorize three Scriptures a day, as it regards their particular problem, whatever it might be, and quote them over and over again, this will bring God on the scene, for God has to abide by His Word.

While the Lord's Supper is most definitely Scriptural, that is, if carried out in the right way, and while memorizing Scriptures is very profitable as well, which I do constantly, still, that is taking something that wasn't meant to be, at least as we're trying to make it, which the Lord will never accept. In fact, all of these religious efforts present themselves as the greatest fault of the Child of God.

While the Lord's Supper is definitely not a work of the flesh, we most definitely turn it into one when we try to make it into something it was never intended to be. When we do this, it is an insult to Christ, and as well, to the Holy Spirit.

THE HOLY SPIRIT AND SPIRITUAL ADULTERY

Whenever our faith is placed in anything other than the Cross of Christ exclusively, we as Believers, in a sense, are living in a state of spiritual adultery. Listen again to Paul. While the following is quite voluminous, still, I think it is profitable for the Believer for us to copy it word for word from THE EXPOSITOR'S STUDY BIBLE.

"Know ye not, Brethren *(Paul is speaking to Believers)*, (for I speak to them who know the Law,) *(he is speaking of the Law of Moses, but it could refer to any type of religious Law)* how that the Law has dominion over a man as long as he lives? *(The Law has dominion as long as he tries to live by Law. Regrettably, not understanding the Cross regarding Sanctification, virtually the entirety of the Church is presently trying to live for God by means of the Law. Let the Believer understand that there are only two places he can be, Grace or Law. If he doesn't understand the Cross as it refers to Sanctification, which is the only means of Victory, he will automatically be under Law, which guarantees failure.)*"

AN ADULTERESS

"**For the woman which has an husband is bound by the Law to** *her* **husband so long as he lives** *(presents Paul using the analogy of the marriage bond)*; **but if the husband be dead, she is loosed from the Law of** *her* **husband** *(meaning that she is free to marry again).*

"**So then if, while** *her* **husband lives, she be married to another man, she shall be called an adulteress** *(in effect, the woman now has two husbands, at least in the Eyes of God; following this analogy, the Holy Spirit through Paul will give us a great truth; many Christians are living a life of spiritual adultery; they are married to Christ, but they are, in effect, serving another husband, 'the Law'; it is quite an analogy!)*: **but if her husband be dead** *(the Law is dead by virtue of Christ having fulfilled the Law in every respect),* **she is free from that Law** *(if the husband dies, the woman is free to marry and serve another; the Law of Moses, being satisfied in Christ, is now dead to the Believer and the Believer is free to serve Christ without the Law having any part or parcel in his life or living)*; **so that she is no adulteress, though she be married to another man** *(presents the Believer as now married to Christ, and no longer under obligation to the Law).*"

MARRIED TO CHRIST

"**Wherefore, my Brethren, you also are become dead**

to the Law *(the Law is not dead per se, but we are dead to the Law because we are dead to its effects; this means that we are not to try to live for God by means of 'Law,' whether the Law of Moses, or religious Laws made up by other men or of ourselves; we are to be dead to all religious Law)* **by the Body of Christ** *(this refers to the Crucifixion of Christ, which satisfied the demands of the broken Law, which we could not satisfy; but Christ did it for us; having fulfilled the Mosaic Law in every respect, the Christian is not obligated to Law in any fashion, only to Christ and what He did at the Cross)*; **that you should be married to another** *(speaking of Christ)*, **even to Him Who is raised from the dead** *(we are raised with Him in Newness of Life, and we should ever understand that Christ has met, does meet, and shall meet our every need; we look to Him exclusively, referring to what He did for us at the Cross)*, **that we should bring forth fruit unto God** *(proper fruit can only be brought forth by the Believer constantly looking to the Cross; in fact, Christ must never be separated from the Work of the Cross; to do so is to produce 'another Jesus' [II Cor. 11:4])*" **(Rom. 7:1-4).**

THAT WHICH GREATLY HINDERS THE HOLY SPIRIT

All of this tells us that any Believer, who places his or her faith in anything except the Cross of Christ exclusively, is being unfaithful to Christ, which means that such a person is living in a state of spiritual adultery. To be sure, that will greatly hinder the Holy Spirit. Thank God, He doesn't leave us in such situations, for all of us have ventured into these areas, but it does hurt greatly.

As Believers, and as stated in the notes, we are married to Christ. We are to be faithful to Him in every respect; however, when we place our faith in anything other than the Cross of Christ, and no matter how good the other thing may be in its own right, the Lord looks at us as having committed and continuing to commit spiritual adultery. In other words, in the Mind and

Eyes of God, it is the same thing as a husband being unfaithful to his wife or a wife being unfaithful to her husband. As anyone should understand, adultery is a most serious thing. In fact, most marriages in the natural sense do not survive such. But, we must also understand that in the spiritual sense, it is just as telling and just as debilitating.

Thank God that the Holy Spirit isn't human. Were He, He would have abandoned us a long time before; however, He is God. As such, He will stay with us as long as He can and will, in fact, do everything He can for us, despite the fact that we are living in a state of spiritual adultery. Let us say it again:

Any Believer, who places his or her faith in anything except the Cross of Christ exclusively, is living in a state of spiritual adultery, which greatly hinders the Holy Spirit, and which is the cause of virtually all failure in the lives of Believers.

Regrettably, the modern Church, for all practical purposes, is Cross illiterate. In other words, we have strayed so far from the Gospel that anymore the modern church hardly knows what the Gospel actually is. In short, the Gospel is, *"Jesus Christ and Him Crucified"* (I Cor. 1:17).

THE CROSS PROVIDES THE LEGAL RIGHT
FOR THE HOLY SPIRIT TO WORK

What do we mean by that statement?

The Work of Christ on the Cross was and is a legal work. Man had sinned against God, which means he owed a debt to God that he simply could not pay. It was a legal debt, and because the Law of God had been broken. Man is a lawbreaker.

For the account to be settled, in other words, for the thing to be made right, the debt would have to be paid. It was legally owed, and as a result, the debt must be legally satisfied. However, in this regard, man finds himself in an acute dilemma. In other words, it's a debt he cannot hope to pay, no matter how hard he tries, but if man is to be salvaged, the debt has got to be paid.

It was paid, and by the Lord Jesus Christ, God's Only Son,

Who gave Himself as a perfect Sacrifice, which God accepted as payment in full.

With the sin debt lifted, thereby paid, at least for all who will believe (Jn. 3:16), this made it possible, and makes it possible, for the Holy Spirit to come into the heart and life of the Believer and there to abide forever (Jn. 14:16-17).

Before the Cross, and because the blood of bulls and goats could not take away sins, the Holy Spirit was limited as to what He could do with, for, and upon Believers. But since the Cross, the way has been opened for Him to function in our hearts and lives in a totally different way. All of this is not because of the great and good things we have done, but because of the great and good thing that the Lord did at the Cross of Calvary. Again, we go back to the Cross!

Now, unequivocally, we are told in the Word of God as to exactly how the Holy Spirit works. In fact, it is labeled a *"Law,"* referring to its legality. It's the way that He works, and the only way that He works, meaning that He will work no other way. Let's see what the Word of God says:

LIFE IN THE SPIRIT

*"**There is** therefore now no condemnation (guilt) to them which are in Christ Jesus (refers back to Rom. 6:3-5 and our being baptized into His Death, which speaks of the Crucifixion), who walk not after the flesh (depending on one's personal strength and ability or great religious efforts in order to overcome sin), but after the Spirit (the Holy Spirit works exclusively within the legal confines of the Finished Work of Christ; our Faith in that Finished Work, i.e., 'the Cross,' guarantees the help of the Holy Spirit, which guarantees Victory).*"

THE LAW OF THE SPIRIT

Now we come to the manner and way in which the Holy

Spirit works and, in fact, meaning that He will work in no other fashion. This is a *"Law."*
Paul said:

> **"For the Law** *(that which we are about to give is a Law of God, devised by the Godhead in eternity past [I Pet. 1:18-20]; this Law, in fact, is 'God's Prescribed Order of Victory')* **of the Spirit** *(Holy Spirit, i.e., 'the way the Spirit works')* **of Life** *(all life comes from Christ, but through the Holy Spirit [Jn. 16:13-14])* **in Christ Jesus** *(any time Paul uses this term or one of its derivatives, he is, without fail, referring to what Christ did at the Cross, which makes this 'life' possible)* **has made me free** *(given me total Victory)* **from the Law of Sin and Death** *(these are the two most powerful Laws in the Universe; the 'Law of the Spirit of Life in Christ Jesus' alone is stronger than the 'Law of Sin and Death'; this means that if the Believer attempts to live for God by any manner other than Faith in Christ and the Cross, he is doomed to failure)"* **(Rom. 8:1-2).**

In closing this Chapter, hopefully, we have given you the manner in which the Holy Spirit works, which is at least one of the single most important factors in the belief system of the Child of God. Understanding this, and we pray that we have made it easily understandable, such a Believer has now learned God's provision of life and living, in other words, how to live a victorious life, victorious over the world, the flesh, and the Devil.

THE REVELATION

The promise of this Revelation was some nine years before it was possessed. As we often say, there is a great distance between the Promise and the Possession.
The year was 1988. It was the month of March, and my whole world had crashed, and I was left with little understanding. How

could it happen? Why did it happen? How was such possible?

The day in question, both Frances and I had stayed home from the office for the purpose of spending the day in prayer. To be sure, we had much to pray about.

Our house is outside the city limits and sits on some twenty acres of land. In those days, whenever I prayed each day, I would walk around the perimeter. At that particular time I was at the back of the property.

Never in all of my life have I experienced such demonic oppression as I did that particular morning. Satan can be very convincing in his accusations. He began to tell me how I had disgraced my family, disgraced my Church, disgraced myself, and above all, had disgraced the Work of God.

If I remember correctly, I had eight hundred dollars in the bank. He suggested to me, *"Take that money and just disappear."* He went on to say, *"You'll be doing the Work of God a service, if you are out of the picture."*

In fact, his oppression became so powerful that I remonstrated to the Lord, *"Lord, You promised that You would not allow anything to come upon us any harder than we could bear, but with every temptation, that You would make a way of escape."*

I then said, *"Lord, I think that You are allowing more than a human being can stand."* I then sobbed out, *"Please help me!"*

THE MOVING OF THE SPIRIT

In all of my life I don't think that I've ever experienced something such as that which happened that particular day. One moment it seemed like there were a thousand pounds on my shoulders, and growing heavier by the moment. And then, all of a sudden, it happened.

The next moment, the Spirit of the Lord covered me. The weight instantly lifted, and it was like I was floating in air. One moment it was impossible, and the next moment, anything was possible. It was like the Lord said, *"That's enough,"* and Satan immediately left.

As I stood there weeping before the Lord, He then spoke to my heart. It was very short and to the point. He said:

"I'm going to show you things about the Holy Spirit you do not now know."

As I stood there thinking about that for a moment, I realized instantly that there were all kinds of things about the Holy Spirit I did not know. He is God, so, how much do we really know? Yet, I realized that the Lord was addressing the situation at hand.

TIME WHICH FOLLOWED

I knew beyond the shadow of a doubt that the Lord had spoken these words to my heart, but there was nothing that happened. Days went into weeks and weeks into months, and still nothing. Oftentimes I thought about it, knowing that the Lord had spoken to me, yet there was nothing I could put my finger on that I knew was the fulfillment of that Promise. In fact, nine years passed. As I've stated, there is a great distance between the Promise and the Possession.

THE REVELATION OF THE CROSS

To fast-forward to 1997, the Revelation that changed my life was to take place at that particular time. Without going into detail, first of all, the Lord showed me the meaning of the sin nature, taking me to Romans, Chapter 6.

A few days later, while in one of the morning prayer meetings, He showed me the solution to the sin nature, saying to me three things, but all very similar. They are:

• The answer for which you seek is found in the Cross.
• The solution for which you seek is found in the Cross.
• The answer for which you seek is found only in the Cross.

Nothing about the Holy Spirit was said, and yet, I knew that whatever the Lord did, the Holy Spirit was very much involved.

However, the Lord did not mention to me the Holy Spirit

at that time, only the Cross. While I was literally ecstatic with joy, so much so that it was like I was in another world, at least for a short period of time, still, there was the nagging question about the Holy Spirit.

If the Cross of Christ were the answer and, in fact, the only answer, where did this leave the Holy Spirit?

I knew that the Holy Spirit had helped me to touch a great portion of the world with the Gospel of Jesus Christ, seeing literally hundreds of thousands brought to a saving knowledge of our Lord. As well, I had seen tens of thousands baptized with the Holy Spirit, for which we give the Lord all the Praise and all the Glory.

I prayed about it very much, but all I could do was leave it with the Lord.

HOW THE HOLY SPIRIT WORKS

Several weeks passed, and rejoicing night and day, I began to teach the Cross over our very small radio network. Then it was only two or three stations, where now it is seventy-eight stations.

At any rate, as we were nearing the conclusion to the program that morning, all of a sudden, I made a statement that shocked me. I had not studied the statement, had not heard the statement, had not read it anywhere, yet, I knew it was true. I have never had anything like this to happen to me before or since.

I made the statement, *"The Holy Spirit works exclusively within the parameters of the Finished Work of Christ, and will not work outside of those parameters."*

As stated, I had never read such a statement, had never heard such a statement, and had not thought about it previously to this moment. I just made the statement and then sat there stunned at what I had said, yet I knew that it was right.

As I paused, Loren Larson, who was seated across the table from me, spoke up, saying, *"Can you give me Scripture for that?"*

Once again, how could I give a Scripture when I didn't even really know what I had said! But then, the Spirit of God began to move upon me exactly as He had a few moments before. He drew my attention to Romans 8:2. I then quoted it:

"The Law of the Spirit of Life in Christ Jesus, has made me free from the Law of Sin and Death." And, once again, I knew it was right.

The program was coming to a conclusion and when it ended, I sat there for a few moments literally stunned at what had taken place.

I then arose and turned to my right to walk out the door in order to leave the Studio, but then, the Spirit of the Lord came on me again, and I stopped.

The Lord spoke to me, saying, *"Do you remember what I told you that day in March, 1988, that I would show you things about the Holy Spirit that you did not then know?"*

I stood there a moment with tears running down my face and said, *"Yes Lord, I remember!"*

He said, *"I have just fulfilled My Promise to you. That which I have given you, you have not previously known."*

In fact, that which the Lord gave to me that morning in 1997 has completely revolutionized my thinking in every respect. I now know how the Holy Spirit works in our hearts and lives. He works exclusively by and through the Cross of Christ. That means, as I have repeatedly stated, that the Cross of Christ must ever be the Object of our Faith.

A NEW TRUTH?

No, it's not a new Truth! It's that which the Lord gave to the Apostle Paul nearly two thousand years ago; however, having said that, it must as well be recognized that this is a Truth that the modern church knows little or nothing about. Considering how important that it is, how all-encompassing it is, it's a great Truth that the Holy Spirit intends, even demands, that all of us know.

"We would see Jesus, for the shadows lengthen,
"Across this little landscape of our life;

"We would see Jesus, our weak Faith to strengthen,
"For the last weariness, the final strife."

"We would see Jesus, the great Rock Foundation,
"Whereon our feet were set with sovereign Grace;
"Not life, nor death, with all their agitation,
"Can thence remove us, if we see His Face."

"We would see Jesus, other lights are paling,
"Which for long years we have rejoiced to see;
"The blessings of our pilgrimage are falling,
"We would not mourn them, for we go to Thee."

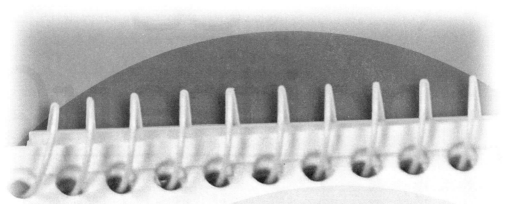

CHAPTER FOUR

Do Believers Receive
The Holy Spirit
At Conversion?

QUESTION:

DO BELIEVERS RECEIVE THE HOLY SPIRIT AT CONVERSION?

ANSWER:

Yes! Believers do receive the Holy Spirit at conversion.

In fact, the Holy Spirit is involved in everything spiritual that happens to us. We cannot be Saved without the Work of the Holy Spirit in our lives respecting conviction, and above all, regeneration.

Concerning the convicting Power of the Holy Spirit, the Word of God says:

HOLY SPIRIT CONVICTION

Jesus said:

"No man can come to Me, except the Father which has sent Me draw him *(the idea is that all initiative toward Salvation is on the part of God toward the sinner and not from the sinner himself; without this 'drawing of the Father,' which is done by the Holy Spirit, no one could come to God, or even have any desire to come to God)*" (Jn. 6:44).

WHAT JESUS TAUGHT ABOUT THE HOLY SPIRIT

Our Lord had more to say about the Holy Spirit the last week of His life than He did the entirety of the balance of His Ministry put together. Why did He wait this long to give His Disciples instructions as it regards the Holy Spirit, which, as is obvious, are extremely important?

Two reasons:

• First of all, He was with them. Whatever they needed, they would go to Him and that he would provide. But, now that He was about to leave, He informed them that the Holy Spirit, in essence, would now take His place. So, understanding that,

He related to them that which was to come.

• Secondly, He did not give them any teaching on the Holy Spirit, to speak of, until these last few days, simply because they would not have understood it anyway. Giving them teaching on this all important subject just before He was crucified left it fresh in their minds, and as well, told them what to expect. When the Holy Spirit came on the Day of Pentecost, with all the Disciples at that time being filled with the Spirit, they easily recalled what the Lord had told them, with the Holy Spirit, Who now abides within them, helping them to understand spiritual things.

Peter is an example. He said:

"**And as I began to speak** *(had gotten a little way into the Message)*, **the Holy Spirit fell on them, as on us at the beginning** *(speaks of Cornelius and his household being baptized with the Spirit, exactly as the Apostles and others had been on the Day of Pentecost)*.

"**Then remembered I the Word of the Lord, how that He said** *(pertains to something that Peter had not mentioned in the actual happening)*, **John indeed baptized with water; but you shall be Baptized with the Holy Spirit** *(Acts 1:5; Mat. 3:11)*" **(Acts 11:15-16).**

THE FUNCTION OF THE HOLY SPIRIT

In His address to His Disciples, our Lord now gives some instructions respecting the Holy Spirit as it regards doctrine, especially pertaining to what Christ did at Calvary. As we have said and continue to say, the Holy Spirit works entirely within the framework of the Finished Work of Christ, i.e., *"the Cross."* In fact, He will not work outside of those parameters. The Cross is what gives Him the legal right and the legal means to do all that He does (Rom. 8:2).

The Text and the notes contained in THE EXPOSITOR'S STUDY BIBLE on this subject are quite voluminous; however, I think it would be helpful to include it all, at least, up to a point.

Jesus said:

PERSECUTION

"These things have I spoken unto you, that you should not be offended *(concerns all the warnings of the coming persecution).*

"They shall put you out of the Synagogues *(religion, which refers to that which man has devised, will not accept Christ and the Cross)*: yes, the time comes, that whosoever kills you will think that he does God service *(speaks of terrible religious deception [I Tim. 4:1]).*

"And these things will they do unto you *(in one way or the other),* because they have not known the Father, nor Me *(despite their claims!).*"

THAT THEY MAY REMEMBER

"But these things have I told you, that when the time shall come, you may remember that I told you of them *(if the world loves us, something is wrong with our testimony).* And these things I said not unto you at the beginning *(the beginning of His Ministry was not the time to reveal these things),* because I was with you *(but now He is about to leave them, so He reveals what is going to happen).*

"But now I go My way to Him Who sent Me *(back to the Father in Heaven)*; and none of you asks Me, Where do You go? *(They are not asking now, simply because it seems they are beginning to understand what He is saying, at least about leaving.)*"

I MUST LEAVE IN ORDER THAT
THE COMFORTER MAY COME

"But because I have said these things unto you, sorrow has filled your heart *(they somewhat understood Him going back to the Father, but still, they didn't understand the coming Resurrection).*

"**Nevertheless I tell you the truth; It is expedient for you that I go away** *(the Mission and Ministry of the Holy Spirit to the Body of Christ depended upon the return of Christ to the Father)*: **for if I go not away, the Comforter** *(Holy Spirit)* **will not come unto you** *(concerns the respective Office Work of both Jesus and the Holy Spirit – Jesus as the Saviour of men, and the Holy Spirit as the Power of the Church)*; **but if I depart, I will send Him unto you** *(a Finished Work on the Cross was demanded of Christ before the Holy Spirit could be sent).*"

THE CONVICTION OF SIN

"**And when He** *(the Holy Spirit)* **is come, He will reprove** *(convict)* **the world of sin** *(the supreme sin of rejecting Christ)*, **and of Righteousness** *(Jesus is Righteousness, and declared so by the Resurrection)*, **and of Judgment** *(Satan was judged at Calvary, and all who follow him are likewise judged)*:

"**Of sin, because they believe not on Me** *(to reject Christ and the Cross is to reject Salvation)*;"

TO CONVICT OF RIGHTEOUSNESS

"**Of Righteousness, because I go to My Father** *(Jesus presented a spotless Righteousness to the Father, namely Himself, which pertained to His Sacrifice at Calvary, that was accepted by God; consequently, that Righteousness is imputed to all who will believe in Him and His Work on the Cross)*, **and you see Me no more** *(meaning that His Work was Finished)*;"

CONVICTED OF JUDGMENT

"**Of Judgment, because the Prince of this world is**

judged *(Satan was completely defeated at Calvary and, thereby, judged as eternally condemned; all who follow him will suffer his fate, the Lake of Fire, and that fate will be forever and forever [Rev. 20:12-15])"* **(Jn. 16:1-11).**

THE WORK OF THE HOLY SPIRIT IS ALWAYS TIED TO THE CROSS

When Jesus said that the Holy Spirit would convict of sin, of Righteousness, and of Judgment, this points explicitly to the Cross.

The major sin of humanity is rejecting Christ and what He did at the Cross in order that man might be Saved. Jesus said, *"because they believe not on Me."* Other than the Lord Jesus Christ, there are no other means of Salvation. And of course, this speaks of what He did at the Cross, which makes Salvation possible for all who will believe (Jn.3:16).

So, the Cross of Christ is placed at the forefront of the Holy Spirit's dealings with man. Always and without exception, as it pertains to Christ, it is *"Who He is,"* which means that He is God manifest in the flesh, in effect, the Son of the Living God, and *"What He did,"* which speaks exclusively of the Cross and the Redemption there furnished, and because Christ there paid the price.

OF RIGHTEOUSNESS

The Holy Spirit screams loudly, one might say, that the only Righteousness that God will recognize is that which is afforded by Christ, due to what He did at the Cross. Upon simple Faith in Christ, a spotless, pure, perfect Righteousness is instantly imputed to the believing sinner (Rom. 5:1-2).

As well, all other proposed righteousness, no matter how religious it might be, is referred to by the Lord as self-righteousness, which God can never accept. All the Righteousness of God, which comes from Jesus Christ and is made possible by the Cross, comes to the believing sinner simply on the basis of simple Faith; however, it must be Faith exclusively in Christ and what Christ has done for us at the Cross.

OF JUDGMENT

Everyone who rejects Christ and the Cross, for the two cannot be separated, will, without fail, experience the Wrath of God.

Satan has already been judged by God, meaning that his eternal destination will be the Lake of Fire (Rev. 20:10). Consequently, all who follow him, meaning that they have rejected the Lord Jesus Christ and what He did at the Cross, will experience the same eternal destination. It is the *"Lake of Fire"* forever and forever.

Let the reader understand that the only thing that stands between man and eternal Hell is the Cross of Jesus Christ. That's a blunt statement, but it happens to be true. And, one might as well say that the only thing that stands between the Church and apostasy is the Cross of the Lord Jesus Christ.

• Christ is the Source of all things we receive from God (Jn. 14:6).

• The Cross of Christ is the Means by which these things are given to us (Rom. 6:3-5; I Cor. 1:17, 18; Gal. 6:14).

• The Cross of Christ as the Object of our Faith, and the only Object of our Faith, is the only manner in which we receive these things which are freely given (Rom. 5:1-2; 6:11, 14; I Cor. 1:17, 23; 2:2).

• The Holy Spirit superintends all of this (Rom. 8:1-2, 10; Eph. 2:13-18).

BORN OF THE SPIRIT

Even though the following has already been given in another Chapter, still, due to its vast significance as it regards how a believing sinner is *"born of the Spirit,"* I feel it appropriate to give it here again as well. Jesus gave this information to Nicodemus, which gives us an idea as to how a person is born of the Spirit. He said:

NICODEMUS

"There was a man of the Pharisees, named Nicodemus *(said to have been one of the three richest men in Jerusalem)*, a Ruler of the Jews *(a member of the Sanhedrin, the ruling body of Israel)*:

"The same came to Jesus by night *(it is not known exactly as to why he came by night)*, and said unto Him, Rabbi, we know that You are a Teacher come from God *(the pronoun 'we' could indicate that Nicodemus represented several members of the Sanhedrin; Nicodemus addresses Christ here as a man, and not as God; the Cross would change him)*: for no man can do these miracles that You do, except God be with Him *(in this, he is correct!)*."

YOU MUST BE BORN-AGAIN

"Jesus answered and said unto him *(presents an answer totally different from that which he expected)*, Verily, verily, I say unto you, Except a man be born again *(the term, 'Born-Again,' means that man has already had a natural birth, but now must have a Spiritual Birth, which comes by Faith in Christ, and what He has done for us at the Cross, and is available to all)*, he cannot see the Kingdom of God *(actually means that without the New Birth, one cannot understand or comprehend the 'Kingdom of God')*.

"Nicodemus said unto Him, How can a man be born when he is old? *(This proclaims this spiritual leader of Israel as having no knowledge at all of what Jesus is saying. Had he truly been 'Born-Again,' he would have understood these terms.)* can he enter the second time into his

mother's womb, and be born? *(It seems he did not know the language of the Prophets concerning circumcision of the heart [Deut. 30:6; Jer. 4:4], and concerning a hard heart and right spirit [Ps. 51:10; Ezek. 36:26-27].)"*

BORN OF WATER AND OF THE SPIRIT

"Jesus answered, Verily, verily, I say unto you, Except a man be born of water and *of* the Spirit *(the phrase, 'born of water,' speaks of the natural birth, which Jesus says in the next Verse, and pertains to a baby being born; being 'Born of the Spirit' speaks of a Spiritual Birth, which is brought about by God Alone; and neither does it speak of Water Baptism)*, **he cannot enter into the Kingdom of God.**

"That which is born of the flesh is flesh *(has to do with the natural birth, and is illustrated, as stated, by the phrase, 'born of water')*; **and that which is born of the Spirit is spirit** *(has to do with that which is solely of God; the one [flesh] has no relationship to the other [Spirit] and cannot be joined)."*

THE MYSTERY OF
THE BORN-AGAIN EXPERIENCE

"Marvel not that I said unto you, You must be born again *(evidently addresses itself to the surprise, which must have been registered on the countenance of Nicodemus)*.

"The wind blows where it lists, and you hear the sound thereof, but cannot tell from where it comes, and whither it goes *(presents the way in which Jesus explains the 'Born-Again' experience; He likens it to the wind which comes and goes, but is impossible to tell exactly how)*: **so is everyone who is born of the Spirit** *(it is a Spiritual Birth, so it cannot be explained intellectually)"* **(Jn. 3:1-8).**

THERE IS A GREAT DIFFERENCE, HOWEVER, IN BEING *"BORN OF THE SPIRIT"* AND BEING *"BAPTIZED WITH THE SPIRIT"*

While the Holy Spirit definitely comes into the heart and life of every Born-Again Believer, and there to abide permanently, still, being *"born of the Spirit,"* is totally different than being *"baptized with the Spirit."*

"Born of the Spirit" pertains to Regeneration.

REGENERATION

The Greek word for Regeneration is *"Palingenesia."* As Paul uses the word in Titus 3:5, it pertains to Spiritual Regeneration. It involves the communication of a new life.

Concerning Regeneration, Vine's Expository Dictionary of New Testament Words says, *"The New Birth and Regeneration do not represent successive stages in spiritual experience, they refer to the same, but view it in different aspects. The New Birth stresses the communication of spiritual life in contrast to antecedent spiritual death; regeneration stresses the inception of a new state of things in contrast with the old."*[1]

Medical science claims that the possibility exists that particular genes in the human make-up can become malformed, thereby, causing particular problems with individuals. We speak of problems such as alcoholism, homosexuality, child molestation, etc. The *"gene"* is an element of the germ plasm that controls transmission of a hereditary character, in other words, the type of personality that one has. It pertains to one's DNA. Medical science concludes that if a malformed gene can be made right or replaced, this would address the perversion caused by the malformed gene, or so they speculate.

The problem, however, is actually not the gene itself, but that which causes the gene to become malformed, that is, if it actually does have a bearing on the personality of an individual.

It is ironic that the word *"Regeneration,"* as used in the

Born-Again experience, actually means to be *"re-gened."* In fact, the *"Born-Again"* experience alone can change an individual, in effect, making of the person *"a new creation."* Paul said:

"Therefore if any man *be* in Christ *(Saved by the Blood)*, *he is* a new creature *(a new creation)*: old things are passed away *(what we were before Salvation)*; behold, all things are become new. *(The old is no longer useable, with everything given to us now by Christ as 'new.')*

"And all things *are* of God *(all these new things)*, Who has reconciled us to Himself by Jesus Christ *(which He was able to do as a result of the Cross)*, and has given to us the Ministry of Reconciliation *(pertains to announcing to men the nature and conditions of this Plan of being Reconciled, which is summed up in the 'preaching of the Cross' [I Cor. 1:21, 23])*;"

THE WORD OF RECONCILIATION

"To wit, that God was in Christ *(by the agency of Christ)*, reconciling the world unto Himself *(represents the Atonement as the work of the Blessed Trinity and the result of love, not of wrath)*, not imputing their trespasses unto them *(refers to the fact that the penalty for these trespasses was imputed to Christ instead)*; and has committed unto us the Word of Reconciliation. *(All Believers are to preach the Cross in one way or the other [I Cor. 1:18])*" (II Cor. 5:17-19).

BAPTIZED WITH THE SPIRIT

As stated, there is a vast difference between being *"born of the Spirit,"* and being *"baptized with the Spirit."* In fact, one cannot be baptized with the Spirit until one has first been *"born of the Spirit."* Concerning that, Jesus said:

"*Even* the Spirit of Truth *(the Greek says, 'The Spirit*

of the Truth,' which refers to the Word of God; actually, He does far more than merely superintend the attribute of Truth, as Christ 'is Truth' [I Jn. 5:6]); **Whom the world cannot receive** *(the Holy Spirit cannot come into the heart of the unbeliever until that person makes Christ his or her Saviour; then He comes in)*, **because it sees Him not, neither knows Him** *(refers to the fact that only Born-Again Believers can understand the Holy Spirit and know Him)*: **but you know Him** *(would have been better translated, 'But you shall get to know Him')*; **for He dwells with you** *(before the Cross)*, **and shall be in you** *(which would take place on the Day of Pentecost and forward, because the sin debt has been forever paid by Christ on the Cross, changing the disposition of everything)*" **(Jn. 14:17).**

Being *"born of the Spirit"* pertains to Regeneration, while being *"baptized with the Spirit"* pertains to power to carry out the Work of the Lord.

THERE IS A VAST DIFFERENCE IN THESE TWO WORKS OF THE SPIRIT

Without the Believer being Baptized with the Spirit, precious little is truly going to be done for the Lord.

The reason?

Those who do not believe in the Baptism with the Holy Spirit with the evidence of speaking with other Tongues, as a rule, have very little moving and operation of the Holy Spirit within their lives. This means that whatever is done generally is man conceived, man birthed, and man operated, which the Lord can never accept. The Lord will only accept that which is conceived by the Holy Spirit and carried out by the Holy Spirit. Yes, the Holy Spirit uses mankind to do this, but it is the Spirit of God Who originates the Plan, whatever the Plan might be.

Being baptized with the Spirit includes the following

operation in one's life:

• The Holy Spirit is a Comforter, i.e., *"Helper"* (Jn. 14:16).

• *"He will guide you into all Truth"* (Jn. 16:13).

• *"He will show you things to come"* (Jn. 16:13).

• *"He shall glorify Christ in the Believer"* (Jn. 16:14).

• *"He shall receive of Mine* (that which Christ has done for us at the Cross), *and shall show it unto you"* (Jn. 16:14).

• *"But you shall receive power, after that the Holy Spirit is come upon you"* (Acts 1:8).

• *"All life is in the Spirit,"* which means there is no life outside of the Spirit (Rom. 8:10).

• The Holy Spirit *"quickens our mortal bodies,"* which means that He gives us power to live a Holy Life, providing our Faith is anchored firmly in Christ and the Cross (Rom. 8:11).

• We are meant to be *"led by the Spirit of God"* (Rom. 8:14).

• The Holy Spirit *"makes intercession for us"* (Rom. 8:26).

• The Holy Spirit functions through us by the means of His Gifts (I Cor. 12:8-11).

• Those baptized with the Spirit have the privilege of praying in other Tongues, which speaks directly to God (I Cor. 14:2).

Salvation is God's greatest gift to the world while the Baptism with the Holy Spirit is His greatest gift to the Church.

"I know not what awaits me,
"God kindly veils my eyes,
"And o'er each step of my onward way,
"He makes new scenes to rise;
"With every joy He sends me comes,
"A sweet and glad surprise."

"One step I see before me,
"'Tis all I need to see,
"The light of Heaven more brightly shines,
"When Earth's illusions flee;
"And sweetly through the silence comes,
"His loving, 'Follow Me!'"

"Oh, blissful lack of wisdom,
"'Tis blessed not to know;
"He holds me with His Own Right Hand,
"And will not let me go,
"And lulls my troubled soul to rest,
"In Him Who loves me so."

"So on I go not knowing;
"I would not if I might;
"I'd rather walk in the dark with God,
"Than go alone in the light;
"I'd rather walk by Faith with Him,
"Than go alone by sight."

CHAPTER FIVE

Is The Baptism With The Holy Spirit An Experience Separate And Distinct From Salvation?

QUESTION:

IS THE BAPTISM WITH THE HOLY SPIRIT AN EXPERIENCE SEPARATE AND DISTINCT FROM SALVATION?

ANSWER:

Yes! The Baptism with the Holy Spirit is an experience separate and distinct from Salvation.

• As stated, one cannot be baptized with the Spirit until one has first been born of the Spirit.

• While the Baptism with the Spirit can be received moments after Salvation, it is not received at Salvation.

• The Baptism with the Spirit does not make one more Saved. As far as Salvation is concerned, Justification by Faith is complete within itself.

There are three things to which I want to call your attention as it regards this all-important aspect of the Baptism with the Holy Spirit. The first one is as follows:

JESUS HAD TO HAVE THE HOLY SPIRIT
TO ACCOMPLISH HIS WORK

If Jesus, the Son of the Living God, God manifest in the flesh, had to have the Holy Spirit to accomplish His Divine purposes, then what about us? Of course, as God, our Lord needed nothing. But, as The Man, Christ Jesus, and functioning as a man, and totally as a man, He had to have the Holy Spirit. And, please understand:

• Jesus, even though never ceasing to be God, not even for one moment, still, functioned not at all as God, but rather, as a man. In other words, every Miracle He performed was done solely by the Power and the Authority of the Holy Spirit. Everything He did in His Ministry was by and through the Spirit. So, concerning this, even as He began His public Ministry, the Scripture says:

THE SPIRIT OF GOD

"And Jesus, when He was baptized *(this was the beginning of His earthly Ministry)*, went up straightway *(immediately)* out of the water *(refers to Baptism by immersion and not by sprinkling)*: and, lo, the Heavens were opened unto Him *(the only One, the Lord Jesus Christ, to Whom the Heavens would be opened)*, and he saw the Spirit of God *(Holy Spirit)* descending like a dove, and lighting upon Him *(John saw a visible form that reminded him of a dove)*:

"And lo a Voice from Heaven, saying *(the Voice of God the Father)*, This is My Beloved Son, in Whom I am well pleased *(the Trinity appears here: the Father speaks, the Spirit descends, and the Son prays [Lk. 3:21])*" (Mat. 3:16-17).

THE LEADING OF THE SPIRIT

Now we are given an example of the function and leading of the Holy Spirit in the Life of Christ, which is meant for us as well. The Scripture says:

"Then *(immediately after the descent of the Holy Spirit upon Him)* was Jesus led up *(urgently led)* of the Spirit *(Holy Spirit)* into the wilderness *(probably close to Jericho)* to be tempted of the Devil *(as the Last Adam, He would be tempted in all points like as we are [Heb. 4:15; I Cor. 15:21-22, 45, 47])*" (Mat. 4:1).

I want to drive home the point that if our Lord in His earthly Ministry had to have the Holy Spirit to empower Him, to lead Him, to guide Him, then don't you think that this need is resident in our lives as well? In fact, and as stated, without the Holy Spirit precious little, if anything, is going to be accomplished for the Lord. Even though, at the expense of being blunt, the truth is, without the Holy Spirit all, no matter the machinery, amounts to nothing.

AN ILLUSTRATION

I once saw an illustration that I think beautifully describes that of which I speak.

Two men in a cartoon were standing in a room looking at a huge machine. The machine stood about twelve feet high and possibly was about twelve feet long. On it were all types of pulleys and sprockets, which were going full force, with all the associated racket and clamor.

One of the men turned to the other and asked, *"What does it make?"*

The other one looked at him and then said, *"Make?"*

In other words, for all of its activity, it made nothing.

That's the way with most of the modern church. It is filled with religious machinery, so to speak, but, in effect, it does absolutely nothing for the Lord. I suppose that's at least one of the reasons that it has been said, *"The doing of religion is one of the most powerful narcotics there is."*

Getting back to the original statement, if our Lord had to have the Holy Spirit in order to carry out His Ministry, then I think it stands to reason that the same need applies to us as well.

THE COMMAND OF OUR LORD

It should quickly be said that the Baptism with the Holy Spirit with the evidence of speaking with other Tongues is not an option. It is that which the Believer must have, that is, if we are to do anything for the Lord. While, of course, this is not necessary for Salvation, it most definitely is necessary for Service.

Concerning this, Jesus said:

"And, being assembled together with *them* (speaks of the time He ascended back to the Father; this was *probably the time of the 'above five hundred' [I Cor. 15:6])*, **Commanded them** *(not a suggestion)* **that they should not depart from Jerusalem** *(the site of the Temple where the Holy Spirit would descend)*, **but wait for the Promise of the Father** *(spoke of the Holy Spirit which had been promised by the Father [Lk. 24:49; Joel, Chpt. 2])*, **which, said *He*, you have heard of Me** *(you have also heard Me say these things [Jn. 7:37-39; 14:12-17, 26; 15:26; 16:7-15])*.

"**For John truly baptized with water** *(merely symbolized the very best Baptism Believers could receive before the Day of Pentecost)*; **but you shall be baptized with the Holy Spirit not many days hence** *(spoke of the coming Day of Pentecost, although Jesus did not use that term at that time)*."

POWER

Our Lord then said:

"**But you shall receive power** *(Miracle-working Power)*, **after that the Holy Spirit is come upon you** *(specifically states that this 'Power' is inherent in the Holy Spirit, and solely in His domain)*: **and you shall be witnesses** *(doesn't mean witnessing to souls, but rather, to one giving one's all in every capacity for Christ, even to the laying down of one's life)* **unto Me** *(without the Baptism with the Holy Spirit, one cannot really know Jesus as one should)* **both in Jerusalem, and in all Judaea, and in Samaria, and unto the uttermost part of the Earth** *(proclaims the Work of God as being worldwide)*" **(Acts 1:4-5, 8).**

THE LAST WORD OF CHRIST TO HIS FOLLOWERS

The last words of anyone should be thought of as important. In fact, the last Words of Christ are of phenomenal magnitude, as should be overly obvious.

In the address given to His Followers just before His Ascension, our Lord could have dealt with many things. He could have dealt with Prophecy, in which, actually, His Disciples endeavored to engage Him. He could have dealt with the coming formation of the Church. He could have dealt with their calling as Apostles. In fact, the list is endless. But, the truth is, in the last address given to His Followers, He chose to address the subject that was the most important, which was the necessity of these Believers being baptized with the Holy Spirit. In fact, He was telling them, *"Don't go try to build Churches, don't go try to witness for Me, don't go try to do anything for Me, until you are first 'baptized with the Holy Spirit.'"* That was the gist of His statement.

If it is to be noticed, He did not suggest to them that they needed the Holy Spirit in order to carry out His work, but rather, *"He commanded them."*

The word *"commanded"* in the Greek is *"paraggello,"* and means *"to give a charge, in essence, a military command."* As stated, it was not a suggestion.

IS THAT COMMAND FOR US PRESENTLY?

That command is most definitely for us presently!

To try to limit this command to that particular time (some two thousand years ago), and to that particular place (Jerusalem), is to do great violence to the Word of God.

Concerning this, Simon Peter said in his Message on the Day of Pentecost:

"But this is that which was spoken by the Prophet Joel *(please notice that Peter did not say, 'this fulfills that spoken by the Prophet Joel,' but rather, 'this is that . . .' meaning that it will continue)*" **(Acts 2:16).**

AS MANY AS THE LORD OUR GOD SHALL CALL

Peter also said the following in his inaugural Message.

"**For the Promise** *(of the Baptism with the Holy Spirit)* **is unto you** *(directed toward the many Jews standing in the Temple listening to Peter that day)*, **and to your children** *(means that this great outpouring did not stop with the initial outpouring, but continues on)*, **and to all who are afar off** *(meaning that it's not only for those in Jerusalem, but the entirety of the world as well)*, **even** **as many as the Lord our God shall call** *(that 'Call' is 'Whosoever will' [Jn. 7:37-39; Rev. 22:17])*" **(Acts 2:39).**

Let us say it again. The Baptism with the Holy Spirit is an experience separate, distinct, and apart from Salvation. While it may be received moments after Salvation, it is not received with Salvation. The Baptism with the Holy Spirit with the evidence of speaking with other Tongues doesn't make one more Saved. It is not for that purpose. It is to give one power to carry out the Works of Christ.

EARMARKS OF THE EARLY CHURCH

If what we refer to presently as *"Church"* is to actually be Church, it's going to have to carry the earmarks of the Early Church given to us in the Book of Acts and the Epistles. If those earmarks are not prevalent, then whatever it is we are referring to as *"Church,"* in fact, isn't Church, at least, that which God recognizes.

The Early Church was conceived by the Holy Spirit. While He used men and women to carry it out, still, the conception was His. Unfortunately, most of that which presently goes under the label of *"Church,"* is not Church at all, but rather, something else, which means that it was conceived by man, or rather, ultimately overtaken by man.

We must ever understand that it is the Holy Spirit Who conceives, Who births, Who builds, using men and women to do such. But, the moment that human hands attempt to take the place of the Holy Spirit, at that moment, the Holy Spirit withdraws.

WHAT WERE THE EARMARKS OF THE EARLY CHURCH?

* Salvation by the Blood of Jesus Christ (Acts 20:28; Rom. 3:25; 5:9; Eph. 1:7; Col. 1:14).
* The Baptism with the Holy Spirit with the evidence of speaking with other Tongues (Acts 2:4; 10:44-48; 19:1-7).
* Divine Healing by the Power of God (Mk. 16:18-20; Acts 3:11; James 5:14-15; I Pet. 2:24).
* The Gifts of the Spirit are in operation (I Cor. 12:1-11).
* The preaching of the Cross which results in Victory over the world, the flesh and the devil (Rom. 6:1-14; 8:1-2, 11; I Cor. 1:17, 18, 23; 2:2; Gal., Chpt. 5; 6:14; Eph. 2:13-18; Col. 2:14-15).
* The Doctrine of the Rapture of the Church (I Thess. 4:13-18; II Thess. 2:7-8; Rev. 1:19; 4:1).
* The Doctrine of the Second Coming (II Thess. 2:1-8; Rev. 19:11-21).
* The Doctrine of the Millennium (Rev. 20:4-6; Isa. 2:1-4; 4:1-6; 11:1-10).
* The Perfect Age to come which will be eternity without end (Rev., Chpts. 21-22).

If Church is to be Church, the great Doctrines mentioned must be preached and practiced and with forthcoming evidence. This is what the Holy Spirit intends.

BIBLE PROOF THAT THE BAPTISM WITH THE HOLY SPIRIT IS AN EXPERIENCE SEPARATE AND APART FROM SALVATION

As we've already stated, the Baptism with the Spirit does not make one more Saved. That's not its intended purpose at all. Its purpose is for Service. It follows Salvation and, as again already stated, one cannot be baptized with the Holy Spirit unless one has first been Saved (Jn. 14:17).

THE DAY OF PENTECOST (ACTS 2:1-4)

The first experience of Believers being baptized with the

Holy Spirit took place on the Day of Pentecost. Now that the Cross was a fact, meaning that all sin had been atoned, and that God had accepted the Sacrifice of Christ, the Holy Spirit could now come in a brand-new dimension. He could now come into the hearts and lives of all Believers, there to dwell forever (Jn. 14:16).

As well, it certainly should be understood that all those on the Day of Pentecost, which included the original Apostles, with Matthias having taken the place of Judas, and even Mary, the Mother of our Lord, were already Saved. Yet, and to which we have previously directed attention, they were commanded by our Lord to be baptized with the Holy Spirit. The Scripture says concerning this:

> "**And when the Day of Pentecost was fully come** *(the Feast of Pentecost, one of the seven great Feasts ordained by God and practiced by Israel yearly; it took place fifty days after Passover)*, **they were all with one accord in one place** *(not the Upper Room where they had been previously meeting, but rather, the Temple [Lk. 24:53; Acts 2:46])*.
>
> "**And suddenly there came a sound from Heaven as of a rushing mighty wind** *(portrays the coming of the Holy Spirit in a new dimension, all made possible by the Cross)*, **and it filled all the house** *(the Temple)* **where they were sitting** *(they were probably in the Court of the Gentiles)*."

BEGAN TO SPEAK WITH OTHER TONGUES

> "**And there appeared unto them cloven tongues like as of fire** *(the only record of such in the New Testament, and was the fulfillment of the Prophecy of John the Baptist concerning Jesus [Mat. 3:11])*, **and it sat upon each of them** *(refers to all who were there, not just the Twelve Apostles; the exact number is not known)*.
>
> "**And they were all filled with the Holy Spirit** *(all were filled, not just the Apostles; due to the Cross, the Holy Spirit*

could now come into the hearts and lives of all Believers to abide permanently [Jn. 14:16]), **and began to speak with other Tongues** *(the initial physical evidence that one has been baptized with the Spirit, and was predicted by the Prophet Isaiah [Isa. 28:9-12], and by Christ [Mk. 16:17; Jn. 15:26; 16:13])*, **as the Spirit gave them utterance** *(meaning they did not initiate this themselves, but that it was initiated by the Spirit; as we shall see, these were languages known somewhere in the world, but not by the speaker)*" **(Acts 2:1-4).**

THE SAMARITANS WHO WERE BAPTIZED WITH THE HOLY SPIRIT (ACTS 8:14-17)

The next great incident of Believers being baptized with the Holy Spirit was the Samaritans. Concerning this group, the Scripture says:

"Then Philip went down to the city of Samaria *(should have been translated, 'a city of Samaria,' which was probably 'Sychem'; this was the Philip of Acts 6:5)*, **and preached Christ unto them** *(refers to him proclaiming Jesus as the Messiah, God manifest in the flesh, and being raised from the dead; he would not have understood much about the Cross at this particular time; that awaiting the conversion of Paul)*.

"And the people with one accord gave heed unto those things which Philip spoke *(proclaims a great acceptance of the Gospel)*, **hearing and seeing the miracles which he did** *(verified the Message he preached)*.

"For unclean spirits, crying with loud voice, came out of many who were possessed *with them (the Name of Jesus was used to cast out demons)*: **and many taken with palsies, and who were lame, were healed.**

"And there was great joy in that city *(when the Message of Christ is accepted, it always brings 'great joy')*.**"**

THE CASE OF SIMON THE SORCERER

"But there was a certain man, called Simon, which beforetime in the same city used sorcery *(pertained to the practice of the rites of the art of the Magi; it is of Satan)*, and bewitched the people of Samaria, giving out that himself was some great one *(it seemed they believed his claims)*:

"To whom they all gave heed, from the least to the greatest *(proclaims that all were duped by his sorceries)*, saying, This man is the great power of God *(they attributed his magic and stunts to being done by the Power of God, when in reality it was of Satan; much in the modern church which claims to be the Power of God falls into the same category)*.

"And to him they had regard, because that of long time he had bewitched them with sorceries *(the word 'bewitched' refers to the fact that the person or persons are deprived of the ability to think or order their thoughts correctly)*."

THEY BELIEVED THE GOSPEL

"But when they believed Philip preaching the things concerning the Kingdom of God *(they now encountered a Power which was greater than the powers of darkness)*, and the Name of Jesus Christ *(Salvation is in that Name and what it refers to, which speaks of the Cross; the very Name 'Jesus' means 'Saviour')*, they were baptized, both men and women *(they were baptized in water after they were Saved, not baptized in order to be Saved)*.

"Then Simon himself believed also *(every evidence is that Simon truly gave his heart and life to the Lord Jesus; the word 'believed' is used here exactly as it was in the previous Verse, which signifies Salvation [Jn. 3:16; Rom. 10:9-13])*: and when he was baptized *(plainly informs us that Philip saw enough evidence of Repentance and Faith in Christ that he baptized Simon exactly as he did the others)*, **he continued with Philip, and wondered, beholding the miracles and signs which were done** *(he watched carefully what Philip was doing, and noted that there was no trickery involved).*"

THEY RECEIVED THE HOLY SPIRIT

The Scripture continues:

"Now when the Apostles which were at Jerusalem heard that Samaria had received the Word of God *(many had been Saved)*, **they sent unto them Peter and John** *(for a reason which we will see)*:

"Who, when they were come down, prayed for them, that they might receive the Holy Spirit *(this was their purpose for coming, and this is how important it is for Believers to be baptized with the Spirit)*:

"(For as yet He *(the Holy Spirit)* **was fallen upon none of them** *(evidently Philip had strongly preached Salvation, but had not preached the Baptism with the Holy Spirit)*: **only they were baptized in the Name of the Lord Jesus.)** *(This is meant to infer that they had been baptized in water, but not the Baptism with the Spirit.)*

"Then laid they *their* hands on them *(presents one of the ways Believers can be baptized with the Spirit, but this is not necessary in order to be filled [Acts 2:4; 10:44-48])*, **and they received the Holy Spirit** *(doesn't give any more information, but we know from Acts 2:4; 10:44-48; 19:1-7 that they also spoke with Tongues)*" **(Acts 8:5-17).**

Any honest interpretation of these Passages proclaims to us the fact that these Samaritans were Saved when they heard Philip preach the Gospel, with them, thereby, accepting Christ. Some days later they were baptized with the Holy Spirit when

Peter and John came to their area, thereby, preaching this great Doctrine. This proves that the Baptism with the Holy Spirit is an experience separate and apart from Salvation. This means that one is baptized with the Holy Spirit after conversion, that is, if this great Doctrine is preached to them, as did Peter and John to the Samaritans.

PAUL'S BAPTISM WITH THE HOLY SPIRIT (ACTS 9:17-18)

The conversion of Paul, at first known as Saul, was, no doubt, one of the greatest conversions in history. In fact, this man's coming to Christ would literally change the complexion of the Church. Concerning his Salvation and Baptism with the Spirit, the Scripture says:

"And Saul, yet breathing out threatenings and slaughter against the Disciples of the Lord *(presents Paul as the Leader of the persecution against the Early Church)*, went unto the High Priest *(if it was A.D. 35, Caiaphas was the High Priest; once again, we see the evil of religion)*,

"And desired of him letters to Damascus to the Synagogues *(proclaims the persecution led by Paul branching out to other cities)*, that if he found any of this way *(portrays the description of the Early Church [Jn. 14:6; Acts 18:25-26; 19:9, 23; 22:4; 24:14, 22])*, whether they were men or women, he might bring them bound unto Jerusalem *(refers to them appearing before the Sanhedrin, the same group that Crucified Christ)*."

THE SALVATION OF PAUL

"And as he journeyed, he came near Damascus *(approximately 175 miles from Jerusalem)*: and suddenly there shined round about him a light from Heaven *(proclaims the appearance of Christ in His Glory)*:

"And he fell to the earth *(implies that the Power of*

God knocked him down), **and heard a voice saying unto him, Saul, Saul, why do you persecute Me?** *(To touch one who belongs to the Lord in a negative way is to touch the Lord!)*

"And he said, Who are You, Lord? *(Paul uses this in the realm of Deity, not merely as respect as some have claimed.)* **And the Lord said, I am Jesus Whom you persecute** *(presents the Lord using the Name that Paul hated)*: ***it is* hard for you to kick against the pricks** *(has reference to sharp goads, which were placed immediately behind the oxen and were attached to the plow; to kick against it would cause sharp pain)***."**

LORD, WHAT WILL YOU HAVE ME DO?

"And he trembling and astonished said *(he was stupefied and astounded)*, **Lord, what will You have me to do?** *(This constitutes the moment that Paul was Saved.)* **And the Lord *said* unto Him, Arise, and go into the city, and it shall be told you what you must do** *(pertains to the Plan of God for Paul, which, in effect, would change the world)*.

"And the men which journeyed with him stood speechless *(they were very much aware that something had happened, but they did not know exactly what)*, **hearing a voice, but seeing no man** *(but Paul saw the Man, and that Man was Christ)***."**

PAUL BLINDED

"And Saul arose from the earth; and when his eyes were opened, he saw no man *(it seems that his eyes had been blinded by the Glory of the Lord)*: **but they led him by the hand, and brought *him* into Damascus** *(Paul, the champion of the persecutors, is now led like the blind man he temporarily is)*.

"And he was three days without sight *(speaks only*

of the physical sense; in fact, for the very first time he was now able to see), **and neither did eat nor drink** *(presents him fasting three days and nights)*.

ANANIAS

"**And there was a certain Disciple at Damascus, named Ananias** *(the word 'Disciple,' as used in the Book of Acts, without exception refers to followers of Christ)*; **and to him said the Lord in a vision, Ananias** *(he actually saw the Lord, but in Vision form)*. **And he said, Behold, I** *am here* **Lord** *(proclaims an extensive familiarity with the Lord, far beyond the normal)*.

"**And the Lord** *said* **unto him, Arise, and go into the street which is called Straight** *(proclaims the street, which still exists even after nearly two thousand years)*, **and enquire in the house of Judas for** *one* **called Saul of Tarsus** *(expresses the name of the man who was the most notorious scourge of the followers of Christ in the world of that time)*: **for, behold, he prays** *(Paul had much to pray about)*,

"**And has seen in a vision a man named Ananias coming in** *(proclaims the second Vision that Paul had in a very short period of time)*, **and putting** *his* **hand on him, that he might receive his sight.**"

A CHOSEN VESSEL UNTO ME

"**Then Ananias answered, Lord, I have heard by many of this man** *(how empty our fears often are! how ignorant we are of where our chief good lies hid! but God knows; let us trust Him)*, **how much evil he has done to Your Saints at Jerusalem** *(but, the Lord has changed this man, and he will become the greatest blessing to the Saints of anyone in history)*:

"**And here he has authority from the Chief Priests to bind all who call on Your Name** *(Paul's evil intentions* *had preceded him; but the Lord invaded those intentions, completely changing them).*

"**But the Lord said unto him, Go your way** *(presents an urgency which demands instant obedience by Ananias)*: **for he is a chosen vessel unto Me** *(it means, 'Divine Selection')*, **to bear My Name before the Gentiles, and Kings, and the Children of Israel** *('Gentiles' are placed first; that was Paul's principal calling).*

"**For I will show him how great things he must suffer for My Name's sake** *(this is altogether different from much of the modern gospel, which, in fact, is no Gospel at all!)*."

THAT HE MIGHT BE FILLED WITH THE HOLY SPIRIT

"**And Ananias went his way, and entered into the house** *(he obeyed the Command of the Lord)*; **and putting his hands on him** *(on Paul)* **said, Brother Saul** *(he addressed Paul in this manner because Paul was already Saved, and had been so for the last three days and nights)*, **the Lord,** *even* **Jesus, Who appeared unto you in the way as you came, has sent me, that you might receive your sight, and be filled with the Holy Spirit** *(this proclaims the fact that one is not baptized with the Holy Spirit at conversion, as many teach; in fact, the Baptism with the Holy Spirit is a separate work of Grace, which takes place after conversion [Acts 2:4; 8:14-17; 19:1-7])*.

"**And immediately there fell from his eyes as it had been scales: and he received sight forthwith, and arose, and was baptized** *(was baptized with water, after he was baptized with the Holy Spirit)*" **(Acts 9:1-18).**

THE SALVATION AND INFILLING OF THE SPIRIT OF CORNELIUS (ACTS 10:44-48)

The account of the Salvation and infilling of the Spirit of Cornelius and those with him presents a turning point in history.

It was the Gospel of Jesus Christ now being presented to the Gentile world. This was about eight years after the Crucifixion, Resurrection, and Ascension of our Lord. We pick up with the Message that Peter preached in the household of Cornelius. The Scripture says:

"Then Peter opened *his* mouth, and said *(proclaims a profound truth, as simple as it was; the Gospel will now break the bounds of Judaism, despite the efforts of man to do otherwise)*, Of a truth I perceive that God is no respecter of persons *(not meant to be implied by Peter that this Truth is new, for it is not [II Sam. 14:14], but up to this time Peter had applied it to Jews only, not Gentiles)*:

"But in every Nation *(the Gospel is for all)* he who fears Him, and works righteousness, is accepted with Him *(the pronoun 'Him' refers to Christ; God accepted the Sacrifice of Christ on the Cross, and all who accept Christ and the Cross are accepted with 'Him')*.

"The Word which *God* sent unto the Children of Israel, preaching peace by Jesus Christ *(this is justifying Peace, which comes instantly upon the acceptance of Christ)*: (He is Lord of all:) *(Jesus Christ is Lord because He has made Salvation possible for all who will believe [Phil. 2:11])*.

"That word, *I say*, you know *(refers to the Life, Ministry, Death, Resurrection, and Ascension of Christ)*, which was published throughout all Judaea, and began from Galilee, after the Baptism which John preached *(John introduced Christ)*;"

THE ANOINTING UPON CHRIST

"How God anointed Jesus of Nazareth with the Holy Spirit and with Power *(as a Man, Christ needed the Holy Spirit, as we certainly do as well! in fact, everything He did was by the Power of the Spirit)*: Who went about doing

good *(everything He did was good)*, **and healing all who were oppressed of the Devil** *(only Christ could do this, and Believers can do such only as Christ empowers them by the Spirit)*; **for God was with Him** *(God is with us only as we are 'with Him')*.

"**And we** *(the Apostles and others)* **are witnesses of all things which He did both in the land of the Jews, and in Jerusalem** *(Jerusalem is inferred because it was the center of religious authority; so they were without excuse)*; **Whom they slew and hanged on a tree** *('they' referred to 'the Sanhedrin,' the religious leaders of Israel)*:"

JESUS WAS RAISED FROM THE DEAD

"**Him God raised up the third day** *(Peter is affirming the Resurrection of Christ)*, **and showed Him openly** *(Jesus revealed Himself after the Resurrection to quite a number of people)*;

"**Not to all the people** *(not to all of Israel)*, **but unto witnesses chosen before of God** *(refers to those who had Faith in Him and believed)*, ***even*** **to us, who did eat and drink with Him after He rose from the dead** *(proclaims that Jesus was not a spirit, or mere apparition, but rather real, physical, and alive)*."

JESUS CHRIST IS THE JUDGE

"**And He Commanded us to preach unto the people** *(presents God's Way of spreading the Gospel)*, **and to testify that it is He which was ordained of God** *to be* **the Judge of the quick** *(living)* **and dead** *(today Jesus is the Saviour, tomorrow He will be the Judge)*.

"**To Him give all the Prophets witness** *(means that He fulfilled all of the Prophecies)*, **that through His Name** *(His Name Alone)* **whosoever** *(anyone in the world)* **believes in Him** *(Believes in Who and What He has done, referring to* *the Cross)* **shall receive remission of sins** *(freedom, deliverance, forgiveness)*.

THE HOLY SPIRIT

"While Peter yet spoke these words *(concerning Believing in Him)*, **the Holy Spirit fell on all them which heard the Word** *(even though we are given very little information here, this is the moment when Cornelius and his household accepted Christ, and were Saved)*.

"And they of the Circumcision *(Jews)* **which believed** *(Believed in Christ)* **were astonished** *(at what they saw the Lord doing, which could not be denied)*, **as many as came with Peter, because that on the Gentiles also was poured out the Gift of the Holy Spirit** *(Cornelius and his household were Saved, and then moments later baptized with the Holy Spirit; it was quite a meeting!)*."

SPEAKING WITH TONGUES

"For they heard them speak with Tongues *(this is the initial, physical evidence that one has been baptized with the Holy Spirit; it always and without exception accompanies the Spirit Baptism)*, **and magnify God** *(means that some of them would stop speaking in Tongues momentarily, and then begin to praise God in their natural language, magnifying His Name)*. **Then answered Peter** *(presents the Apostle about to take another step)*,

"Can any man forbid water, that these should not be baptized *(they had accepted Christ and had been baptized with the Spirit, so now they should be baptized in water, which they were)*, **which have received the Holy Spirit as well as we?** *(Multiple millions of Gentiles since that day have been baptized with the Holy Spirit.)*

"And he Commanded them to be baptized in the Name of the Lord *(simply means, 'by the Authority of the*

Lord'). **Then prayed they him to tarry certain days** *(which he possibly did!)*" **(Acts 10:34-48).**

THE REASON THE LORD DID IT THIS WAY

The next Chapter proclaims some of the leaders in Jerusalem somewhat skeptical of what Peter had done by going into the house of a Gentile, etc. But, when Peter explained to them what had happened, they readily accepted his testimony.

That more than likely is the reason the Lord baptized Cornelius and those with him immediately after they were Saved. Had Peter explained to those in Jerusalem that Cornelius and his household had accepted Christ, the skepticism of those in Jerusalem may have continued. However, when he told them that, as well, they had been baptized with the Holy Spirit with the evidence of speaking with other Tongues, in fact, exactly as the Apostles had received, they then had no argument left.

THE EPHESIAN DISCIPLES FILLED WITH THE SPIRIT (ACTS 19:1-7)

This is the last of five accounts in the Book of Acts of Believers being baptized with the Holy Spirit. I think the accounts unquestionably show that the Baptism with the Holy Spirit is an experience different from Salvation, and, as we have repeatedly stated, the Baptism with the Spirit is not for one to be Saved, that already having occurred. This experience is that one may have power. And, as we have also stated, without this experience, as given to us in the Book of Acts, there is not going to be very much truly done for the Lord Jesus Christ. Concerning these Ephesian Disciples, the Word says:

"And it came to pass, that, while Apollos was at Corinth *(pertains to Acts 18:27)*, Paul having passed through the upper coasts came to Ephesus *(refers back to Acts 18:23)*: and finding certain Disciples *(they were followers of Christ, but deficient in their understanding),* **"He said unto them, Have you received the Holy Spirit since you believed?** *(In the Greek, this is literally, 'having believed, did you receive?' We know these men were already Saved because every time the word 'Disciples' is used in the Book of Acts, it refers to individuals who have accepted Christ. Paul could tell that these individuals, although Saved, had not yet been baptized with the Holy Spirit.)* **And they said unto him, We have not so much as heard whether there be any Holy Spirit** *(doesn't mean that they didn't know of the existence of the Holy Spirit, but they were not aware that the Age of the Spirit had come, and that Believers could literally be baptized with Him; at Salvation, the Holy Spirit baptizes Believing sinners into Christ; at the Spirit Baptism, Jesus baptizes Believers into the Holy Spirit [Mat. 3:11]).*

"And he said unto them, Unto what then were you baptized? *(After asking about the Holy Spirit Baptism, Paul was met with a blank stare, so to speak.)* **And they said, Unto John's Baptism** *(this was the Baptism of Repentance).***"**

JOHN'S BAPTISM

"Then said Paul, John verily baptized with the Baptism of Repentance *(which, in effect, was all that could be done at that particular time),* **saying unto the people, that they should believe on Him which should come after him, that is, on Christ Jesus** *(proclaims John the Baptist lifting up Jesus as the Saviour of mankind).*

"When they heard *this* *(no doubt, Paul said much more; however, the evidence is they instantly believed and accepted what Paul said, and they then desired what he said),* **they were baptized in the Name of the Lord Jesus** *(means, 'by the authority of the Lord Jesus'; the only Baptismal formula in the Word of God is Mat. 28:19).***"**

THE HOLY SPIRIT CAME ON THEM

"**And when Paul had laid *his* hands upon them** *(constitutes a Biblical principle [Acts 8:17; 9:17-18])*, **the Holy Spirit came on them** *(refers to them being baptized with the Holy Spirit)*; **and they spoke with Tongues, and prophesied** *(proclaims Tongues as the initial physical evidence that one has been baptized with the Holy Spirit; sometimes there is prophesying at that time, and sometimes not [Acts 8:17; 9:17; 10:46])*.

"**And all the men were about twelve** *(it seems that no women were involved at this particular time)*" (**Acts 19:1-7**).

Again we emphasize the fact that the Word of God is unequivocally clear in the fact that the Baptism with the Holy Spirit is an experience that follows Salvation. Believers are definitely born of the Spirit at Salvation, which means, in essence, that they do receive the Holy Spirit; however, as we've also said any number of times, there is a vast difference in being *"born of the Spirit,"* and *"baptized with the Spirit."* Of course, as is obvious, being *"born of the Spirit"* is the greatest thing that could ever happen to anyone. But, if one wants to be of service to the Lord, one is going to have to be, as well, *"baptized with the Spirit."*

"When this passing world is done,
"When has sunk yon glorious sun,
"When we stand with Christ on high,
"Looking o'er life's history;
"Then, Lord, shall I fully know,
"Not till then how much I owe."

"When I stand before the Throne,
"Dressed in beauty not my own,
"When I see You as You are,
"Love You with unsinning heart;

"Then, Lord, shall I fully know,
"Not till then how much I owe."

"Even on Earth, as through a glass,
"Darkly, let Your Glory pass;
"Make forgiveness feel so sweet;
"Make Your Spirit's help so meet;
"Even on Earth, Lord, make me know,
"Something of how much I owe."

"Chosen not for good in me,
"Wakened up from wrath to flee;
"Hidden in the Saviour's side,
"By the Spirit sanctified;
"Teach me, Lord, on Earth to show,
"By my love, how much I owe."

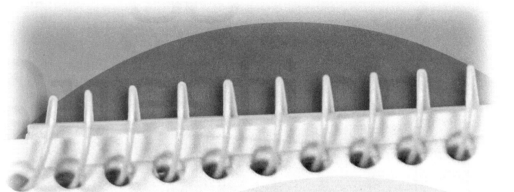

CHAPTER SIX

What Is The Initial Physical Evidence, If Any, Of Being Baptized With The Holy Spirit?

QUESTION:

WHAT IS THE INITIAL PHYSICAL EVIDENCE, IF ANY, OF BEING BAPTIZED WITH THE HOLY SPIRIT?

ANSWER:

While there are many evidences of being baptized with the Spirit, the initial physical evidence that one has been baptized with the Spirit is speaking with other Tongues as the Spirit of God gives the utterance.

As well, if one hasn't spoken with other Tongues, one has not been baptized with the Holy Spirit. The experience they have had, if any, may definitely have been from the Lord and may have been greatly wonderful, still, the Bible bears it out that speaking with other Tongues is the initial physical evidence that one has been baptized with the Spirit. There is no other evidence given in the Word of God. As we go along, especially when we get to the infilling of the Apostle Paul, we will prove from the Word of God that all experiences other than speaking with other Tongues, as wonderful as they may be in their own right, and as much as they may be from the Lord, still, aren't evidence of being baptized with the Spirit.

Let's see what the Word of God says about the matter.

THE SECOND CHAPTER OF ACTS

Luke wrote, saying:

"And they were all filled with the Holy Spirit *(all were filled, not just the Apostles; due to the Cross, the Holy Spirit could now come into the hearts and lives of all Believers to abide permanently [Jn. 14:16])*, and began to speak with other Tongues *(the initial physical evidence that one has been baptized with the Spirit, and was predicted by the Prophet Isaiah [Isa. 28:9-12], and by Christ [Mk. 16:17;*

Jn. 15:26; 16:13]), **as the Spirit gave them utterance**
*(meaning they did not initiate this themselves, but that it was
initiated by the Spirit; as we shall see, these were languages
known somewhere in the world, but not by the speaker)*"
(Acts 2:4).

THE WAY THE SENTENCE IS STRUCTURED

When it said, *"and they were all filled with the Holy Spirit,"*
part of the emphasis is on the word *"all."* As well, the word
"all," as it is here used, can also be transferred to the next phrase
making it read, *"and all began to speak with other Tongues."*

There is no hint that those on the Day of Pentecost, ever how
many there were, who were filled with the Spirit, received it any
other way than by the action of *"speaking with other Tongues."*

Some have claimed that some receive by speaking with
Tongues, but with others, there is another type of evidence.
That is not borne out in the Word of God. If the Holy Spirit
were going to function in that manner, this would have been the
time to have done so. But the sentence structure is such, with
the evidence overwhelming, that when all of these people were
filled with the Spirit, all of them spoke with other Tongues.

(In another Chapter we will deal with the question as to how
that Tongues are beneficial!)

THE EIGHTH CHAPTER OF ACTS

When the account was given of the Samaritans receiving
the Holy Spirit, nothing is said as to how they received. It just
simply said, *"Who, when they were come down, prayed for them,
that they might receive the Holy Spirit"* (Acts 8:15).

However, there is other evidence in this account that tells us
they did speak with other Tongues. Let's see what the Bible says.

Even though Simon the Sorcerer, it seems, was genuinely
Saved under the Ministry of Philip, still, when Peter and John
came to Samaria and preached the Doctrine of the Baptism

with the Holy Spirit to the Samaritans, Simon was enamored by what he saw and heard. It seems, at least in his mind, that he reverted back to his old custom of sorcery. The Scripture says concerning this:

THE SINFUL PROPOSAL

"And when Simon saw that through laying on of the Apostles' hands the Holy Spirit was given *(what did he see? he saw and heard them speak with Tongues)*, he offered them money *(he would not have offered money for the mere laying on of hands)*,

"Saying, Give me also this power, that on whomsoever I lay hands, he may receive the Holy Spirit *(money cannot purchase these Gifts, or anything else of God for that matter)*.

"But Peter said unto him, Your money perish with you, because you have thought that the Gift of God may be purchased with money *(every Preacher must be extra careful that money not be made a part of the equation; God has nothing for sale; everything He has is a 'Gift' [Jn. 3:16])*."

LOGOS

"You have neither part nor lot in this matter *(the word 'matter' in the Greek, as it is used here, is 'Logos,' and means 'a word or speech'; Peter is referring to these Believers speaking with other Tongues)*: for your heart is not right in the Sight of God *(self-will is the cause of the evil heart)*.

"Repent therefore of this your wickedness *(proclaims just how bad the sin was, but yet that hope is offered)*, and pray God, if perhaps the thought of your heart may be forgiven you *(tells us that God Alone could remedy this situation, and He always will upon proper Repentance, which says that He is right and I am wrong)*.

"For I perceive *(refers to the Holy Spirit informing Peter of the exact cause, and not mere symptoms)* that you are in the gall of bitterness *(condition of extreme wickedness)*, and *in* the bond of iniquity *(a bondage of greed for money, power, and control over other men)*.

"Then answered Simon, and said, Pray ye to the Lord for me *(suggests a right attitude on the part of Simon)*, that none of these things which you have spoken come upon me *(has reference to him potentially perishing, that is if he remained on that particular course)*" (Acts 8:18-24).

THE NINTH CHAPTER OF ACTS

Once again, the Scriptural account of Paul being *"filled with the Holy Spirit"* gives us no information whatsoever as to what exactly happened. The Scripture merely says:

"And Ananias went his way, and entered into the house *(he obeyed the Command of the Lord)*; and putting his hands on him *(on Paul)* said, Brother Saul *(he addressed Paul in this manner because Paul was already Saved, and had been so for the last three days and nights)*, the Lord, *even* Jesus, Who appeared unto you in the way as you came, has sent me, that you might receive your sight, and be filled with the Holy Spirit *(this proclaims the fact that one is not baptized with the Holy Spirit at conversion, as many teach; in fact, the Baptism with the Holy Spirit is a separate work of Grace, which takes place after conversion [Acts 2:4; 8:14-17; 19:1-7])*" (Acts 9:17).

UNSCRIPTURAL DIRECTION

Ever since the Latter Rain outpouring, so to speak, which commenced at approximately the turn of the Twentieth Century, fulfilling the Prophecy of Joel (Joel 2:23), there have been many and varied responses to this outpouring.

(The *"Former Rain,"* again so-called, took place beginning on the Day of Pentecost and continued during the time of the Early Church. In fact, there were people who continued to be filled with the Spirit all down through the centuries of the Church Age. However, due to the fact that the Church eventually apostatized, ultimately morphing into the Roman Catholic system, this great Message, along with the Message of Salvation, for all practical purposes, ceased to be preached. If the Word of whatever subject in the Bible is not proclaimed, then people will not receive that which is promised.)

Since the Latter Rain outpouring, there have been many and varied responses to what the Lord has done. Some of the responses were and are:

• Some few accepted it, and continue to do so, who are the ones who have touched, and are touching, the world for Christ.

• Some have claimed that one can be baptized with the Spirit with Tongues or without Tongues.

• Others have claimed that while speaking in Tongues was real, it passed away with the Apostles, meaning that those who claim presently to be filled and, thereby, speak with other Tongues are only deceiving themselves.

• Some openly and bluntly claim that the Baptism with the Holy Spirit and speaking with other Tongues is of the Devil. Such a direction is perilously close to blaspheming the Holy Spirit if, in fact, the line has not already been crossed.

THE EXPERIENCES OF THE APOSTLE PAUL

The Scripture is emphatically clear that Paul was *"filled with the Holy Spirit"* as Ananias laid hands on him and prayed for him some three days after he was Saved on the road to Damascus. As should be obvious, the great Apostle had tremendous experiences in his conversion experience. Some of them are:

• The Scripture says, *"And suddenly there shined round about him a light from Heaven"* (Acts 9:3). This was quite an experience, as would be obvious. Yet, this great light shining about him was not the Baptism with the Holy Spirit, as wonderful as this experience was.

• The Scripture then says, *"And he fell to the earth"* (Acts 9:4). This means literally that the Power of God was so great on him at that time that he could no longer stand and, thereby, fell to the ground. Some believe that he was on a horse, but the Scripture does not say. At any rate, his falling to the earth was a manifestation of the Power of God, but still, he wasn't baptized with the Holy Spirit.

• Then he heard the Voice of Christ *"saying unto him, Saul, Saul, why do you persecute Me?"* (Acts 9:4). The Scripture doesn't say that Paul literally saw the Lord, but it most definitely does say that he heard the Voice of our Lord. As should be obvious, this was quite an experience, but this didn't mean that Paul was then baptized with the Holy Spirit.

• Then the Lord gave Paul direction after the Jew from Tarsus had accepted Him as *"Lord,"* saying unto him, *"Arise, and go into the city, and it shall be told you what you must do"* (Acts 9:6). Despite having this tremendous direction given to him, and by none other than the Lord, still, he wasn't at the time baptized with the Spirit.

All of these things that Paul experienced were wonderful, to say the least, and most definitely were from the Lord and of the Lord, but none of these things were the Baptism with the Holy Spirit.

Now, many, many Christians would think if they had these types of experiences, it should be construed as having been baptized with the Holy Spirit. It doesn't! Despite all of these things happening to him, still, the Lord told Ananias to go to where Paul was and pray for him, *"that he might receive his sight, and be filled with the Holy Spirit,"* which he was!

While we dare not minimize these wonderful things which happened to Paul, again, it should be clear that these experiences were not the Baptism with the Holy Spirit.

And yet, there are many people presently who think that

any experience from the Lord of similar nature, whatever it might be, constitutes being baptized with the Spirit. Let us say it again:

Whenever a Believer is baptized with the Holy Spirit, that Believer will speak with other Tongues. If not, while what they have received may definitely be a blessing from the Lord, still, it is not the Baptism with the Holy Spirit.

THE TENTH CHAPTER OF ACTS

The Scripture says concerning Cornelius and those with him:

"**While Peter yet spoke these words** (*concerning Believing in Him*)**, the Holy Spirit fell on all them which heard the Word** (*even though we are given very little information here, this is the moment when Cornelius and his household accepted Christ, and were Saved*)**.

"**And they of the Circumcision** (*Jews*) **which believed** (*Believed in Christ*) **were astonished** (*at what they saw the Lord doing, which could not be denied*)**, as many as came with Peter, because that on the Gentiles also was poured out the Gift of the Holy Spirit** (*Cornelius and his house-hold were Saved, and then moments later baptized with the Holy Spirit; it was quite a meeting!*)**.

"**For they heard them speak with Tongues** (*this is the initial, physical evidence that one has been baptized with the Holy Spirit; it always and without exception accompanies the Spirit Baptism*)**, and magnify God** (*means that some of them would stop speaking in Tongues momentarily, and then begin to praise God in their natural language, magnifying His Name*)**" (Acts 10:44-46).

Emphatically the Scripture states, *"for they heard them speak with Tongues."*

In the Eleventh Chapter of Acts, Peter, explaining this situation, which was momentous, to say the least, told the Elders in Jerusalem:

"**And as I began to speak** *(had gotten a little way into the Message),* **the Holy Spirit fell on them, as on us at the beginning** *(speaks of Cornelius and his household being baptized with the Spirit, exactly as the Apostles and others had been on the Day of Pentecost).*

"**Then remembered I the Word of the Lord, how that He said** *(pertains to something that Peter had not mentioned in the actual happening),* **John indeed baptized with water; but you shall be Baptized with the Holy Spirit** *(Acts 1:5; Mat. 3:11).*"

THE LIKE GIFT

"**Forasmuch then as God gave them** *(the Gentiles)* **the like Gift** *(Salvation and the Holy Spirit Baptism)* **as *He did*** **unto us, who believed on the Lord Jesus Christ** *(the requirement);* **what was I, that I could withstand God?** *(To not go would be to disobey God)*" **(Acts 11:15-17).**

Once again, the emphasis is placed on the fact that all speak with other Tongues when they are baptized with the Holy Spirit. If not, while they may definitely have been blessed and blessed greatly by the Lord, still, they have not been baptized with the Holy Spirit.

THE NINETEENTH CHAPTER OF ACTS

The happenings at Ephesus, as recorded in this Nineteenth Chapter, took place about twenty-five years after the Day of Pentecost. The account given in this Nineteenth Chapter proclaims the fact that Paul, *"finding certain Disciples"* in that particular city, seemed to feel in his spirit that they, although Saved, had not been baptized with the Holy Spirit. So, he asked them, *"Have you received the Holy Spirit since you believed?"*

Some have claimed that these individuals were not even Saved. That is incorrect. Two factors tell us differently. They are:

• The phrase given in the King James, *"Have you received the Holy Spirit since you believed?,"* in the Greek literally says, *"Having believed, did you receive?"* The Scripture plainly tells us that if we believe on the Lord Jesus Christ, we will be Saved (Jn. 3:16; Acts 16:31). So, these individuals were Believers, meaning that they had already been Saved, but they had not yet been baptized with the Holy Spirit. Once again, this totally refutes the idea that at conversion one is also filled with the Spirit at the same time, etc.

• The Scripture as well refers to these individuals as *"Disciples."* Every time this word is used in the Book of Acts, it refers to followers of Christ and infers their Salvation.

Something else should be said in regard to this. It was instantly recognizable to Paul that even though these people were Saved, still, he knew they had not been filled with the Spirit. This is the case almost on a worldwide basis. Upon meeting other Believers whom one does not really even know, perhaps has never met, in talking with them a few moments, it becomes quickly obvious as to whether they are Spirit-filled or not.

The Scripture says:

> **"And when Paul had laid** *his* **hands upon them** *(constitutes a Biblical principle [Acts 8:17; 9:17-18])*, **the Holy Spirit came on them** *(refers to them being baptized with the Holy Spirit)*; **and they spoke with Tongues, and prophesied** *(proclaims Tongues as the initial physical evidence that one has been baptized with the Holy Spirit; sometimes there is prophesying at that time, and sometimes not [Acts 8:17; 9:17; 10:46])*" **(Acts 19:6).**

Five times the account is given in the Book of Acts of Believers being baptized with the Holy Spirit. Four of those times the Scripture is emphatic that they spoke with Tongues. The only time that it doesn't say is in the Ninth Chapter of Acts as it regards the infilling of the Apostle Paul; however, it doesn't really tell us at all how he was filled, just that Ananias was to pray for him, which he did.

But Paul did say in his First Epistle to the Church at Corinth, in giving them instructions as it regards how that Tongues are to be used, *"I thank my God, I speak with Tongues more than you all"* (I Cor. 14:18).

As well, the Apostle was not speaking of his linguistic ability of being able to speak two or three languages, which most Jews then could do. He was speaking, as the entirety of the context bears out, about him worshipping the Lord in Tongues, a language he did not know but spoke as the Spirit of God moved on him.

THE PROPHECY OF ISAIAH

Paul quoted the great Millennial Prophet Isaiah as it regards how that Tongues would be rejected. Isaiah said, and Paul quotes:

"In the Law it is written, With men of other tongues and other lips will I speak unto this people; and yet for all that will they not hear Me, saith the Lord" (Isa. 28:ll, I Cor. 14:21). This predicts that many, if not most, would refuse to heed this which is of the Lord.

If we want to follow the Word of the Lord, we will have to admit that the Bible teaches that speaking with other Tongues as the Spirit of God gives the utterance is the initial, physical evidence that one has been baptized with the Holy Spirit and, in fact, is the only initial physical evidence.

"The great Physician now is near,
"The sympathizing Jesus;
"He speaks the drooping heart to cheer,
"O hear the Voice of Jesus."

"Your many sins are all forgiven,
"Oh! Hear the Voice of Jesus;

"Go on your way in peace to Heaven,
"And wear a crown with Jesus."

"All glory to the dying Lamb,
"I now believe in Jesus;
"I love the blessed Saviour's Name,
"I love the Name of Jesus."

"His Name dispels my guilt and fear,
"No, no other Jesus;
"Oh! How my soul delights to hear,
"The charming Name of Jesus."

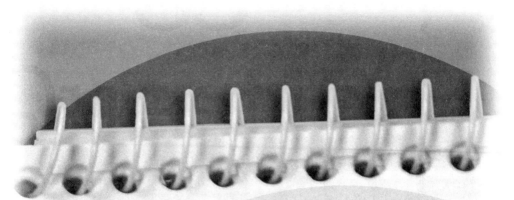

CHAPTER SEVEN

What Is The Value In Speaking With Other Tongues?

QUESTION:

WHAT IS THE VALUE IN SPEAKING WITH OTHER TONGUES?

ANSWER:

There is much value in speaking with other Tongues, even as we shall show from the Scriptures. To be sure, the Lord doesn't do anything that is of no value. In fact, everything He does is freighted with value, with profit, with help, and of every description. In this Chapter we will show you from the Word of God the value of speaking with other Tongues, proof which is undeniable. That's one of the reasons the Apostle Paul said, as it regards this wonderful gift, *"I would that you all spoke with Tongues . . ."* (I Cor. 14:5).

TONGUES, AS USED BY THE HOLY SPIRIT, ARE LANGUAGES KNOWN SOMEWHERE IN THE WORLD, BUT NOT BY THE SPEAKER

It is a very dangerous thing to refer to Tongues, as is done by some, as incoherent babble or gibberish, etc. In fact, even as we will prove from the Word of God, Tongues are languages known and spoken somewhere in the world, but not by the speaker. In fact, the Holy Spirit went into great detail to prove this fact, and did so even on the Day of Pentecost.

On that great day when many were baptized with the Holy Spirit, in fact, all who obeyed the Lord, the Holy Spirit went into detail to prove the fact that what these people were speaking, even though they did not know or understand what they were saying, were, in fact, languages known somewhere in the world. The account is as follows:

"OUT OF EVERY NATION UNDER HEAVEN"

"And there were dwelling at Jerusalem Jews, devout

men, out of every nation under Heaven *(Jews were then scattered all over the Roman World, with thousands coming in from every nation to keep the Feast).*

"Now when this was noised abroad *(multitudes who were in the Temple heard and saw the proceedings and, as well, began to tell others),* **the multitude came together** *(what was happening attracted a multitude),* **and was confounded, because that every man heard them speak in his own language** *(means that these onlooking Jews heard these people speaking in many different languages, in fact, languages of the nations of their residence, wherever that might have been, proving that this was not gibberish or babble as some claim)."*

ALL ARE GALILAEANS

"And they were all amazed and marveled *(mostly centered upon this speaking with other Tongues),* **saying one to another, Behold, are not all these which speak Galilaeans?** *(This means that the Galilaean accent was peculiar and well-known [Mk. 14:70; Lk. 22:59]).*

"And how hear we every man in our own tongue, wherein we were born? *(This proves once again that this was not babble, mere chatter, or gibberish, but rather a language known somewhere in the world, but not by the speaker.)"*

DIFFERENT TONGUES

"Parthians, and Medes, and Elamites, and the dwellers in Mesopotamia, and in Judaea, and Cappadocia, in Pontus, and Asia,

"Phrygia, and Pamphylia, in Egypt, and in the parts of Libya about Cyrene, and strangers of Rome, Jews and proselytes,

"Cretes and Arabians, we do hear them speak in our tongues the wonderful Works of God *(this tells us what speaking in Tongues actually is, a recitation of the*

'Wonderful Works of God')."

SOME WERE AMAZED AND SOME MOCKED

"**And they were all amazed, and were in doubt** *(should have been translated, 'and were perplexed'; they had no rational answer to their perplexity)*, **saying one to another, What does this mean?** *(This was asking more in wonder than demanding an answer.)*

"**Others mocking said** *(they scoffed; whether by gesture or word, they jeered at the Testimony of this given by the Holy Spirit)*, **These men are full of new wine** *(was actually an accusation that they were drunk, i.e., 'intoxicated'; some were amazed and some 'mocked,' which continues to be done even unto this hour)*."

"THIS IS THAT . . . SPOKEN BY THE PROPHET JOEL"

"**But Peter, standing up with the Eleven, lifted up his voice, and said unto them** *(Peter will now preach the inaugural Message of the Church on that Day of Pentecost)*, **You men of Judaea, and all you who dwell at Jerusalem, be this known unto you, and hearken to my words** *(the Message was probably delivered on Solomon's Porch, a part of the Court of the Gentiles; it was where debates and such like were commonly conducted)*:

"**For these are not drunken, as you suppose** *(in effect, says they are drunk, but not in the common manner)*, **seeing it is *but* the third hour of the day** *(9 a.m.)*.

"**But this is that which was spoken by the Prophet Joel** *(please notice that Peter did not say, 'this fulfills that spoken by the Prophet Joel,' but rather, 'this is that . . .' meaning that it will continue)*."

THE POURED OUT SPIRIT

"**And it shall come to pass in the last days, saith**

God (*proclaims these 'last days' as beginning on the Day of Pentecost, and continuing through the coming Great Tribulation*), **I will pour out of My Spirit upon all flesh** (*speaks of all people everywhere and, therefore, not limited to some particular geographical location; as well, it is not limited respecting race, color, or creed*): **and your sons and your daughters shall prophesy** (*includes both genders*), **and your young men shall see visions, and your old men shall dream dreams** (*all given by the Holy Spirit; the Hebrew language insinuates, 'both your young men and old men shall see Visions, and both your old men and young men shall dream Dreams'; it applies to both genders as well*):

"**And on My servants and on My handmaidens I will pour out in those days of My Spirit** (*is meant purposely to address two classes of people who had been given very little status in the past, slaves and women*); **and they shall prophesy.** (*Pertains to one of the 'Gifts of the Spirit' [I Cor. 12:8-10]*)" (**Acts 2:5-18**).

Now, many have asked the question as to what good it does anyone to speak with other Tongues. People who ask such questions, despite their claims, know little or nothing about the Moving and Operation of the Holy Spirit. Everything they do is by and through the flesh, which is never of God. Let's see what the Bible says about the value of speaking with other Tongues, in other words, how it helps the individual, help I might quickly add, which is desperately needed by all of us.

"A SOUND FROM HEAVEN"

"And suddenly there came a sound from Heaven as of a rushing mighty wind" (Acts 2:2).

This *"sound from Heaven"* is undeniably linked with the coming of the Holy Spirit evidenced by speaking with other Tongues. So, anything of this nature that is from Heaven, to be sure, is most profitable for the individual who has the privilege of experiencing such. That which is from Heaven I most definitely want and desire. And, we are here told that speaking with other Tongues has its origin in that which is from Heaven.

GREAT JOY

Peter said, *"For these are not drunken, as you suppose, seeing it is but the third hour of the day"* (Acts 2:15). In truth, these Galilaeans were drunk, but it was not on intoxicating beverage but, rather, the Joy of the Lord. Anything that will bring this type of joy, and the Baptism with the Holy Spirit with the evidence of speaking with other Tongues will do exactly that, is extremely worthwhile. In fact, alcoholic beverage and certain types of drugs are given as substitutes by Satan trying to imitate that which the Lord does through the Spirit. To be sure, we need this joy, which the Holy Spirit Alone can provide.

Unfortunately, much of modern Christendom knows precious little about the Joy of the Lord, and it's because they know very little about the Holy Spirit. As a result, their experience with the Lord leaves much to be desired.

"SPOKEN BY THE PROPHET JOEL"

Peter also said, *"But this is that which was spoken by the Prophet Joel"* (Acts 2:16).

Joel prophesied this which Peter quoted nearly eight hundred years before Christ. So, if anyone wants to know what it is, *"this is that . . .,"* meaning, at that time it was not ending but, in fact, just beginning. It continues unto this hour. So, everyone who is baptized with the Holy Spirit and speaks with other Tongues as the Spirit of God gives the utterance can say with Peter, *"this is that. . . ."*

Something prophesied nearly eight hundred years before Christ and then coming to pass beautifully on the Day of Pentecost, and which continues unto this hour, which the Scripture bears out, that I greatly want and desire.

SPEAKS UNTO GOD

Paul said, *"For he who speaks in an unknown Tongue speaks not unto men, but unto God . . ."* (I Cor. 14:2).

Plainly and clearly, we are told here that anyone and everyone who speaks in other Tongues speaks *"unto God."* If we think about that a few moments, that is a very heady thing. Anything designed by the Lord, which is for our benefit and which speaks directly to Him, has got to be valuable indeed! When one worships in Tongues, one does not have to wonder if the Lord is hearing him. We are here unequivocally told that He most definitely does. What a privilege!

PERSONAL EDIFICATION

"He who speaks in an unknown tongue edifies himself . . ." (I Cor. 14:4).

All of us need Spiritual edification, and we are here plainly told that when we speak with other Tongues, in other words, worship the Lord in Tongues, which we should do on a daily basis, this is personal edification. In other words, it builds us up, strengthens us, helps us, etc. As stated, it's something all of us need and is available to all who will freely and readily accept it.

"THE WONDERFUL WORKS OF GOD"

The onlookers said, *"We do hear them speak in our tongues the wonderful Works of God"* (Acts 2:11).

So, we are here told as to exactly what speaking in Tongues actually is. It is a recitation of the *"wonderful Works of God,"* which is something extremely important, as should be obvious.

No doubt, speaking with other Tongues recites the great happenings of the Lord given to us in His Word and, as well, things which have taken place in our own lives. I should think that anyone would recognize the fact, at least anyone who is truly Saved, that to recite these great happenings, and to do so on a constant basis, is a wonderful thing to be able to do. Speaking with other Tongues does exactly that.

TONGUES ARE FOR A SIGN TO UNBELIEVERS

Paul said, *"Wherefore Tongues are for a sign, not to them who believe, but to them who believe not"* (I Cor. 14:22).

How is this so when virtually all unbelievers know absolutely nothing about speaking with other Tongues?

The idea is not that they know it and understand that it is a sign to them, but rather, this great Gift being given tells the whole world that these are the last days. And, if these *"last days"* began on the Day of Pentecost, and they most definitely did, then it should stand to reason that we are now living in the last of the last days. This means that every time one speaks in Tongues, whomever he may be, and wherever he may be, especially now, this is the Lord telling us and, in fact, the entirety of the world, that's it's about over.

This especially refers to the Latter Rain outpouring which began at about the turn of the Twentieth Century. That being the case, speaking with other Tongues becomes prophetically very important.

A *"REST"* AND A *"REFRESHING"*

The great Prophet Isaiah said, and some seven hundred and fifty years before Christ, and I quote from THE EXPOSITOR'S STUDY BIBLE:

"For with stammering lips and another tongue will He speak to this people. *(The phrase, 'stammering lips,' refers to a proper language being spoken, but yet the people hearing it would not understand it. Paul quoted this same*

Passage as it regards the Gift of Tongues as a sign to unbelievers [I Cor. 14:21-22]. Oftentimes, the Holy Spirit used strange circumstances to present Prophecy proclaiming tremendously important coming events, even as this Prophecy does.

"Such also was the Prophecy given through Isaiah of the Birth of Christ through a 'virgin' [Isa. 7:14]. The occasion would be the unbelief, ridicule, and scorn of wicked Ahaz.

"Therefore, it seems that the Holy Spirit designed both these Prophecies [the Virgin Birth of Christ and the Baptism with the Holy Spirit], to occasion Faith in Believers and unbelief in mockers!)

"To whom He said, This is the rest wherewith you may cause the weary to rest; and this is the refreshing: yet they would not hear. *(Coupled with Verse 11, this tells us that speaking with other Tongues brings about a 'rest' from the tiredness of the journey of life. As well, speaking with other Tongues brings about a 'refreshing,' which rejuvenates the person. Many people ask, 'What good is there in speaking with other Tongues?' This mentioned by Isaiah presents two Blessings, of which there are many. Regrettably, despite this tremendous gift given to the people of God, at least to those who will believe, like Judah of old, most 'will not hear,' even as Paul quoted Isaiah [I Cor. 14:21])"* **(Isa. 28:11-12).**

WE, AS BELIEVERS, DESPERATELY NEED THIS *"REST"* AND *"REFRESHING"*

And this is the way, worshipping the Lord in other Tongues, which provides this *"rest"* **and** *"refreshing."* **Unfortunately, far too many modern Believers have become hooked on prescription drugs, trying to bring about that which the Lord Alone can do. Regrettably, most Believers, even those who are baptized with the Holy Spirit and who speak with other Tongues, at least occasionally, little know its worth and value. So, little knowing**

or understanding such, the *"need"* is attempted to be met by the methods of the world, which never succeeds.

While we certainly do not expect the world to understand this, we do, in fact, have the right to expect Believers to understand it, but regrettably, most don't!

As a Believer, and especially considering the vicissitudes, difficulties, and burdens of life and living, I need this *"rest"* and *"refreshing"* which is provided by the Lord. I need *"rest"* from the journey and *"refreshing"* to continue the journey. Worshipping the Lord in other Tongues provides that *"rest"* and *"refreshing."*

"Lord, I hear of showers of Blessing,
"You are scattering full and free,
"Showers the thirsty land refreshing:
"Let some drops now fall on me."

"Pass me not, O gracious Father!
"Sinful though my heart may be;
"You might lead me, but the rather,
"Let Your Mercy fall on me."

"Pass me not, O tender Saviour!
"Let me love and cling to Thee:
"I am longing for Your Favor;
"While You are Calling, call for me."

"Pass me not, O mighty Spirit!
"You can make the blind to see;
"Witness of Jesus' merit,
"Speak the Word of power to me."

"Love of God, so pure and changeless!
"Blood of Christ, so rich and free!
"Grace of God, so strong and boundless!
"Magnify them all in me."

"Pass me not! Your lost one bringing,
"Bind my heart, O Lord, to Thee:
"While the streams of life are springing,
"Blessing others, oh bless me."

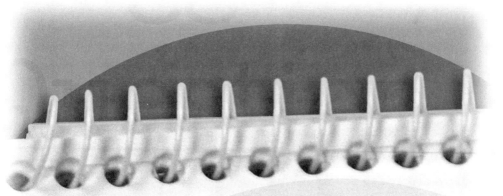

CHAPTER EIGHT

What Is The Anointing Of The Holy Spirit?

QUESTION:

WHAT IS THE ANOINTING OF THE HOLY SPIRIT?

ANSWER:

The Anointing of the Holy Spirit is simply the Presence of God on a person to enable that person to preach, teach, sing, pray, witness, etc. It can be, and is meant to be, on any Believer, preacher, or otherwise. In other words, any Believer can be anointed by the Holy Spirit and, in fact, is intended to be anointed by the Holy Spirit.

A COMFORTER

Jesus said, and concerning the Holy Spirit:

"**And I will pray the Father, and He shall give you another Comforter** *('Parakletos,' which means 'One called to the side of another to help')*, **that He may abide with you forever** *(before the Cross, the Holy Spirit could only help a few individuals, and then only for a period of time; since the Cross, He lives in the hearts and lives of all Believers, and does so forever)*" **(Jn. 14:16).**

This *"help,"* which the Holy Spirit gives us, is the anointing to carry out the task at hand, whatever it might be.

NO LIMITATIONS

We must understand that there are no limitations as it regards this anointing. As stated, it is meant for all Believers, and is meant to be of service to us in every capacity of our life and living, whatever that might be.

We must also understand that the Anointing of the Holy Spirit is not some strange thing that only pertains to a few individuals, but rather, that it is meant to be part and parcel for every Believer, whoever they might be, and wherever they might be. We all need the Anointing of the Holy Spirit in everything we do.

Every time I preach, I ask the Lord to anoint me to deliver the Message which He has anointed me to receive. When I give an Altar Call, I ask for the Anointing of the Spirit to give that invitation. In fact, I want the Leading, Guidance, and Help of the Holy Spirit in every single thing I do, because I need it desperately.

A HELPER

If it is to be noticed, the manner in which the Holy Spirit helps us is that we do our part, and then He will help us with the rest. He will not take charge of our lives, thereby, doing for us what we can do for ourselves. There is a reason for that.

The Holy Spirit is meant to develop us in the Lord. He wants us to grow in Grace and the knowledge of the Lord. We cannot do that if He does everything for us; however, we must, above all, understand that without His Help, we're not going to get anything done. While our part is required, it alone will accomplish nothing for the Lord, yet, the Holy Spirit insists that we do that part, which is to make ourselves a willing agent through which He may work.

The Holy Spirit will not preach for me, but He will help me preach. He will not sing for me, but He will help me sing. He will not do my praying for me, but He most definitely will help me to pray. He will not make my decisions for me, but He will help me to make the right decisions. All of that is the Anointing of the Spirit, i.e., the Presence of God on the individual.

THE ANOINTING OF THE HOLY SPIRIT ON OUR LORD

As God, as should be obvious, Jesus did not need the Anointing; however, as the Man Christ Jesus, He most definitely did need the Anointing, i.e., *"the help,"* of the Holy Spirit. If He, the Lord of Glory, the Son of the Living God, the Saviour of man, needed the Anointing of the Holy Spirit, I am absolutely certain that we most definitely need that Anointing.

The Scripture says of Him:

"And He taught in their Synagogues, being glorified of all *(this was the beginning; it would soon change)*.

"And He came to Nazareth, where He had been brought up *(makes vivid the fact that Jesus was Very Man, even as He was Very God)*: and, as His custom was *(in our language presently He was faithful to Church)*, He went into the Synagogue on the Sabbath Day, and stood up for to read *(it was common to ask visitors to expound on the Word)*.

"And there was delivered unto Him the Book *(Scroll)* of the Prophet Isaiah. And when He had opened the Book, He found the place where it was written *(Isa. 61:1)*."

"THE SPIRIT OF THE LORD" UPON CHRIST

"The Spirit of the Lord *is* upon Me *(we learn here of the absolute necessity of the Person and Work of the Holy Spirit within our lives)*, because He has anointed Me *(Jesus is the ultimate Anointed One; consequently, the Anointing of the Holy Spirit actually belongs to Christ, and the Anointing we have actually comes by His Authority [Jn.16:14])* to preach the Gospel to the poor *(the poor in spirit)*; He has sent Me to heal the brokenhearted *(sin breaks the heart, or else is responsible for it being broken; only Jesus can heal this malady)*, to preach Deliverance to the captives *(if it is to be noticed, He didn't say to 'deliver the captives,' but rather, 'preach Deliverance,' which refers to the Cross [Jn. 8:32])*, and recovering of sight to the blind *(the Gospel opens the eyes of those who are spiritually blind)*, to set at liberty them who are bruised *(the vicissitudes of life at times place a person in a mental or spiritual prison; the Lord Alone, and through what He did at the Cross, can open this prison door)*,

"**To preach the acceptable Year of the Lord** *(it is believed that the day on which Jesus delivered this Message was the first day of the Year of Jubilee)*" **(Lk.4:15-19).**

HOW DOES ONE HAVE THIS ANOINTING?

Under the New Covenant it is meant, as stated, for every single Believer on Earth to have the Anointing of the Holy Spirit. Yet, for the full flow of this Anointing to be prevalent, the person must first of all be baptized with the Holy Spirit with the evidence of speaking with other Tongues. While there can be a measure of Anointing without this experience, its full measure cannot be known and experienced without the Believer first being baptized with the Spirit. In fact, there can be precious little Leading and Guidance of the Spirit and precious little Help of the Spirit in any capacity unless the individual is first baptized with the Holy Spirit, and as we have repeatedly stated, with the evidence of speaking with other Tongues.

The Lord *"helping"* us, as He does as Comforter, and *"anointing"* us, constitutes that which is basically the same. His Help is His Anointing, etc. For the Lord to help us and for the Holy Spirit to be to us as He desires to be, there must be consecration on the part of the Believer. While this definitely cannot be earned or merited, still, at the same time, *"they who hunger and thirst after Righteousness shall be filled"* (Mat. 5:6).

We should understand that the Holy Spirit wants to help us as Believers in all things that we do. If the person is a carpenter by trade, the Holy Spirit wants to help that person be a better carpenter. If the Believer is a truck driver, or a teacher, or whatever, the Holy Spirit wants to help that person, which He most definitely will do, if we will desire that help and, thereby, avidly seek the Lord for such help.

Unfortunately, some Believers have been led to believe that

the Anointing of the Holy Spirit is for preachers only; however, the Bible simply tells us, *"And these signs shall follow them who believe . . ."* (Mk. 16:17). The only requirement is to be a *"Believer."*

THE CROSS OF CHRIST AND THE HOLY SPIRIT

While a full understanding of the Cross of Christ, which in reality is an understanding of the New Covenant, is not absolutely necessary in order to be anointed by the Lord, this knowledge will greatly enhance the Anointing, as should be obvious. When one is *"walking after the Spirit,"* and doing so constantly, which means they are not *"walking after the flesh,"* the Holy Spirit most definitely has greater liberty to work as He desires to work.

In truth, the Anointing of the Holy Spirit can rest with individuals from the moment they are Saved, but especially from the moment they are baptized with the Holy Spirit. However, as would be obvious, such a Believer, a babe in the Lord, which means we make many mistakes and go in many wrong directions, still has the Holy Spirit's help, i.e., *"anointing."* In other words, the Holy Spirit doesn't wait until we are mature in the Lord before He begins to anoint us. Thank the Lord for that; otherwise, not a single Believer could be used of the Lord.

Yet, when Light is given, it is intended that the Believer walk in that Light. If not, such grieves the Holy Spirit, and His Help in such a situation will become less and less.

A PERSONAL EXPERIENCE

Since the Lord began to open up to me the Message of the Cross in 1997, which He continues unto this hour, I have found a much greater freedom in prayer, a much greater understanding of the Word of God, and I believe a greater Anointing to preach and to teach, in fact, a greater Anointing in everything I do for Him. That doesn't mean that His Anointing before

1997 was insufficient. There is nothing about the Holy Spirit that is insufficient, which includes everything He does. It must always be remembered that the Holy Spirit works with us from an attitude and position of perfection on His Part, even though we only *"know in part."* With the Holy Spirit everything is a process of Spiritual Growth. We must remember that many times He works with us, not according to the spiritual level of maturity we presently occupy, but rather, according to the Spiritual Growth we are soon to experience. He can do that because He is God and, therefore, knows all things, past, present, and future.

PROPERLY EXPERIENCING SPIRITUAL GROWTH

Inasmuch as the Cross of Christ is that which makes possible the working of the Holy Spirit within our lives, it is imperative that the Cross of Christ be the sole Object of our Faith (Rom. 5:1-2; 6:1-14; I Cor. 1:17-18, 23; 2:2). The Holy Spirit wants to help us a whole lot more than He is able to do because of our wrong direction. If our doctrine is wrong, that greatly hinders Him. If our attitude and motives are wrong, that greatly hinders Him. If we insist on having our way, this presents a tremendous problem with Him. Thank God, under those circumstances, as debilitating as it might be for Him, He, thankfully, doesn't leave us. He'll work with us, try to speak to us, and try to show us, all without forcing the issue, which He could readily do if He so desired; however, as we've already stated, force is not His Way. He wants sole possession of us and in every capacity, but, it is sole possession that we must give Him, for He, as stated, will not take it by force.

To sum up, the Anointing of the Holy Spirit is actually the *"help"* the Lord gives us as our Comforter. As well, it is *"help"* in every capacity, that is, if we will only allow it to be. This Anointing or help is available to every single Believer and in every single capacity of life and living. The Anointing is simply the Presence of God functioning in our hearts and lives, helping us to do whatever needs to be done. As we have also stated, for this to be as it ought to be, the Believer must first be baptized with the Holy Spirit with the evidence of speaking with other Tongues. Without that, there is precious little Anointing. As well, the Baptism with the Holy Spirit, although making such available, does not necessarily mean that the Anointing of the Spirit will function in one's life. On our part there must be a hunger and a thirst after Righteousness; there must be a desire to have the Leading and Guidance of the Holy Spirit in all that we do. As well, I personally think that such a Believer must have a proper prayer life for the Anointing to function and operate as it should. Whatever is truly done for the Lord is always, in some way, accompanied by the Anointing of the Holy Spirit.

"Behold, what love, what boundless love,
"The Father has bestowed,
"O and sinners lost, that we should be,
"Now called the sons of God!"

"No longer far from Him, but now,
"By Precious Blood made nigh;
"Accepted in the well-beloved,
"Near to God's Heart we lie."

"What we in Glory soon shall be,
"It does not yet appear;
"But when our Precious Lord we see,
"We shall His Image bear."

"With such a blessed hope in view,
"We would more holy be,
"More like our risen, glorious Lord,
"Whose Face we soon shall see."

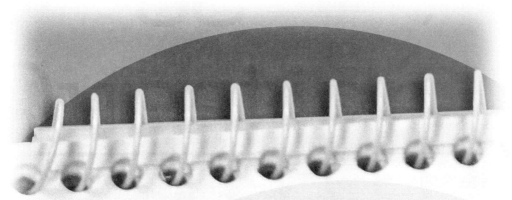

CHAPTER NINE

Brother Swaggart, What Are The Gifts Of The Spirit?

QUESTION:

BROTHER SWAGGART, WHAT ARE THE GIFTS OF THE SPIRIT?

ANSWER:

The Gifts of the Spirit pertain to Gifts listed in I Corinthians 12:8-10. Only Spirit-filled people can have these Gifts, and we speak of those who have been baptized with the Holy Spirit with the evidence of speaking with other Tongues. I have never heard of anyone exercising one of these Gifts who wasn't baptized with the Holy Spirit. In fact, most who do not subscribe to the Spirit Baptism claim that these Gifts stopped with the death of the original Apostles. And then those who do lend some type of idea that they exist today explain them totally in the natural realm. In other words, the *"Gifts of Healing(s)"* pertain to doctors and nurses, with the gift of *"the Word of Wisdom,"* which they erroneously label as the *"Gift of Wisdom,"* as being possessed by elderly Christians who have a lot of experience. In other words, everything is explained in the natural, taking it out from the Domain of the Holy Spirit. Of course, none of that is Scripturally correct.

In this Chapter we hope to shed some light on what these Gifts are, and how they operate.

CAN PREACHERS BESTOW THESE GIFTS ON OTHERS?

No! Preachers cannot bestow Gifts of the Spirit on others. These are *"Gifts of the Spirit,"* and not gifts of man. He Alone can bestow these Gifts as He Alone can empower these Gifts.

The Word of God concerning this question plainly states:

"But all these work that one and the selfsame Spirit *(refers to the fact that all the abilities and powers of the*

Gifts are produced and operated by the energy of the Spirit), **dividing to every man severally as He** *(the Holy Spirit)* **will.** *(All the distribution is within the discretion of the Holy Spirit, which means that men or women cannot impart Gifts to other individuals. That is the domain of the Spirit Alone!)*" **(I Cor. 12:11).**

If it is to be noticed, the Scripture plainly says, *"Dividing to every man severally as He (the Holy Spirit) will,"* **not as man wills.**

Unfortunately, in the last few decades there have been seminars and meetings of various types where it was claimed that certain preachers could bestow Gifts on others, etc.

One of the biggest sins of Believers is to intrude into the Office Work of the Holy Spirit, which is His Domain Alone. Neither in the Book of Acts nor the Epistles, which is the proclamation of the Early Church and the Doctrine by which the Early Church was founded, will you find any of the Apostles, even the Apostle Paul, bestowing Gifts of the Spirit on others.

Some have tried to force Romans 1:11 into this arena; however, Paul is not there talking about Gifts of the Spirit as it pertains to the nine Gifts. What was he talking about?

THE ESTABLISHING OF BELIEVERS

The great Apostle said:

"First, I thank my God through Jesus Christ for you all, that your Faith is spoken of throughout the whole world *(speaks of the Roman Empire)*.

"For God is my witness, Whom I serve with my spirit *(his human spirit)* in the Gospel of His Son *(Jesus Christ and Him Crucified)*, that without ceasing I make mention of you always in my prayers *(Paul had a strong prayer life)*;

"Making request *(has to do with seeking the Lord about a certain thing, in this case the privilege of ministering to the Church at Rome)*, if by any means now at length I might have a prosperous journey by the Will of God to come unto you *(Acts, Chpts. 27 and 28, record that journey; it was very prosperous spiritually, but not prosperous in other ways)*.

"For I long to see you, that I may impart unto you some Spiritual Gift *(does not mean, as some think, that Paul could impart one or more of the nine Gifts of the Spirit, but rather speaks of explaining to them more perfectly the Word of God)*, to the end you may be established *(Spiritual Gifts, as valuable as they are, do not establish anyone; it is the Truth of the Word which establishes, and that alone [Jn. 8:32])*" (Rom. 1:8-11).

THREE GROUPS

Even though we will explain these Gifts exactly as they are given in the Scripture, still, to help us understand them a little better, they can be sectioned in groups of three. They are:

Three Gifts that reveal something:
- The Word of Wisdom
- The Word of Knowledge
- Discerning of spirits

Three Gifts which do something:
- Faith
- Gifts of Healing(s)
- Working of Miracles

Three Gifts that say something:
- Prophecy
- Diverse kinds of Tongues
- Interpretation of Tongues

"I WOULD NOT HAVE YOU IGNORANT"

It is clear and plain in the Word of God that the Lord wants us to understand these Gifts, what they are, how they function, how they operate, etc. That being the case, we should eagerly desire this information. Concerning this, the Scripture says:

"Now concerning Spiritual *Gifts*, Brethren *(in this case, this has to do with the nine Gifts of the Spirit outlined in Verses 8 through 10)*, I would not have you ignorant *(proclaims the Spirit of God, through Paul, saying He wanted the entirety of the Church to know about these Gifts)*.

"You know that you were Gentiles *(meaning that, before their conversion, they had no knowledge of God)*, carried away unto these dumb idols, even as you were led. *(They were primarily led by superstition and witchcraft.)*

"Wherefore I give you to understand, that no man speaking by the Spirit of God calls Jesus accursed *(the True Spirit of God would never do such a thing; so those who did such were not of God)*: and *that* no man can say that Jesus is the Lord, but by the Holy Spirit. *(Any other manner will be incorrect. It is the Holy Spirit Alone, Who reveals the Lordship of Christ to the Believer.)*"

"DIVERSITIES" AND *"DIFFERENCES"*

"Now there are diversities of Gifts *(different types of Gifts)*, but the same Spirit *(all of this means the Holy Spirit never contradicts Himself)*.

"And there are differences of Administrations *(different Services, Ministries, Offices)*, but the same Lord. *(Christ is the One Who assigns the different Ministries, with the Holy Spirit then carrying out the function. As well, Christ never contradicts Himself.)*

"And there are diversities of Operations *(different ways the Gifts work)*, but it is the same God which works all in all *(has reference to the fact it is God the Father Who energizes all things and all ways)*" (I Cor. 12:1-6).

THESE GIFTS ARE A BLESSING

The Scripture says:

"But the manifestation of the Spirit *(pertains to that which the Gifts make manifest or reveal)* is given to every man to profit withal. *(If the Gifts are allowed to function properly, which they definitely will if the Holy Spirit has His Way, all will profit)*" **(I Cor. 12:7).**

Now, let's take the Gifts one by one, hopefully, to shed more light on these Blessings given to us by the Holy Spirit.

"THE WORD OF WISDOM"

"For to one is given by the Spirit *(proclaims the Holy Spirit as being the One Who carries out the instructions of Christ, relative to who gets what)* the Word of Wisdom *(pertains to information concerning the future, whether of people, places, or things)* . . ." **(I Cor. 12:8).**

If it is to be noted, it is not the Gift of Wisdom, but rather, *"the Word of Wisdom."* It means that the Lord gives us some information about a particular subject regarding the future, whether of people, places, or things, but only a small amount.

As well, we should quickly add that some of these Gifts work in tandem with each other. In other words, several of the Gifts may be in Operation at one time about one particular subject, which, no doubt, happens many times. In fact, the illustration I'm about to give incorporated the *"Word of Knowledge"* and the *"Word of Wisdom."* I could give many illustrations, but I think the one that we will now give will serve the purpose.

THE WHITE HOUSE

If I remember correctly, the year was 1987. At any rate, it was during the Reagan Administration.

The White House called and asked if I would come to Washington where I would meet with two other preachers, only one with whom I was acquainted. The reason for the request pertained to two Baptist preachers in the State of Nebraska, I think it was, who had been put in jail because they refused to subject their private Christian school to certain demands made by the state, which they felt violated their conscience, etc.

I had read about the situation in the newspapers, but beyond that had no knowledge of the situation and was not acquainted with the preachers. At any rate, wondering how in the world that we could be of any help, I consented to go.

THE MEETING IN WASHINGTON

The day of the meeting I arrived according to instructions and was taken to a particular room where the meeting would be held in the Old Executive Office Building, I believe it is called. Once again, if I remember correctly, it is situated near the Capitol.

When I went into the room with the two other preachers, I found it packed to capacity. Most of the President's Cabinet was there. I was seated next to Ed Meese, the Attorney General of the United States. Directly across from me was Jim Baker, the Secretary of State. Next to him was Jim McFarland, the National Security Advisor. The balance of the room was filled with lawyers. In fact, at the table where we were seated, there must have been eight or ten lawyers, along with scores standing around the wall.

Mr. Baker spoke first, outlining the situation, making the statement that it was deplorable to see preachers of the Gospel put in jail for obeying their conscience. He then went on to say that the White House would do anything to help get these men released, providing it was legal and did not embarrass the President. The lawyers made some statements, as well as the other two preachers. At about that time, possibly about an hour into the meeting, Mr. Meese, the Attorney General, spoke up and made a statement concerning the legalities of the problem.

THE LORD SPOKE TO MY HEART

While the other two preachers had made some remarks, I

had not said anything, wondering why they called us there and what help we might be, which, in my mind, was none at all.

As Mr. Meese began to speak, the Lord, all of a sudden, began to speak to my heart. He told me exactly what to say which, if carried out, would immediately bring about the release from jail of these two preachers.

To say that I was nervous would be a gross understatement. Finally, Mr. Meese finished with his statement, and the Lord spoke to my heart and said, *"Now is the time."*

When Mr. Meese finished speaking, there was silence for a moment, and then I spoke up. Of course, every head turned toward me, wondering what I would say.

I asked the question exactly as the Lord had spoken to my heart. The question was, *"Isn't the President supposed to make a speech tonight that will cover the nation?"*

Mr. Baker immediately replied and said, *"Well, yes, he is!"*

I then said, *"Why not have the President mention this situation in Nebraska, which will call attention to the matter, and will probably shame the officials in this city to the extent that they will immediately release these preachers!"*

When I finished, there was a silence that gripped the room. All of a sudden, one of the principal lawyers, actually a Constitutional lawyer who was seated at the head of the table, jumped up, slammed his fist on the table and said, *"That will work."* He then added, *"Why didn't I think of that!"*

Mr. McFarland spoke up then and said, *"Yes, the President is making a speech tonight, and I am writing the speech. I know exactly what to say."*

With that, the meeting ended.

THE PRESIDENT OF THE UNITED STATES

That night President Reagan made the speech as scheduled and in the body of the speech mentioned the situation in Nebraska, as to the shame of preachers in America being put in jail for trying to obey their conscience.

The next morning they were released. It was all because of a Word of Knowledge linked with a Word of Wisdom. The Word of Knowledge had to do with information needed then, and the Word of Wisdom came into play as it regarded what the future would hold, namely the next morning when they would be released.

HOW THESE GIFTS WORKED

Had I thought on this subject before this meeting?

Not really because I knew next to nothing about the situation. In other words, what I spoke to these men that day, which resulted in the release of these preachers, had not entered my mind at all before the Lord began to speak to me at the exact time that He did. To be frank, I personally contributed absolutely nothing to that which was stated. The Lord, as simple as it turned out to be, but which no one else thought of, told me exactly what to say and how to say it.

I've had the Lord do that with me any number of times down through the years, but at the same time, there have been times that I pleaded for a Word from the Lord in this capacity, concerning needs that I thought were very important, but with nothing being given. It might be quickly added that these Gifts are not worked at will. In other words, the person cannot turn it on or turn it off. This is strictly the Domain of the Holy Spirit, Who will function as He so desires and when He so desires.

THE WORD OF KNOWLEDGE

"... To another the Word of Knowledge *(concerns the past or the present, relative to persons, places, or things; it is to be noted that it's 'the Word of,' which means a small amount)* by the same Spirit *(it is the Holy Spirit Who functions in all of these Gifts)*" (I Cor. 12:8).

If it is to be noticed, the *"Word of Wisdom"* pertains to

information concerning the future, while the *"Word of Knowledge"* pertains to information concerning the past or the present.

Once again, I could give any number of illustrations, but I think the following will explain this Gift.

A CONSTRUCTION PROJECT

The first office we constructed in Baton Rouge relative to the Ministry was located in the south central part of the city. Our present offices are located on the south side.

The year was probably about 1973 or 1974. The Ministry was growing by leaps and bounds, and we were adding an addition to our present structure.

The engineers had drawn the plans for the addition, and the day before a big truck had delivered the concrete beams that would span the building, with a big crane brought out on this particular day to erect the beams in place.

There were several engineers there that morning with all of the equipment ready to go.

One of the city engineers walked over to me at a given point in time, actually when the crane was about ready to put up the first beam. He said to me, *"Reverend Swaggart, we've got a problem."* He then said, *"We can't put this beam up here as this building is now constructed. If we do, the wall on which one side will be placed could give way with the entire structure falling down."*

I stood there looking at him for a few moments and then stated, *"Well, I guess we'll have to get the engineers to draw up another plan that will accommodate this of which you speak."*

He then said, *"Yes, you can do that; however, these concrete beams cannot remain where they are. In fact,"* he went on to say, *"they are designed with a particular type of stress, and if they are not placed in the position for which they are designed, they will probably crack, making them unusable."*

I tried to absorb all that he said, knowing that tens of thousands of dollars of God's money were at stake.

THE LORD SPOKE TO ME

He walked over, conferring with other engineers, and I walked to the back of the structure where I could hopefully pray for just a moment to try to get the Mind of the Lord as to what to do.

Let me make it perfectly clear that I have absolutely no experience whatsoever in construction. In other words, I had absolutely no knowledge whatsoever about the things he was telling me.

I stood at the back of the building alone, asking the Lord what we could do. Instantly, it happened.

The Lord told me to go back to the engineer and to propose to him the following solution.

I walked over to where two or three of them were standing discussing the matter. At the opportune time I said to them, *"If we put two by tens on top of that wall, bolt them securely to where they will spread out the weight, won't that take care of the problem?"*

This was what the Lord had told me to ask. Now, please understand, as I've already stated, I know absolutely nothing about construction regarding engineering or anything else of this type.

Those engineers stood there a moment looking at me, and finally, one turned to the other one and said, *"You know, I believe that will work."*

We had someone go to the hardware immediately and purchase the required two by tens. When he came back, they bolted them to the top of that wall. About an hour later, the big crane picked up the first one and laid it in place, followed by all the rest of them.

Once again I walked to the back of the building, and I was weeping. Of course, it was not for sorrow but for joy; however, at any rate, one of the engineers saw me and hastily walked over to where I was.

He said, *"Reverend Swaggart, don't worry, everything is*

alright now. We've got it under control."

I didn't say anything to him, but I was rejoicing over what the Lord had just done, which, of course, saved the Ministry tens of thousands of dollars.

What the Lord gave me that day was a *"Word of Knowledge"* concerning the problem. He didn't give me a course on engineering. He didn't give me any knowledge as it regarded what all of this was about, only that which He told me to do. Once again, it was so simple, and yet, the engineers, who work with these types of things all the time, did not at all think of what was suggested.

FAITH

"To another Faith *(special Faith)* by the same Spirit . . ." (I Cor. 12:9).

The *"Faith"* here addressed is not the same as Saving Faith spoken of in Romans 12:3. Neither is it Faith that is a *"Fruit of the Spirit"* (Gal. 5:22).

The *"Faith"* here listed as a Gift of the Spirit is a special Faith which, I believe, is given by the Holy Spirit to every person who has, at the same time, been assigned a particular task which, in the natural, is impossible.

As it regards this Ministry (Jimmy Swaggart Ministries), this special Faith is something that we have to use every single day. We almost never have the funds to do what God has called us to do, meaning that we have to believe Him even day-by-day. It's not a one-time affair that happens once in a while, but, as stated, it is daily. We have to believe that the Lord is going to meet the need and see us through because He has called us to do what we are doing. However, it takes a special Faith to believe this.

When the Lord calls someone to do something, even as He has called this Evangelist for World Evangelism, I believe that He also calls a great number of people to join in this endeavor in order that it be carried out. In other words, I believe the people of our Church (Family Worship Center) are just as called of God as I am. I believe that those who support us are just as called of God as I am as it regards this Ministry. They may live many hundreds or even thousands of miles from Baton Rouge, yet, they are blessed and helped by our telecasts and/or the radio programs, as well as the publications and the music, etc. This includes many of you holding this book in your hands. Along with this Call, you have been given, as well, this special Faith to believe God with me.

YOU HAVE BEEN PLACED HERE BY THE LORD

In other words, your place and position, as it regards this Work and Ministry, are not an accident. You have been placed here by the Lord. As we take this Gospel, this Message of the Cross, to a hurting, dying world, you will have a part in every soul that's Saved, every life that is changed, every Believer baptized with the Spirit, every sick body healed, every bondage of darkness broken, etc. Furthermore, I believe we can say without fear of Scriptural contradiction that every single person in the world, who has been baptized with the Holy Spirit, has Gifts of the Spirit latent within their hearts and lives, waiting to be developed. In other words, the Lord wants to use you in particular Gifts, awaiting only your consecration regarding the matter. Therefore, you should tell the Lord that you want these Gifts to Operate in your life, that is, whatever Gifts He would desire to work through you. I don't believe the Scripture teaches that these Gifts are only for a select few. I believe they are for every single Spirit-filled Believer.

I made mention to our congregation at Family Worship Center a short time ago that, considering the tremendous obstacles, which we have had to overcome as it regards this Ministry, we could not have done it were it not for Gifts which are Operating in the hearts and lives of many of our people. Some of these Gifts, like Faith, are not obvious to others; nevertheless, they are there, and they are working.

To be frank, as it regards many of the Gifts which are not vocal, I feel that many Spirit-filled Believers are used in these Gifts when, most of the time, they don't even know or understand that these things are happening. Nevertheless, they are! One of the reasons that so little is understood about these Gifts is simply the fact that the subject matter is not taught as it ought to be. Once again, I remind the reader that the Holy Spirit has said, *"I would not have you ignorant,"* concerning these things which are so very important (I Cor. 12:1).

GIFTS OF HEALINGS

"... To another the Gifts of Healing(s) *(prayer for the sick)* by the same Spirit" (I Cor. 12:9).

If it is to be noticed, both words, *"Gifts"* and *"Healings,"* are in the plural. In the King James Version, *"Healings"* is not in the plural, but rather, in the singular. However, in the original Text, even as Paul wrote it, both words are plural.
Why?
One thing is certain. Whatever the Holy Spirit did was for a purpose and is very important. He did nothing and does nothing that can be construed as insignificant. And yet, I've read or heard precious little that attempted to define the plurality of these words. Momentarily, I will give what I feel the plurality means.
It should be understood that any Believer can pray for the sick. The Scripture clearly states, *"And these signs shall follow them who believe . . . they shall lay hands on the sick, and they shall recover"* (Mk. 16:17-18). So, every Believer is admonished to pray for the sick and expect the Lord to heal; however, the fact is, for those who definitely have *"Gifts of Healing(s),"* many more healings will be brought about than otherwise.
As it regards the plurality of the words *"Gifts"* and *"Healings,"* I believe that such was done by the Holy Spirit for the following reason.

VARIOUS HEALINGS

Many times, those who have Gifts of Healing(s) will see more healings regarding certain types of diseases than they will other types. It's as though the Lord gives them a special Faith for a certain disease, etc. In other words, they will see many more healings of that particular malady than anything else. Then, there are some to whom the Lord gives a greater anointing, it seems, and they will have Faith for several different types of diseases, which refers to the plurality of the words *"Gifts"* and *"Healing(s)."*

And yet, as it referred to our Lord, no disease or sickness stood in His way, not even death. The Scripture says of Him:

"**For He Whom God has sent speaks the Words of God** *(refers to Christ Who always spoke the Mind of God and, thereby, the Word of God)*: **for God gives not the Spirit by measure** *unto Him (refers to the fact that all others, whomever they may have been and even the very greatest, while having the Holy Spirit, did so by 'measure,' which was not so with Jesus; He had the Spirit in totality, hence, the constant healings and miracles)*" (**Jn. 3:34**).

This means that the Holy Spirit could function in Him as no Believer simply because Christ was Perfect, while all Believers are imperfect.

As well, the Scripture says of Christ, *"You love Righteousness, and hate wickedness: therefore God, Your God, has anointed You with the oil of gladness above Your fellows"* (Ps. 45:7).

All of this states that, whereas we are limited, irrespective as to how much the Lord may use one of us, the Lord of Glory, as is obvious, was unlimited.

A PERSONAL HEALING

When Frances and I first began in Evangelistic work in the

mid-1950's, the great Divine Healing Revivals were beginning to sweep the world. I remember that Gordon Lindsay, editor of the very influential Voice of Healing Magazine, wrote many books on this phenomenon that was taking place, with one of them being, *"Bible Days Are Here Again"*. Countless times I would look at that title, even after I had read the book, and weep for joy. Truly, the Lord was pouring out His Spirit all over the world. The Lord was using frail, imperfect, individuals to once again proclaim the Might and the Power of our Lord Jesus Christ. Giant tents were being constructed, actually the biggest in the world, and being filled to capacity with people who had *"never seen it in this manner before."*

Frances and I were in a meeting in the Lindale Assembly Of God Church in Houston, Texas, pastored by James McKeehan. He was one of the Godliest men that I ever had the privilege to know.

We were at a breakfast of sorts one of the mornings while we were there. Brother McKeehan came up to me and said, *"Brother Swaggart, there's someone here I want you to meet."*

I looked up and standing before me was an elderly gentlemen, frail of build and short of stature. I stood to my feet to shake hands with him when Brother McKeehan said, *"Brother Swaggart, this is Raymond T. Richey."*

I stood there for a few moments, unable to speak. This man had been used of God as possibly few men in history. The Lord most definitely gave him the Gifts of Healing(s), along with the Working of Miracles, and, no doubt, other Gifts as well. He had witnessed and experienced one of the mightiest Moves of God in the world. That's the reason that my tongue would not speak when I stood before him. And yet, he was so very gracious and kind with such a humble demeanor, so much so, in fact, that I will never forget that moment.

A MIGHTY HEALING

I would like to relate just one incident from the thousands, which occurred under this man's Ministry and scores of others like him. I had the privilege of knowing a particular preacher, some years older than I, who had been graciously used of the Lord.

He was of Italian descent, thereby, his entire family knew nothing but Catholicism as it regarded church. This was back in the 1940's, and he found that his mother, although still young of years, was dying with cancer. In fact, her situation was terminal, having been sent home from the hospital to die.

One particular morning, the newspaper boy threw into their yard, by mistake, a newspaper. They did not subscribe to the newspaper in Houston, Texas, simply because they were too poor, he said, to afford the subscription.

At any rate, he picked up the paper, took it inside, and somewhere in the body of that paper he saw a big half page ad that stated, or words to this effect, *"DIVINE HEALING REVIVAL."* It went on to state that blinded eyes were being opened and diseases were being healed, even cancer. When he and his mother saw those words, something leaped within their hearts.

Now, they were Catholic, and in those days Catholics did not go to protestant churches. In fact, they had never been in a protestant church in their lives; irrespective, he resolved somehow to get his mother to the meeting that was being conducted at the Richey Temple in Houston.

She was so sick that she could little walk, but she somehow managed to get to the service. Sure enough, it was like something they had never been in in all of their lives.

If I remember the illustration correctly, they were singing and, oh, what singing it was. They had never heard anything like that in the Catholic Church. And then, all of a sudden, it happened!

A MIRACLE OF HEALING

His mother, even though she had never felt the Spirit of God in all of her life before now, all of a sudden stood to her feet and began to raise her hands and say, *"I feel it, I feel it, I feel it."* That night she was gloriously and miraculously healed by the Power of God. In other words, when she went home that night, she was no longer a Catholic, no longer unsaved, and no longer sick.

The young man in question, her son, became a preacher of the Gospel, and his mother lived many years thereafter. That was just one of the thousands of healings that took place under the Ministry of Raymond T. Richey.

Brother Roccaforte, for that was the Brother's name whose mother was miraculously healed, preached a meeting at our Church in Ferriday, Louisiana. Under his Ministry, my mother and dad were brought to Christ, along with my grandfather and grandmother as well. In our little Church, he gave the testimony one particular night that I've just given to you.

PERSONAL HEALING

When I was ten years old, I came down with a certain type of sickness which the doctors could not diagnose. Even though I was taken to the doctor several times, and even though they ran all types of tests, they couldn't find the problem.

I stayed nauseous constantly and at times would just pass out, in other words, go unconscious.

This happened several times while I was in school with the principal calling my parents each time to come and get me.

The last time it happened, the principal told my Dad, *"If something isn't done for Jimmy, you are going to have to take him out of school."* Then he said this, *"We don't want him dying on our hands."*

I was prayed for any number of times by our Pastor, who had been influenced greatly, even in an indirect way, by the Ministry of Brother Richey. So, our Pastor and my parents, plus all in our Church, definitely believed in Divine Healing. In other words, they firmly believed that our Lord still heals the sick. Nevertheless, despite the fact of being prayed for again and again, I wasn't healed, but rather grew worse.

I look back now, and I believe that it was Satan who was trying to kill me, knowing that the Lord would use us to touch much of this world with the Gospel.

At any rate, the day of my healing came, but my healing came in a very strange way.

After the Sunday Service that day, my mother and dad were to take the Pastor and his wife out to lunch, but first, they would go by the home of one of the parishioners who was ill in order to pray for him.

I remember us walking into the small framed dwelling, going to the back room, and praying for the Brother in question. We all came back to the front room, and I was standing near the door with my Dad and the Pastor, Brother Culbreth, standing on the other side of the small room.

Brother Culbreth still had the bottle of oil in his hands, which he had just used in praying for our dear Brother. My Dad spoke up, saying, *"Brother Culbreth, would you anoint Jimmy with oil and pray for him again,"* and then he added, *"If something isn't done, we're going to have to take him out of school."*

In my mind's eye, I still see Brother Culbreth walking across the room with a smile on his face and quickly anointing me with oil. The moment he laid his hands on my head it happened.

I felt something like a ball of flame, actually about the size of a softball, that started at the top of my head and slowly went down my back and all through my body, and I knew, even beyond the shadow of a doubt, that I was healed.

I was never bothered with that problem again. And, in fact, I have been sick very little in my life since that day.

Now, I had been prayed for, as stated, any number of times by the Pastor, by my parents, and by others in our Church, all to no avail. Why did the Lord do it this way?

That I cannot answer; however, this I do know:

1. I'm so glad that my parents believed in Divine Healing. Were that not the case, I probably wouldn't be alive today.

2. I'm glad they didn't get discouraged and quit when they prayed for me many times previously, and I wasn't healed. They

kept believing, and they kept praying for me. Thank God for that!

3. I'm glad that Jesus Christ still heals today just exactly as He did that Sunday afternoon in 1945, and exactly as He did in His Earthly Ministry. It is, *"Jesus Christ the same yesterday, today, and forever"* (Heb. 13:8).

THE WORKING OF MIRACLES

"To another the working of Miracles" (I Cor. 12:10). As we have stated, many of these Gifts work in tandem. In other words, for one to have the Gift of *"working of Miracles,"* at the same time, one would have to have the Gift of *"Faith,"* as well as the *"Gifts of Healing(s)."*

I personally believe that there are many more Miracles taking place presently than any of us dare realize. Anytime the Lord answers prayer for us, more than likely, He has to perform Miracles, even though they may not be seen by us, in order for that prayer to be answered. As Believers, we should ask the Lord for Miracles, and we should believe for Miracles, whatever the need might be.

Many times we are prone to label something as a *"Healing,"* when in reality it has been a *"Miracle."* However, it is not that important that we properly define all that the Lord has done and is doing. The main thing is that we believe Him, have Faith in Him, and understand that all of these great things did not pass away with the Apostles but, are still active presently, at least for those who will believe.

I tell our people at Family Worship Center, and those who are a part of this Ministry by radio or by television, or by whatever means, and wherever they may be in this world, that we should be a people who expects God to do great and mighty things. We should get up every morning with a spirit of expectation as to what the Lord is going to wondrously do that particular day. We should go to bed at night with a spirit of expectation, believing Him for great and mighty things. I believe in a God of Might and Miracles. I believe in a God Who answers prayer.

I believe in a God Who still does great and mighty things. I believe in a God Who is waiting for His People to believe Him, to step out in Faith, and to claim the treasure-house of Heaven. What I'm about to give is from the Old Covenant; however, anything that the Lord promised under the Old Covenant, He will do even much more under the New Covenant, because our *"Lord is the Mediator of a Better Covenant, which is established upon better Promises"* (Heb. 8:6).

Below is what the Lord told Moses under the Old Covenant, and it goes for us presently as well. In other words, what I'm about to give, you as a Believer, can have, and ought to have, if you will simply believe God. He said, first of all, the condition.

THE CONDITION

"And it shall come to pass, if you shall hearken diligently unto the Voice of the LORD your God, to observe and to do all His Commandments which I command you this day, that the LORD your God will set you on high above all nations of the Earth" (Deut. 28:1).

Now, all of us may look at this particular Passage and immediately understand that we haven't done all *"His Commandments,"* which should be overly obvious. However, what is so wonderful under the New Covenant, which makes it so much better than the Old, is that our Lord Jesus Christ has, in fact, observed and done every single Commandment and has done them perfectly. And then, we must understand that He has done it all on our behalf. In other words, my Faith and your Faith in Him and what He did for us at the Cross automatically gives us His Perfection. So, when the Lord looks at us, He looks at us in the Light of the Lord Jesus Christ and marks us down as *"perfect."* By Faith, we are what He is, and because He has taken what we were, and I speak of our terrible fallen condition, and atoned for it all at Calvary's Cross. What we were, we no longer are, and what He is, we now are, all by Faith.

Now, the following is what we can have in Christ Jesus, and

we can have it now.

ALL THESE BLESSINGS SHALL COME ON YOU, AND OVERTAKE YOU

The Scripture says:

"And all these Blessings shall come on you, and overtake you, if you shall hearken unto the Voice of the LORD your God *(the Blessings will be so abundant that they will literally chase down the people of God)*" **(Deut. 28:2).**

This means that if you turn to the left, you will be blessed; if you turn to the right, you will be blessed; if you walk ahead, you will be blessed; and, if you lag behind, you will be blessed. And, you will be blessed so much that one Blessing won't be used up until another Blessing overtakes you. One can only shout, *"Hallelujah!"*

THE LORD SHALL COMMAND THE BLESSING UPON YOU

"The LORD shall command the Blessing upon you in your storehouses, and in all that you set your hand unto; and He shall bless you in the land which the LORD your God gives you *(when the Command from the Lord is given, nothing can stop that Command)*" **(Deut. 28:8).**

When the Lord commands something, to be sure, it is going to happen. You ought to say to yourself right now, and believe it with all of your heart, that *"the Lord is right now commanding His Blessing upon me."*

"AND THE LORD SHALL MAKE YOU PLENTIFUL IN GOODS"

"And the LORD shall make you plentiful in goods,

in the fruit of your body, and in the fruit of your cattle, and in the fruit of your ground, in the land which the LORD swore unto your fathers to give you *(everything will be bountiful)*" **(Deut. 28:11).**

How much can we have? The answer is instant, *"plenty!"*

"THE LORD SHALL OPEN UNTO YOU HIS GOOD TREASURE"

"The LORD shall open unto you His good Treasure, the heaven to give the rain unto your land in His season, and to bless all the work of your hand: and you shall lend unto many nations, and you shall not borrow *(the treasure-house of Heaven will be opened to you)*" **(Deut. 28:12).**

I think we can imagine that the treasure-house of Heaven is bountiful indeed! And now He tells us that He will on our behalf, *"open unto you His good Treasure."* Believe it and receive it!

"AND THE LORD SHALL MAKE YOU THE HEAD, AND NOT THE TAIL"

"And the LORD shall make you the head, and not the tail; and you shall be above only, and you shall not be beneath; if that you hearken unto the Commandments of the LORD your God, which I command you this day, to observe and to do them *(again, obedience is set before us as the condition)*" **(Deut. 28:13).**

As we have stated, our Lord has already perfectly kept every single *"Commandment,"* and has done so all on our behalf. Our Faith in Him and what He did for us at the Cross gives us all of this, which was promised to Israel of old, and which Promise continues unto this very hour to Spiritual Israel, which pertains to all who will believe.

I believe!

PROPHECY

"To another Prophecy" (I Cor. 12:10).

The Gift of Prophecy is for *"Edification,"* which means *"to build up,"* and *"Exhortation,"* which means *"to implore,"* and *"Comfort,"* which means *"to console"* (I Cor. 14:3).

The Bible student must understand that having the Gift of Prophecy doesn't mean that the person stands in the Office of the Prophet. While all who stand in the Office of the Prophet have the Gift of *"Prophecy,"* as well as the Gifts of *"Word of Wisdom and Word of Knowledge,"* and *"discerning of spirits,"* still, those who have these particular Gifts do not at all stand in the Office of the Prophet. In other words, just because a Believer has these Gifts, he doesn't automatically fill the Office of the Prophet.

THE OFFICE OF THE PROPHET

To be frank, there is no relationship whatsoever, in the pure sense of the word, of the Office of the Prophet and those who have the Gift of Prophecy, etc. The Office of the Prophet is one of the fivefold Ministry Gifts (Eph. 4:11).

The one who stands in the Office of the Prophet is used by the Lord to *"foretell"* and *"forthtell."* And yet, most of the Ministry of the God-called Prophet is to serve in the capacity of *"forthtelling."* That means that the Prophet serves as a Preacher of Righteousness in order to call the Church to Repentance. Actually, John the Baptist, who Jesus referred to as the greatest Prophet born of woman, served precious little in the arena of *"foretelling,"* which speaks of dealing with the future. Almost all of his Ministry was in the realm of *"forthtelling,"* which was to call Israel to Repentance.

THE GIFT OF PROPHECY

Many times Believers get the Office of the Prophet and the Gift of Prophecy confused. They are two different things altogether. As we have stated, only a tiny few who have the Gift of Prophecy, at the same time, stand in the Office of the Prophet.

Those who have the Gift of Prophecy are used of the Lord to edify the Body of Christ by their utterances, to exhort the Body of Christ to live right, and to comfort Believers.

When someone who claims to have the Gift of Prophecy pronounces doom and gloom on the congregation, such cannot be construed as being Scriptural. As would be obvious, such does not edify, does not exhort, and does not comfort. Paul said, *"He who Prophesies edifies the Church"* (I Cor. 14:4).

As well, Paul said, *"The spirits of the Prophets are subject to the Prophets"* (I Cor. 14:32).

What did he mean by that?

He meant that if an individual claims to be compelled to blurt out at any time whatever he thinks that God has given him, that person is out of order. The Holy Spirit works with the spirit of a person with both deciding when is the right time for an utterance to be given.

As an example, if the Lord is anointing me to preach, He is not going to anoint somebody else to interrupt what I'm saying with a Word of Prophecy or Tongues, etc., as Scriptural and right as those things may be in their own capacity.

Down through the years, many times the Lord has been anointing me greatly to preach, with such registering powerfully with the congregation. And then, because of the anointing that was on me and, as well, on the entirety of the congregation, somebody would feel that they had to give out an utterance in Tongues or Prophecy at that particular time, which was not a help, but rather, a hindrance. Once again, *"the spirits of the Prophets are subject to the Prophets,"* meaning that the Lord does not compel anyone to do anything.

Now, there have been times when I've been preaching that the Lord would move on someone to give an utterance in Tongues, which was meant to be interpreted, or a word of Prophecy, and it was right, Scriptural, and correct. But, once again, if a person who is used by the Lord in these capacities will ask the Lord to help them to be used at the right time, the Lord will honor that request.

These Gifts are a great blessing to the Church, if they are used correctly; however, to be used correctly, the person who has these Gifts must be consecrated to the Lord. I'm glad that I can say that virtually all of the Gifts are in Operation in Family Worship Center, for which we are so thankful to the Lord. At the same time, I cannot remember when one of the Gifts has been used out of place. Our people are led by the Spirit, and if one is led by the Spirit, one will conduct oneself correctly. In fact, the entirety of the Fourteenth Chapter of I Corinthians is given over by the Apostle Paul to instruct the Church as to how the three vocal gifts of Prophecy, Tongues, and Interpretation of Tongues are to be used.

IS PREACHING PROPHECY?

In the truest sense of the word, no, preaching is not Prophecy! And yet, at the same time, at times during the body of preaching, there very definitely can be a word of Prophecy given. Let me give you an example.

THE FORMER SOVIET UNION

Frances and I, along with Jim Woolsey, who had set up the meetings, in 1985 were in what was then known as the Soviet Union for a series of meetings. I preached in Moscow, in Siberia, and in Minsk.

I ministered in a Pentecostal Church in Minsk on a Sunday morning. The place was filled to absolute capacity. In fact, it was right in the midst of the message, as the Spirit of God moved powerfully over that congregation, that my interpreter, a KGB agent, was wondrously Saved.

As I delivered a particular statement and then paused for him to interpret it, he said nothing. I turned around and looked at him, and tears were rolling down his cheeks. At that moment he gave his heart to Christ.

Right in the middle of this message the Lord spoke through me by Prophecy, which was also a Word of Wisdom.

I made the statement that the Gospel of Jesus Christ was going to go into every city, every town, and every village in the Soviet Union. When I said those words, I knew they were from the Lord, but they were so powerful and so far sweeping that it scared me.

When the Service ended and Frances and I and others were going back to the hotel, I mentioned to her about this incident.

I thought in my mind and my spirit, how in the world could this be done, the Gospel of Jesus Christ going to every city, town, and village in the Soviet Union? This was an atheistic country that did not believe in God. But, I knew that it was of the Lord, and somehow He would bring it to pass.

JIM WOOLSEY

Jim Woolsey was in charge of placing our Telecast all over the world in country after country with it translated into various languages.

He came into my office in the latter part of 1988 and said, *"Brother Swaggart, I believe that it's possible for us to go on television in Latvia."* This was one of the Soviet Republics. He went on to say that we would have to translate the program into Russian, but he thought it could be done. I told him to go ahead, but I will have to confess that I was somewhat skeptical in my spirit.

However, the Lord helped him to do just that, to get the program on in the capital city of Latvia, and the Lord used it mightily.

A few weeks later he came into my office again, and again said, *"Brother Swaggart, I believe I can get our telecast on T.V.1 out of Moscow."*

Now, T.V.1 in Moscow was the world's largest television

network, incorporating over 7,000 stations, reaching every city, town, and village in the Soviet Union. Actually, it was the propaganda channel for Communism, which meant that it covered every nook and cranny of one-sixth of the world's land surface. I will never forget my reaction when he told me that. I honestly didn't believe he could do such a thing. But again, I told him to proceed. I did not know where we would find the money to pay for it, but I knew it was the Lord.

In the latter part of 1988, if I remember correctly, he was able to place the telecast, translated into Russian, on T.V.1 out of Moscow. To say that it was a Miracle of the Lord would be a gross understatement.

For over two years we broadcast over this network, covering the entirety of the Soviet Union, exactly that which the Lord had spoken in the midst of the message which I delivered that Sunday morning in Minsk.

A CONFIRMATION OF THE WORD OF GOD

A particular religious denomination here in the States claimed that we were lying about being on television in what was then known as the Soviet Union. One brother who was supporting our work, which support we desperately needed, I might quickly add, believed this lie and quit supporting.

But, as he told me later, he did not feel right in his spirit about what he had done. So, on one particular day he specifically asked the Lord to show him if Brother Swaggart were telling the truth, or if he were lying about being on television in the Soviet Union.

The very next day, if I remember correctly, he picked up the local newspaper and was thumbing through it and came upon an article that had been reprinted from the prestigious Washington Post. It was written by a lady reporter who worked for the Post, and who had travelled extensively in Russia and had done so for the purpose of writing this article about the changes which were taking place in that great country.

Down in the body of the article, which was quite long, and which had nothing to do with Jesus Christ, the lady wrote, *"And by the way, I could not get away from Jimmy Swaggart. Everywhere I went, in every city, I saw his telecast."*

When he read that statement, he said to me in a letter, or it was over the phone, I don't remember which, *"Brother Swaggart, I turned cold all over."* He went to the post office immediately and sent a gift, asking the Lord, as well, to forgive him.

When that Word was given in the midst of that message that Sunday morning in Minsk, it looked, for all practical purposes, to be absolutely impossible. How in the world, in the midst of monolithic Soviet Union, could the Gospel of Jesus Christ go into every city, town, and village? But it did, and it was because the Lord orchestrated every bit of it.

I will have to say one more thing regarding this. It was not my Faith that brought about this tremendous Miracle of God, but rather, the Faith of Jim Woolsey. He probably made forty trips to Moscow working on this project before he finally got the approval of the powers that be for us to go on the air. But, he knew what the Lord had said, and he persevered, which opened the door for one of the greatest Moves of God that the world has ever known, for which we give the Lord all the Praise and all the Glory.

DISCERNING OF SPIRITS

The Scripture says, *"To another discerning of spirits"* (I Cor. 12:10).

Discerning of spirits refers to the following:
• Human spirits;
• Demon spirits; and,
• The Holy Spirit.

This is not the Gift of Discernment, but rather, the Gift of *"discerning of spirits."*

It is true that when a person comes to Christ, their capacity of discernment increases greatly, which it definitely should;

however, this is not what the Holy Spirit is here addressing.

FALSE DOCTRINE

One of the reasons that so many modern Christians are falling for so much false doctrine is that there is so little *"discerning of spirits"* in Operation at this present time. As a Minister of the Gospel, oftentimes I will watch Christians fall for things that are so obviously wrong, yet, they seem to not know any better. The modern church, due to falling away from the Administration of the Holy Spirit, has come to the place that it little understands the difference in evil spirits and the Holy Spirit. That is tragic! But, it is true. Entire religious denominations are being led astray and, I might quickly add, denominations which once had the Flow and Moving of the Holy Spirit.

I read a letter the other day written by a leader in a Full Gospel denomination, so-called, who was castigating this Ministry (Jimmy Swaggart Ministries), and extolling the greatness of the Purpose Driven Life system. The tragedy is, this leader in that denomination didn't even have enough spirituality to know and understand that the Purpose Driven Life scheme is totally of man, which means it is not at all of God. He did not have enough discernment to know that, much less the Gift of *"discerning of spirits."* When Believers, so-called, begin to stray from the Word of God, which must be the criteria for all things, then the Working, Moving, and Operation of the Holy Spirit begins to fall by the wayside as well. That's the tragedy with modern Pentecostal denominations. For the most part, they have embraced humanistic psychology, which means they cannot at the same time have the Moving and Working of the Holy Spirit. Either one cancels out the other. If you are going to embrace humanistic psychology, you cannot have at the same time the Holy Spirit. If you follow the Ways of the Spirit, you will not want or desire the ways of humanistic psychology. The two are antithetical, meaning, *"being in direct and unequivocal opposition."*

AN EXAMPLE

Some years ago, Frances and I were in a particular city in a crusade. It was Saturday night.

After the service ended, Frances motioned for me to come to where she was, as she was speaking with two people, a man and his wife.

We walked over to a place to where we could have a little privacy, and Frances mentioned to me that this couple was having marriage difficulties. I did not know them and neither did Frances.

At any rate, as we were standing there listening to them, all of a sudden, the Lord spoke to my heart and told me what the problem was. I discerned the spirit of lying in the dear lady who stood before me. Now, the Lord does not reveal these kinds of things to me often, but that night, He did.

I called her to the side, out of earshot of her husband. I then said to her, *"Sister, your marriage is in trouble, in serious trouble, because you are being unfaithful to your husband."*

Her eyes grew wide in astonishment because she knew that I did not know her or anything about her. I said, *"You are having an affair with another man."*

She dropped her head and began to sob, admitting that it was true. I then said to her that she would have to tell her husband of this problem and repent before God, and that it must be broken off instantly.

We then went back to where Frances and the lady's husband were standing. I said nothing to him, leaving it up to her and to her discretion. Frances and I prayed with them, and they left.

I received a letter from her some weeks later. She told me how that she had done exactly what I said, repented before God, broke off the thing, and had related everything to her husband. She went on to tell me that it looked like their marriage was going to be saved.

Now, in that particular episode, not only was *"discerning of spirits"* in Operation, as I discerned a lying spirit in this dear lady, but also, a *"Word of Knowledge,"* which related the situation that had been happening and was happening then, and also a *"Word of Wisdom,"* which stated what she must do and how that it would turn out alright if she obeyed the Lord.

As we have already stated, many times these Gifts work in tandem with each other.

DIFFERENT KINDS OF TONGUES

"To another diverse kinds of Tongues" (I Cor. 12:10).

The *"kinds of Tongues"* refer to different languages but unknown by the speaker. This is proven, as we have already stated, from Acts 2:5-13.

It must be understood that Paul is speaking here of the *"Gift of Tongues,"* and not the Tongues that are used in our everyday prayer language and worship. Many non-Believers get this confused, thinking that anytime a person speaks in Tongues, it's supposed to be interpreted, and if it's not interpreted, that proves it's not real. They totally misunderstand the situation.

In fact, one might say for the sake of clarification, that there are two types of Tongues. They are:

• The Tongues that one receives when one is baptized with the Holy Spirit. They are to continue to use these Tongues, praying in the Spirit and worshipping in the Spirit, which they should do on a daily basis. However, even though anything and everything that God does for us is a *"Gift,"* still, Paul is speaking in this Twelfth Chapter of I Corinthians of the nine Gifts of the Spirit. In other words, he delineates these Gifts as it regards these particular nine Spiritual Gifts, one might say. What I'm saying is, our prayer language is not the Gift of Tongues of which Paul here speaks. It's not meant to be interpreted and, in fact, is not to be interpreted. It is simply worship of the Lord, which within itself, and as we also have explained in another Chapter, is extremely beneficial to the Child of God.

• The Gift of Tongues is that which Paul is here address-ing. In fact, he goes into detail in the Fourteenth Chapter as to how this Gift is to be used. In other words, speaking with other

Tongues, whether in worship or whether as a Gift, is explained in the Fourteenth Chapter of I Corinthians. He says the following:

1. For the Gift of Tongues to be as helpful as the Gift of Prophecy, Interpretation of Tongues must be brought into play as well.

2. When it is time to preach to the congregation or to teach the congregation, one certainly should not try to do so in Tongues because, as would be obvious, the people would not understand what is being said. That's the reason the Apostle said, *"So likewise ye, except you utter by the tongue words easy to be understood, how shall it be known what is spoken?"* (I Cor. 14:9). What was taking place was the following.

Many of the Corinthians, not knowing or understanding how the Gifts should operate in the services, that is, when they came together to worship the Lord, were blurting out in Tongues, and doing so constantly, which hindered the service. Paul went on to say that while the one speaking may be blessed, no one else is (I Cor. 14:16-17).

3. Inasmuch as *"the spirits of the Prophets are subject to the Prophets,"* meaning that no one is forced by the Lord to do anything, if one feels he has a message that is to be given to the Church, he should wait till the appropriate time (I Cor. 14:32).

4. And, when the utterance is given and properly interpreted, with both being from the Lord, it will *"speak unto men to Edification, Exhortation, and Comfort"* (I Cor. 14:3).

"THE INTERPRETATION OF TONGUES"

Paul said, *"To another the interpretation of Tongues"* (I Cor. 12:10). As we've already stated, it's only utterances that are given in Church Services, and given at the appropriate time, which are to be interpreted and, in fact, are meant by the Lord to be interpreted.

And, we must remember, this is an interpretation and not a translation. These are two different things. It is the Gift of *"interpretation of Tongues,"* and not the gift of *"translation of Tongues."*

Concerning this Gift, the following should be noted:

• Tongues and interpretation of Tongues equal Prophecy regarding significance.

Paul said:

> "I would that you all spoke with Tongues *(refers here in this instance to one's prayer and worship language)*, but rather that you Prophesied *(now reverts to this particular Gift of the Spirit)*: for greater *is* he who Prophesies than he who speaks with Tongues, except he Interpret, that the Church may receive Edifying" (I Cor. 14:5).

• The one who has the Gift of Tongues, meant to be uttered in public services and interpreted, the Scripture says he should also *"pray that he may interpret,"* in other words, pray that the Lord would give him, as well, the Gift of Interpretation of Tongues (I Cor. 14:13). This is for the obvious reason. If it is a small assembly and the person with a Gift of Tongues has to depend on someone else, the other person being the interpreter, and that person is not present, this presents a problem. So, the one with the Gift of Tongues should pray that the Lord would use him or her as well, as it regards the interpretation of Tongues. In fact, this is the ideal!

• In a public service, the Holy Spirit through Paul said that utterances should be limited *"by two, or at the most by three,"* meaning the individuals who are giving the utterances in Tongues, which are meant to be interpreted (I Cor. 14:27).

• If there is no interpreter present, the individual is to *"keep silence in the Church; and let him speak to himself, and to God"* (I Cor. 14:28).

TO PROFIT WITHAL

Again we go back to the words of Paul as he introduced the Gifts. He said:

"**But the manifestation of the Spirit** *(pertains to that which the Gifts make manifest or reveal)* **is given to every man to profit withal.** *(If the Gifts are allowed to function properly, which they definitely will if the Holy Spirit has His Way, the entirety of the Church will profit, which of course, is the intention of the Holy Spirit)*" **(I Cor. 12:7).**

"The Master comes! He calls for thee,
"Go forth at His Almighty Word;
"Obedient to His last Command;
"And tell to those who never heard,
"Who sit in deepest shades of night,
"That Christ has come to give them light!"

"The Master calls! Arise and go;
"How blessed His Messenger to be!
"He Who has given you liberty,
"Now bids you set the captives free,
"Proclaim His mighty Power to save,
"Who for the world His Life-Blood gave."

"The Master calls! Shall not the heart,
"In warm responsive love reply,
"Lord, here am I, send me, send me,
"Your willing slave, to live or die;
"And an instrument unfit indeed,
"Yet You will give me what I need."

"And if you cannot go, yet bring,
"An offering of a willing heart;
"Then, though you tarry at home,
"Your God shall give you to your part.
"The messengers of peace upbear,
"In ceaseless and prevailing prayer."

"Short is the time for service true,

"For soon shall dawn that glorious day,
"When, all the Harvest gathered in,
"Each faithful heart shall hear Him say,
"'My Child, well done! Your toil is o'er;
"Enter My Joy forevermore.'"

CHAPTER TEN

How Is The "Fruit Of The Spirit" Developed In Our Lives?

QUESTION:

HOW IS THE "FRUIT OF THE SPIRIT" DEVELOPED IN OUR LIVES?

ANSWER:

Inasmuch as the Holy Spirit works exclusively within the parameters of the Finished Work of Christ, i.e., the Cross, the *"Fruit of the Spirit"* can be developed only on the premise of the Believer placing his or her Faith exclusively in the Cross of Christ.

THE *"FRUIT OF THE SPIRIT"*

"But the Fruit of the Spirit *(are not 'fruits' but rather 'Fruit'; they are to be looked at as a 'whole,' which means they grow equally)* is love, joy, peace, longsuffering, gentleness, goodness, Faith,

"Meekness, temperance: against such there is no Law. *(Against such there doesn't need to be a Law. But let the Reader understand that this 'Fruit' is of the 'Holy Spirit,' and not of man. It can only develop as we are 'led of the Spirit.' And we can only be led by the Spirit by making the Cross the Object of our Faith)*" (Gal. 5:22-23).

THE PRINCIPAL WORK OF THE HOLY SPIRIT

The Believer must understand that whatever needs to be done in our lives cannot be done by human ability or instrumentality but only by the Holy Spirit. He Alone can make us what we ought to be. In fact, this is one of the principal reasons for His coming into our hearts and lives to abide, and in actuality, to abide forever (Jn. 14:16). Of all the things He does in our hearts and lives, the development of Fruit is, no doubt, His greatest Work. That Fruit is, as we have already stated, *"love, joy, peace, longsuffering, gentleness, goodness, Faith, meekness, temperance"* (Gal. 5:22-23).

The Greek word for fruit is *"Karpos,"* and in this case refers metaphorically to works or deeds as being the fruit of the visible expression of power working inwardly and invisibly, the character of the fruit being evidence of the character of the power producing it (Mat. 7:16). As the visible expressions of hidden lusts are the works of the flesh, so the invisible Power of the Holy Spirit in those who are brought into living union with Christ produces the *"Fruit of the Spirit,"* the singular form suggesting the unity of the character of the Lord as produced in us. (Explanation derived from Vine's Expository Dictionary of New Testament Words.)

IT IS THE *"FRUIT OF THE SPIRIT"* AND NOT THE FRUIT OF MAN

Man cannot develop this Fruit; it can only be developed by the Holy Spirit. There is nothing in the world worse than a fake joy, a fake meekness, a fake love, etc. Yet, when man attempts to develop such himself, such is the result.

As well, there is some evidence in the structure of the words, *"Fruit of the Spirit,"* that the Fruit does not grow haphazardly, that is, one above the other, but all grow equally, or all do not grow at all. In other words, there is no such thing as one having more of the Fruit of love than he does the Fruit of peace, or the Fruit of temperance, but not the Fruit of gentleness, etc. Whatever amount of meekness one has, or joy, etc., he has a like amount of all the other of the Fruit.

I personally believe that this is the greatest Work that the Holy Spirit can carry out in one's life. Of all the things that He does, the development of His Fruit is, I think, the greatest of all. This is what real Christianity actually is.

HOW DOES THE *"FRUIT OF THE SPIRIT"* GROW?

Spiritual Growth is not an automatic thing. While the *"Fruit of the Spirit"* cannot be developed by man, it most definitely can be cultivated by man. This refers to providing the proper spiritual soil in which this can grow. And how can this be done?

THE CROSS

On the heels of Paul listing the *"Fruit of the Spirit,"* he also makes the following statement:

"And they who are Christ's have Crucified the flesh with the affections and lusts. *(This can be done only by the Believer understanding it was carried out by Christ at the Cross, and our being 'Baptized into His Death' [Rom. 6:3-5]. That being the case, and as repeatedly stated, the Cross must ever be the Object of our Faith, which alone will bring about these results.)*"

WALKING IN THE SPIRIT

"If we live in the Spirit, let us also walk in the Spirit *('walk' refers to our lifestyle; this Passage declares both life and Holiness to be the Work of the Holy Spirit; He operates Salvation and He operates Sanctification; both are realized on the Principle of Faith, and that refers to the Cross ever being the Object of our Faith; many know they have received Spiritual Life, as it regards Salvation through Faith, but they think they can only secure Sanctification by the means of works; this is a great error; it never brings Victory; believing in Christ and the Cross for Sanctification, as well as for Justification, introduces one into a life of power and Victory, which is the only way it can be accomplished.)*
"Let us not be desirous of vain Glory *(which is a sign that one is functioning according to Law, i.e., 'the flesh')*, provoking one another *(self-righteousness)*, envying one another. *(These are works of the flesh, and will manifest themselves if our Faith is in things other than the Cross)*"
(Gal. 5:24-26).

If one doesn't walk in the Spirit, one is going to be controlled by the flesh, with the works of the flesh being made manifest in one's life. To portray the two, *"Fruit of the Spirit"* and works of the flesh, they must be placed in juxtaposition.

JUXTAPOSITION

Let us say it again. If the Believer doesn't follow the Word of God as it regards righteous living, which is Faith exclusively in the Cross of Christ, the *"Fruit of the Spirit"* cannot be developed in such a life. The end result will be *"the works of the flesh."* So, Paul places these two in juxtaposition.

THE WORKS OF THE FLESH

"Now the works of the flesh are manifest, which are *these (if one attempts to function by means of Law of any nature, the 'works of the flesh' will be manifested in one's life)*; Adultery, fornication, uncleanness, lasciviousness,

"Idolatry, witchcraft, hatred, variance, emulations, wrath, strife, seditions, heresies,

"Envyings, murders, drunkenness, revelings, and such like *(if one is walking after the flesh [Rom. 8:1], one or more of these sins will manifest themselves in one's life; the only way, and I mean the only way, one can walk in perpetual Victory is to understand that everything we receive from God comes to us by means of the Cross; consequently, the Cross must ever be the Object of our Faith; this being the case, the Holy Spirit, Who works exclusively within the confines of the Sacrifice of Christ, will exert His mighty Power on our behalf, which will enable us to live a Holy life)*: of the which I tell you before, as I have also told *you* in time past *(refers to the fact that the Apostle was not afraid to name specific sins)*, that they which do such things shall not inherit the Kingdom of God. *(This tells us in no uncertain terms that if our Faith is not everlastingly in Christ and the*

Cross, we simply won't make it. God doesn't have two ways of Salvation and Victory, only one, and that is 'Jesus Christ and Him Crucified')" **(Gal. 5:19-21).**

CULTIVATION

The cultivation that is needed by the Believer in order that the *"Fruit of the Spirit"* will have a wholesome environment in which to grow, the Believer's Faith must be exclusively in Christ and what Christ has done for us at the Cross. As well, one should remember, Fruit grows, meaning that it's not an automatic thing. Also, it doesn't grow quickly, but rather, very slowly. In fact, this great Work of the Holy Spirit in our lives, as it regards the development of this Fruit, is a lifelong project.

The cultivation process has to do with the Object of our Faith, which must be the Cross of Christ. That being the case, the Holy Spirit, Who Alone can develop His Fruit within our lives, can then function as He desires to function; however, if our Faith is in anything other than Christ and the Cross, the development of all Fruit simply grinds to a halt.

Our Lord in the Fifteenth Chapter of John proclaims to us how the process works. He said the following:

THE *"FATHER IS THE HUSBANDMAN"*

"I Am the True Vine *(the True Israel, as He is the True Church, and the True Man; more specifically, He Alone is the Source of Life)*, and My Father is the Husbandman *(refers to God the Father not simply as the Vinedresser, but also the Owner, so to speak).*

"Every branch *(Believer)* in Me *(to have Salvation, we must be 'in Christ,' which refers to trusting in what He did at the Cross)* that bears not fruit *(the Holy Spirit Alone can bring forth fruit within our lives, and He does such through the Finished Work of Christ, which demands that the Cross ever be the Object of our Faith)* He takes away *(if the Believer refuses the Cross, ultimately, he will be taken out of the Body of Christ)***: and every** *branch* **that bears fruit** *(has some understanding of Christ and the Cross)***, He purges it** *(uses whatever means necessary to make the Cross the total Object of one's Faith)***, that it may bring forth more fruit** *(only when the Cross becomes the total Object of one's Faith can the Holy Spirit perform His Work of bringing forth proper fruit [Rom. 8:1-2, 11])***."**

EXCEPT YOU *"ABIDE IN ME"*

"Now you are clean through the Word which I have spoken unto you *(the answer, as always, is found in the Word of God; the Story of the Bible is 'Jesus Christ and Him Crucified')***.**

"Abide in Me *(look to Him exclusively, and what He has done for us at the Cross)***, and I in you** *(if we properly abide in Him, which we can only do by ever making the Cross the Object of our Faith, then He will abide in us without fail)***. As the branch** *(Believer)* **cannot bear fruit of itself** *(one cannot sanctify oneself! It is impossible!)***, except it abide in the Vine** *(abiding in Him refers to the fact that we understand that every solution we seek, for whatever the need might be, is found only in Christ and the Cross; we must never separate Christ from the Cross [I Cor. 1:23; 2:2])***; no more can you, except you abide in Me."**

BRINGING *"FORTH MUCH FRUIT"*

"I am the Vine *(not the Church, not a particular Preacher, not even a particular Doctrine, but Christ Alone)***, you** *are* **the branches** *(Believers)***: he who abides in Me, and I in him, the same brings forth much fruit** *(let us say it again; the Believer must understand that everything we receive from God comes to us exclusively through Christ and the Cross; that being the case, the Cross must ever be the*

Object of our Faith; then the Holy Spirit can develop fruit within our lives; it can be done no other way!): **for without Me** *(what He did for us at the Cross)* **you can do nothing** *(the Believer should read that phrase over and over)*."

"WITHERED"

"**If a man abide not in Me** *(refuses to accept the Cross, which means he is serving 'another Jesus' [II Cor. 11:4])*, **he is cast forth as a branch** *(is removed from the Source of Life)*, **and is withered** *(without proper Faith in Christ and the Cross, the Believer ultimately withers)*; **and men gather them, and cast** *them* **into the fire, and they are burned** *(the implication is striking! If proper Faith in Christ and the Cross is not maintained, the ultimate result is eternal Hell)*."

ABIDING IN CHRIST

"**If you abide in Me** *(keep your Faith anchored in Christ and the Cross)*, **and My Words abide in you** *(in fact, the entirety of the Word of God is the Story of 'Christ and the Cross')*, **you shall ask what you will, and it shall be done unto you** *(proper Faith in Christ and the Cross desires only the Will of God, which Will is guaranteed now to be carried forth)*."

GLORIFYING THE FATHER

"**Herein is My Father Glorified** *(that Believers totally and completely place their Faith exclusively in Christ and the Cross)*, **that you bear much fruit** *(meaning that Jesus did not die in vain, but that His Death on the Cross will result in 'much fruit')*; **so shall you be My Disciples** *(Lk. 9:23-24)*."

"LOVE"

"**As the Father has loved Me** *(the Heavenly Father*

loves us accordingly, as we abide in Christ), **so have I loved you** *(the Good Shepherd gives His Life for the sheep)*: **continue ye in My Love** *(we can continue in His Love, only as we continue in our Faith, which must ever have the Cross as its Object)*."

THE KEEPING OF HIS *"COMMANDMENTS"*

"**If you keep My Commandments** *(this can be done only by the Holy Spirit working within us, which He does according to our Faith in Christ and the Cross)*, **you shall abide in My Love** *(this can be done only in the manner stated)*; **even as I have kept My Father's Commandments, and abide in His Love** *(the Father's Commandment regarding Christ was that He was to go to the Cross [Mat. 16:21-24]; His Commandment to us is that we ever make Christ and the Cross Alone the Object of our Faith [Jn. 6:53])*."

"JOY"

"**These things have I spoken unto you, that My Joy might remain in you** *(His Joy remains in us, only as our Faith is properly placed in Him and the Cross)*, **and *that* your joy might be full** *(the Christian cannot know 'full joy' until He properly understands the Cross, which means that he then properly understands Christ)*."

A *"FRIEND"* OF CHRIST

"**This is My Commandment, That you love one another** *(we can only do so through a proper understanding of the Cross)*, **as I have loved you** *(He loved us enough to give His Life for us)*.

"**Greater love has no man that this** *(the epitome of love)*, **that a man lay down his life for his friends** *(this portrays the Cross, as is obvious)*.

"You are My friends *(consequently, I lay down My Life for you)*, **if you do whatsoever I Command you** *(as stated, we can only do what He Commands, as we allow the Holy Spirit latitude within our lives, which is done by ever making the Cross the Object of our Faith)*.

"Henceforth I call you not servants *(Faith in Christ and the Cross Alone can lift the Believer to a new status)*; **for the servant knows not what his lord does** *(with faith improperly placed, the Lord cannot confide in us)*: **but I have called you friends; for all things that I have heard of My Father I have made known unto you** *(therefore, we have no excuse!)*."

"THAT YOUR FRUIT SHOULD REMAIN"

"You have not chosen Me, but I have chosen you *(it is not really that we find the Lord; the truth is, He finds us)*, **and ordained you** *(has chosen us for a purpose)*, **that you should go and bring forth fruit** *(as stated, we can only do this by ever looking to the Cross [Gal. 6:14])*, **and *that* your fruit should remain** *(as our Faith remains in the Cross, the fruit will remain)*: **that whatsoever you shall ask of the Father in My Name** *(using His Name always refers to the Victory He won at the Cross)*, **He may give it you.**

"These things I Command you, that you love one another *(if Faith is improperly placed, there is no love, even as there can be no love)*" **(Jn. 15:1-17).**

There is no life in which the Holy Spirit cannot bring forth His Fruit; however, it must be done God's Way, which, as always, is the Way of the Cross (Gal. 6:14; I Cor. 1:17-18, 23; 2:2).

> *"Beloved, let us love:*
> *"Love is of God;*
> *"In God Alone is love,*
> *"It's true abode."*

"Beloved, let us love:
"For they who love,
"They only are His Sons,
"Born from above."

"Beloved, let us love:
"For love is rest,
"And he who loves not,
"Abides unblest."

"Beloved, let us love:
"In love is light,
"And he who loves not,
"Dwells in night."

"Beloved, let us love:
"For only thus,
"Shall we behold that God,
"Who loves us."

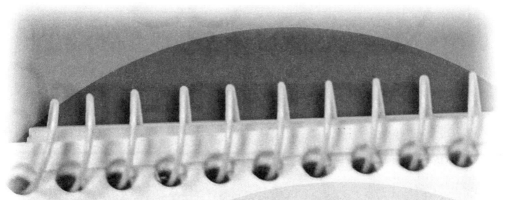

CHAPTER ELEVEN

What Is Blaspheming The Holy Spirit?

QUESTION:

WHAT IS BLASPHEMING THE HOLY SPIRIT?

ANSWER:

Blasphemy against the Holy Spirit carries with it the awful pronouncement that the sinner is *"guilty of an eternal sin,"* which cannot be forgiven. This means that he cannot be Saved. It is with full knowledge speaking detrimentally of the Holy Spirit or His Work. The seriousness of this sin is unparalleled, as should be obvious. We will address the following:
- Who is the Holy Spirit?
- Who can blaspheme the Holy Spirit?
- What happens when one blasphemes the Holy Spirit?
- Can one blaspheme the Holy Spirit in ignorance?

WHO IS THE HOLY SPIRIT?

The Holy Spirit is God. We believe the Bible teaches that there is one God, but manifest in Three Persons, *"God the Father, God the Son, and God the Holy Spirit."* These Three are One, in essence, in unity, and in purpose, but not in number. The Scripture says:

"**For there are Three Who bear record in Heaven** *(the Law has ever required the Testimony of two or three witnesses [Deut. 17:6; 19:15; Mat. 18:16; II Cor. 13:1])*, **the Father, the Word** *(Jesus Christ is the Word [Jn. 1:1])*, **and the Holy Spirit: and these Three are One.** *(The only sense three can be one is in essence and unity, as is clear in Jn. 17:11, 21-23.)*
"**And there are Three Who bear witness in Earth** *(as in Heaven, so on Earth)*, **the Spirit, and the Water, and the Blood** *(speaks of the Holy Spirit; the Humanity of Christ [water], while never ceasing to be Deity, and the Atonement,*

i.e., 'the Cross'): **and these Three agree in One.** *(These Three agree that Christ is Very Man while at the same time being Very God, Who died on the Cross to redeem fallen humanity)*" **(I Jn. 5:7-8).**

"THAT THEY MAY BE ONE, AS WE ARE"

Concerning the Three in One, Jesus said:

"**And now I am no more in the world** *(speaks of His Mission being finished, with Him returning to the Father shortly)*, **but these are in the world** *(speaks of a hostile environment, with God Alone able to keep them)*, **and I come to You** *(the Ascension)*. **Holy Father, keep through Your Own Name those whom You have given Me** *(this would be done by the means of the Cross, and our Faith in that Finished Work)*, **that they may be one, as We** *are. (One in love and unity)*" **(Jn. 17:11).**

"ONE IN US"

Jesus also stated:

"**Neither pray I for these alone** *(Jesus is speaking not only of His present Disciples, but the multitudes in all ages who would believe their Testimony)*, **but for them also which should believe on Me through their Word** *(has reference to the fact that all must take the Word to others)*;

"**That they all may be One** *(again He prays for unity among Believers, which can only be brought about by Love)*; **as You, Father,** *are* **in Me** *(unity and 'Communion')*, **and I in You** *(unity and 'Purpose')*, **that they also may be One in Us** *(the pronoun 'Us' proclaims the Trinity)*: **that the world may believe that You have sent Me** *(proclaims the Father sending the Son into the world to save the world, and the Son sending His Disciples into the world for the* *same purpose).*

"**And the glory which You gave Me I have given them** *(unity and 'Glory')*; **that they may be one, even as We are One** *(one in 'Communion,' 'Purpose,' and 'Glory')*:

"**I in them, and You in Me** *(spoken distinctly by Christ; Jesus is the mediating link of relation between the Father and Believers)*, **that they may be made perfect in one.** *(All of this can be done only through the Cross)* . . ." **(Jn. 17:20-23).**

PERSONAL PRONOUNS

Jesus, when speaking of the Holy Spirit, used personal pronouns about Him, proving the Personality of the Holy Spirit. This means that the Holy Spirit is not merely an emanation from the Father, in other words, the Father's Spirit. He is a Person in His own right. Read carefully that which Jesus said of Him:

"Howbeit when 'He,' the Spirit of Truth, is come, 'He' will guide you into all Truth: for 'He' shall not speak of 'Himself;' but whatsoever 'He' shall hear, that shall 'He' speak: and 'He' will show you things to come" **(Jn. 16:13).**

Jesus would not have used personal pronouns about a mere emanation, even though from God the Father. No! The Holy Spirit is a Person, the same as the Father and the Son are Persons, and by the word *"Person,"* **we mean that each has a Personality of His Own.**

The Holy Spirit is the One Who deals with the unsaved person and as well, with the Believer. As such, He can be *"grieved"* **(Eph. 4:30); and, at least on one occasion, He was seen of John the Baptist (Mat. 3:16). The** *"Spirit"* **can speak to people and, in fact, does so very often (Acts 8:29). The Spirit of God can, as well, be** *"quenched"* **(I Thess. 5:19).**

God the Father and God the Son basically do whatever it is They desire to do, irrespective as to what men may think; however, when it comes to the Holy Spirit, Who Alone brings

us the Word of God, in other words, that for which Jesus died, He can be accepted or rejected. If the person doesn't want Him, He will not remain. Concerning that, the Scripture says:

"And the Glory of the LORD went up from the midst of the city, and stood upon the mountain which is on the east side of the city. *('The mountain which is on the east side of the city' is the Mount of Olivet. 'And the Glory of the LORD went up from the midst of the city,' denotes a reluctance to leave. However, the Holy Spirit is no longer wanted or desired; therefore, He has no choice but to leave.*

"Having reluctantly left the Temple, the Glory then forsook the city, lingering for a while with sorrowing Love upon this Mountain. But the Glory returned to that Mount, veiled in the sinless flesh of the Messiah; once more Love looked upon the Beloved but rebellious City and wept over it [Lk. 19:41].

"A few weeks later, Christ ascended from that same Mountain; and yet, in a future day, in the Glory of His Second Advent, His Feet shall stand, once again, upon it [Zech. 14:4]. Then shall Israel have one heart and a new spirit)" **(Ezek. 11:23).**

THE RETURN OF THE *"HOLY SPIRIT"*

Beautifully enough, Ezekiel saw in the future the return of the Holy Spirit to Israel, which has not happened even as of yet, but most definitely will happen exactly as the great Prophet saw such. He said:

"Afterward He brought me to the Gate, even the Gate that looks toward the east *(this Chapter is glorious indeed, inasmuch as it heralds the return of the Holy Spirit to the Millennial Temple and, therefore, to Israel. Ezekiel saw Him leave [Ezek. 11:23], and now he sees Him return. Atonement, as the eternal foundation of God's Relationship with man, is the keynote of this Chapter, which will occasion the Coming of the Spirit. As stated, this will be at the beginning of the Kingdom Age)*:

"**And, behold, the Glory of the God of Israel came from the way of the east: and His Voice was like a noise of many waters: and the Earth shined with His Glory.** *(Israel rejected Him and so He left! Now Israel has been washed and cleansed by the Blood of the Lamb and, therefore, He returns.)*"

THE *"VISION"*

"**And it was according to the appearance of the Vision which I saw, even according to the Vision that I saw when I came to destroy the city: and the Visions were like the Vision that I saw by the River Chebar; and I fell upon my face.** *(Taking the latter phrase first, 'And I fell upon my face,' one is left with the proper position in the Presence of the Lord of Glory. The phrase, 'That I saw when I came to destroy the city,' does not mean that Ezekiel personally destroyed it, but that he was the announcer of this tragic event!*

"The idea of Ezekiel's terminology is that as God, in the past, had shown Himself as One of Justice and Judgment by overturning and destroying the old, likewise, He will now exhibit Himself as a God of Grace and Mercy by condescending to establish His Abode in the new. Consequently, Ezekiel saw the destruction and the restoration, and in a manner unlike any other Prophet before or since!)"

"**And the Glory of the LORD came into the House by the way of the Gate whose prospect is toward the east** *(comes into the newly built Millennial Temple).*

"**So the Spirit took me up, and brought me into the Inner Court; and, behold, the Glory of the LORD filled the House.** *(The Lord is now entering into and taking possession of the 'House,' as formerly He had entered into and taken possession of the Tabernacle and the Temple of old*

[Ex. 40:34-35; I Ki. 8:10-11])" **(Ezek. 43:1-5).**

As stated, Ezekiel in a Vision saw the Holy Spirit leave the Temple in Jerusalem because He was no longer wanted or desired. This was approximately five hundred years before Christ. The City and the Temple were completely destroyed very shortly thereafter. As well, in another Vision, the great Prophet saw the Holy Spirit return, which will be to the Millennial Temple, and which has not taken place even yet, but will do so very shortly after the Second Coming of the Lord Jesus Christ.

WHO CAN BLASPHEME THE HOLY SPIRIT?

The only ones who can blaspheme the Holy Spirit are those who make a profession of religion exactly as the Pharisees of old, but who have actually never been Saved, or those who have truly been Saved, but through their own volition, have turned their backs upon the Lord and now speak disparagingly of His Moving and Operation.

I do not find in the Word of God that a person who has never made any profession of religion can blaspheme the Holy Spirit. If remarks are made by such individuals about the Holy Spirit, as oftentimes happens, it is done in ignorance, simply because such people don't know enough about the Holy Spirit to blaspheme Him.

CAN A PERSON DESIRE TO BE SAVED, BUT CANNOT DUE TO THE FACT THAT THEY HAVE SPOKEN AGAINST THE HOLY SPIRIT IN TIMES PAST?

Anyone who desires to be Saved can be Saved. In fact, the very idea of the desire to come to the Lord is placed there by the Holy Spirit. That is the Holy Spirit drawing the person to Christ. Concerning this, Jesus said:

"No man can come to Me, except the Father which has

sent Me draw him. *(The idea is that all initiative toward Salvation is on the part of God toward the sinner and not from the sinner himself; without this 'drawing of the Father,' which is done by the Holy Spirit, no one could come to God, or even have any desire to come to God)* . . ." **(Jn. 6:44).**

The Holy Spirit would not draw one to Christ and at the same time refuse Salvation to the individual.

As a child, I did hear some preachers preach particular sermons and claim that individuals had said something about the Holy Spirit, and now they wanted to be Saved, and would try to be Saved, but could not be Saved, meaning they were lost forever. None of that is Biblical. Let us say it again.

Any inclination toward God in any fashion by anyone is always placed there by the Holy Spirit. He does not play games. If He proposes Salvation for anyone, to be sure, that person can be Saved, if he will only believe (Jn. 3:16).

WILL A PERSON KNOW WHEN HE HAS BLASPHEMED THE HOLY SPIRIT?

No! The person will not know when he has blasphemed the Holy Spirit.

Such professors of religion will continue to claim their erroneous way, and at the same time, greatly oppose the right way, all the time thinking they are right. A perfect case in point is the Pharisees.

This was the major religious party in Israel at the time of Christ. They claimed to be fundamentalists, in other words, to believe all of the Bible, which in that day consisted of Genesis through Malachi. They claimed to be the spiritual guides of the people by contrast to the Sadducees, who little believed in anything. They had impeccable reputations in Israel; however, reputation is what other people think about you, while character is what God knows about you. They were extremely self-righteous. In fact, it was self-righteousness which nailed

Christ to the Cross.

A few of them accepted Christ (Nicodemus was one), but the truth is, most of them hated Him with a passion. This means that it was not the thieves, the drunks, or the libertines who crucified Christ, but rather, the religious leaders of that time.

Let's see what they did, which will prove to be a startling example of blaspheming the Holy Spirit, and then let's see what Jesus said about them.

THE MIRACLES PERFORMED BY CHRIST

The Scriptures say:

"But when Jesus knew it *(refers to the plotting of the Pharisees and Herodians against Him)*, **He withdrew Himself from thence** *(went to another town)*: **and great multitudes followed Him, and He healed them all** *('all' is emphatic, meaning that not one single person left without healing)*;

"**And charged them that they should not make Him known** *(He would not allow the fame of His Miracles to hinder His Purpose of offering up Himself as a Sacrifice for sin; the latter was His real Mission)*:

"**That it might be fulfilled which was spoken by Isaiah the Prophet, saying** *(Isaiah is quoted in the Gospels more than any other Prophet)*,

I WILL PUT THE HOLY SPIRIT UPON HIM

"**Behold My Servant** *(He was the Father's Servant)*, **Whom I have chosen** *(chosen by God and not man, hence rejected by man)*; **My Beloved, in Whom My soul is well pleased** *(to please God and not man, should be the goal of every Believer)*: **I will put My Spirit upon Him** *(Holy Spirit)*, **and He shall show judgment to the Gentiles** *(speaks of the coming Church, which is made up virtually* *of Gentiles).*

"**He shall not strive, nor cry** *(will not demand His rights)*; **neither shall any man hear His Voice in the streets** *(He never promoted Himself).*

"**A bruised reed shall He not break, and smoking flax shall He not quench** *(even though they rejected Him, He will not give up on Israel),* **till He send forth judgment unto victory** *(Israel will accept Him at the Second Coming).*

"**And in His Name shall the Gentiles trust** *(His Name means 'Saviour,' and even though the Jews rejected Him, the Gentiles accepted Him).*"

"IS NOT THIS THE SON OF DAVID?"

"**Then was brought unto Him one possessed with a devil** *(demon),* **blind, and dumb** *(the man represented Israel and, in fact, all of mankind):* **and He healed him, insomuch that the blind and the dumb both spoke and saw** *(those who are 'Born-Again' can now Spiritually speak and Spiritually see).*

"**And all the people were amazed, and said, Is not this the Son of David?** *(Had their religious leaders properly led them, the people of Israel would have accepted Christ.)*"

THE *"PHARISEES"*

"**But when the Pharisees heard it** *(heard what the people were saying about Jesus being the Son of David, which He was),* **they said, This** *fellow (the Pharisees never referred to Him even one time by His Name)* **does not cast out devils** *(demons),* **but by Beelzebub the prince of the devils** *(they didn't deny His Power, but claimed that it was of Satan).*

"**And Jesus knew their thoughts** *(revealed to Him by the Holy Spirit),* **and said unto them, Every kingdom divided against itself is brought to desolation; and every city or**

house divided against itself shall not stand *(the idea of the statement is that Satan does not oppose himself! He does not possess one with an evil spirit and then cast out that spirit)***."**

"BY THE SPIRIT OF GOD"

"And if Satan cast out Satan, he is divided against himself; how shall then his kingdom stand? *(Jesus admits here that Satan has a kingdom, which is the kingdom of darkness.)*

"And if I by Beelzebub cast out devils *(demons)***, by whom do your children cast *them* out?** *(The Pharisees and their disciples claimed to cast out demons, but in reality, they didn't; because they were as well of Satan.)* **therefore they shall be your judges** *(the word 'children' refers to the disciples of the Pharisees; Jesus by posing this question did not deny or affirm that they, in fact, actually did cast out demons; He was using the statement only as argument to prove His point).*

"But if I cast out devils *(demons)* **by the Spirit of God** *(Jesus did not cast out demons because He was God, but as a man filled with the Spirit)***, then the Kingdom of God is come unto you** *(this placed the Pharisees in an untenable position; if the Spirit of God were actually helping Him and He had already made it clear that such could not be done without the Spirit of God, then they must admit that He is the Messiah; their accusation backfired on them!)***."**

ONE IS EITHER WITH CHRIST OR AGAINST CHRIST

"Or else how can one enter into a strong man's house *(Satan is pictured here as strong – stronger than men)***, and spoil his goods** *(which Jesus did at the Cross)***, except he first bind the strong man?** *(Only Jesus could bind this strong man.)* **and then he will spoil his house** *(at Calvary*

Satan was totally defeated [Col. 2:14-15]).

"**He who is not with Me is against Me** *(it is impossible to take a neutral position regarding Christ; the word 'against' denotes intense opposition)*; **and he who gathers not with Me scatters abroad** *(refers to the Truth that one cannot be with 'Christ' and 'against' His true servants; the presence of Immanuel tests everything and everybody)*."

WHAT HAPPENS WHEN ONE BLASPHEMES THE HOLY SPIRIT?

"**Wherefore I say unto you** *(addressing the most fearsome statement)*, **All manner of sin and blasphemy shall be forgiven unto men** *(that is if they properly confess the sin to the Lord [I Jn. 1:9])*: **but the blasphemy against the Holy Spirit shall not be forgiven unto men** *(when they accused Him of casting out demons by the power of Satan, when in reality He was doing so by the Power of the Holy Spirit, they blasphemed the Spirit of God; blaspheming the Holy Spirit can only be committed, as stated, by someone who professes to know the Lord, as the Pharisees of old, or else has once known Him, and then turned against Him; the unredeemed, who have never known the Lord, cannot blaspheme the Holy Spirit simply because they have no true knowledge of the Spirit)*."

FORGIVENESS

"**And whosoever speaks a word against the Son of Man, it shall be forgiven him** *(once again, if forgiveness is sought)*: **but whosoever speaks against the Holy Spirit, it shall not be forgiven him, neither in this world, neither in the *world* to come** *(such a person is doomed! However, the statements do not mean that a backslider cannot come back to the Lord; but they do mean that one who has actually blasphemed the Holy Spirit will have no desire to come* *to the Lord, and thereby to Truth, but in fact, will continue to oppose Him; anyone who desires to come to the Lord, again as stated, which desire is placed there by the Holy Spirit, can do so [Rev. 22:17])*" **(Mat. 12:15-32).**

CAN ONE BLASPHEME THE HOLY SPIRIT IN IGNORANCE?

Yes, one can blaspheme the Holy Spirit in ignorance!

However, even though the blasphemy is committed, the Holy Spirit, because of the ignorance of the individual, will not hold one responsible. Paul said of himself:

"And I thank Christ Jesus our Lord, Who has enabled me *(presents the One Who calls and blesses)***, for that He counted me faithful, putting me into the Ministry** *(the Lord knew Paul would be faithful, and that the Gospel committed to him would not be compromised)***;**

"Who was before a blasphemer, and a persecutor, and injurious *(what he was before he was Saved)***: but I obtained Mercy, because I did** *it* **ignorantly in unbelief** *(could be translated, 'I was shown Mercy because, being ignorant, I acted in unbelief')***.**

"And the Grace of our Lord was exceeding abundant *(proclaims that which God stands ready to give to any honest and earnest seeker)* **with Faith and Love which is in Christ Jesus** *(presents that which was produced in Paul, as a result of the Grace of God)***" (I Tim. 1:12-14).**

However, having said that, had Paul rejected Christ when our Lord appeared to him on the road to Damascus he, no doubt, would have been eternally lost. God is patient, gracious, kind, and longsuffering, not willing that any should perish, but that all should come to Repentance; however, with each rejection of the Lord, the person is driven deeper into unbelief, which, if continued, will see the person eternally lost.

BELIEVERS REJECTING CHRIST AND
GOING INTO APOSTASY

Many Jews of Paul's day had accepted Christ, but by which acceptance a great price was exacted. They were ostracized from their families, at least if their families did not accept Christ. This means they were banished, and if met on the street, would not even be recognized. In fact, in some cases, a funeral was conducted, and the person who had accepted Christ was treated as though he were dead.

Many Jews became disillusioned and greatly discouraged because of this, with some of them returning to Judaism, which means they had to repudiate Christ. Paul addresses this head-on in both the Sixth and Tenth Chapters of Hebrews. We will address ourselves to the Sixth Chapter only. We will copy directly from THE EXPOSITOR'S STUDY BIBLE.

The great Apostle wrote and said:

"**Therefore leaving the Principles of the Doctrine of Christ** *(speaks of the 'first principles,' which refers to the Old Testament; Christ is the Centerpiece of the entirety of the Bible)*, **let us go on unto perfection** *(speaks of the New Testament Sacrifice, the Lord Jesus, and the Testament He inaugurated with His Work on the Cross)*; **not laying again the Foundation of Repentance from dead works** *(refers to these Jewish Christians going back to the Old Sacrificial system, etc.)*, **and of Faith toward God** *(refers to Faith toward God in the realm of the Old Testament Way, which God will not accept now inasmuch as Jesus has fulfilled the Old Testament Law)*."

OLD TESTAMENT DOCTRINES

"**Of the Doctrine of Baptisms** *(should have been translated, 'the Doctrine of Washings'; this concerned the many 'washings' contained in the Old Testament Sacrificial* *system)*, **and of laying on of hands** *(goes back to the Levitical Offerings of the Old Testament; when the person brought the animal for sacrifice, he had to lay his hands on the head of the innocent victim, confessing his sins, thereby transferring them to the innocent animal which would be slain [Lev. 16:21])*, **and of Resurrection of the dead** *(refers to Resurrection as taught in the Old Testament; there, this Doctrine was very incomplete, even as all Doctrine in the Old Testament was incomplete; the true meaning could not be given until after the Cross and the Resurrection of Christ, which the Lord gave to Paul [I Cor., Chpt. 15])*, **and of Eternal Judgment.** *(In the Old Testament, the Lord was looked at more so as a Judge than anything else. Since the Cross, He is looked at more as the Saviour.)*"

"ONCE ENLIGHTENED"

"**And this will we do** *(in other words, if we don't do this [refers to going on to the perfection of Christ], the results will be disastrous)*, **if God permit.** *(This refers to the fact that all dependence must be in Christ and the Cross. God will not allow any other type of Faith.)*

"**For** *it is* **impossible for those who were once enlightened** *(refers to those who have accepted the Light of the Gospel, which means accepting Christ and His great Sacrifice)*, **and have tasted of the Heavenly Gift** *(pertains to Christ and what He did at the Cross)*, **and were made partakers of the Holy Spirit** *(which takes place when a person comes to Christ).*"

"THE GOOD WORD OF GOD"

"**And have tasted the good Word of God** *(is not language that is used of an impenitent sinner, as some claim; the unsaved have no relish whatsoever for the Truth of God, and see no beauty in it)*, **and the powers of the world to**

come *(refers to the Work of the Holy Spirit within hearts and lives, which the unsaved cannot have or know).*"

CRUCIFYING AFRESH THE SON OF GOD

"**If they shall fall away** *(should have been translated, 'and having fallen away')*, **to renew them again unto Repentance** *('again' states they had once repented, but have now turned their backs on Christ)*; **seeing they crucify to themselves the Son of God afresh** *(means they no longer believe what Christ did at the Cross, actually concluding Him to be an imposter; the only way any person can truly repent is to place his Faith in Christ and the Cross; if that is denied, there is no Repentance)*, **and put** *Him* **to an open shame** *(means to hold Christ up to public ridicule; Paul wrote this Epistle because some Christian Jews were going back into Judaism, or seriously contemplating doing so)*" **(Heb. 6:1-6).**

WERE THESE JEWS BLASPHEMING
THE HOLY SPIRIT?

Quite possibly some of them were blaspheming the Holy Spirit, meaning that the Lord judged each person individually, as He always does.

However, these Passages do not mean, as some have claimed, that if a person backslides, i.e., *"falls away,"* he cannot come back to Christ. To be sure, if he remains in a state of denial and unbelief, he will be eternally lost. Any person who refuses to believe Christ cannot engage Repentance. As the Scripture says, *"It is impossible!"* But, if that person will renew his Faith in Christ and plead for Mercy and Grace, such a person will always be forgiven by the Lord.

Acceptance by the Lord in every case is always predicated on the individual placing his or her Faith exclusively in Christ and what Christ has done for us at the Cross. That and that alone ensures Salvation. For one to remove one's faith from Christ and the Cross to something else, and if it remains there, it guarantees that such a person will be eternally lost. All Salvation is predicated totally and wholly on Faith in Christ and the price He paid at Calvary in order that we might be Saved (Jn. 3:16; Rom., Chpts. 4-5; Eph. 2:13-18).

"They come and go, the seasons fair,
"And bring their spoil to vale and hill;
"But oh! There is waiting in the air,
"And a passionate hope the Spirit fills.
"Why does He tarry, the absent Lord?
"When shall the Kingdom be restored,
"And Earth and Heaven, with one accord,
"Ring out the cry that the King comes?"

"The floods have lifted up their voice,
"The King has come to His Own, His Own!
"The little hills and vales rejoice,
"His right is to take the crown.
"Sleepers, awake, and meet Him first;
"Now let the marriage hymn outburst,
"And powers of darkness flee, disperse:
"What will it be when the King comes!"

"A ransom Earth breaks forth in song.
"Her sin-stained ages overpast;
"Her yearning, Lord, how long, how long?
"Exchanged for joy at last, at last,
"Angels carry the Royal Command;
"Peace beams forth throughout all the lands;
"The trees of the fields shall clap their hands,
"What will it be when the King comes!"

"Now Zion's hill, with glory crowned,
"Uplifts her head with joy once more:

"And Zion's King, once scorned, disowned,
"Extends her rule from shore to shore.
"Sing, for the land her Lord regains!
"Sing, for the Son of David reigns!
"And living streams overflow her plains:
"What will it be when the King comes!"

"Oh, brothers, stand as men that wait,
"The dawn is purpling in the east,
"And banners wave from Heaven's Gate,
"The conflict now, but soon the feast!
"Mercy and Truth shall meet again;
"Worthy the Lamb that once was slain!
"We can suffer now, He will know us then:
"What will it be when the King comes!"

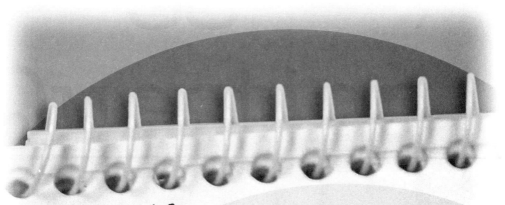

CHAPTER TWELVE

What Is "Spiritual Adultery" And How Does It Affect The Holy Spirit?

QUESTION:

WHAT IS "SPIRITUAL ADULTERY" AND HOW DOES IT AFFECT THE HOLY SPIRIT?

ANSWER:

All Believers are married to Christ. We are to look to Him exclusively for all things, whatever that may be. This means that our Faith is to be in Christ and the Cross and nothing else. Failing that means that our Faith is in something else, and even though the something else may be good in its own right, still, it is not Faith in Christ and the Cross, which means that such a Believer is being unfaithful to Christ, which is *"spiritual adultery."* To be sure, such affects the Holy Spirit greatly. While He doesn't leave us, and thank God for that, still, He is greatly hindered.

Considering that the Holy Spirit works exclusively within the parameters of the Finished Work of Christ, meaning that it is the Cross of Christ that gives Him the legal right to do all that He does, we start to see how serious all of this is.

The Lord doesn't require very much of us, but He does require one thing, and that is that our Faith be exclusively in Christ and what Christ has done for us at the Cross.

EVERYTHING COMES THROUGH THE CROSS

The Believer must understand that while Christ is the Source of all things from God, it is the Cross that is the Means by which all of these things are given to us. To receive them, whatever they might be, the Cross of Christ must ever be the Object of our Faith. *"Spiritual adultery,"* i.e., *"unfaithfulness,"* is a serious sin, to say the least. Whether we realize it or not, this type of unfaithfulness actually says that the Cross of Christ was not enough and needs something added. One can well imagine, considering the price that Christ paid, how great this insult is.

THE WORD OF GOD

Paul explains this in the first five Verses of the Seventh Chapter of Romans. He said:

"**Know you not, Brethren** *(Paul is speaking to Believers)***, (for I speak to them who know the Law,)** *(he is speaking of the Law of Moses, but it could refer to any type of religious Law)* **how that the Law has dominion over a man as long as he lives?** *(The Law has dominion as long as he tries to live by Law. Regrettably, not understanding the Cross regarding Sanctification, virtually the entirety of the church is presently trying to live for God by means of the Law. Let the Believer understand that there are only two places he can be, Grace or Law. If he doesn't understand the Cross as it refers to Sanctification, which is the only means of Victory, he will automatically be under Law, which guarantees failure.)*"

THE MARRIAGE BOND

"**For the woman which has an husband is bound by the Law to *her* husband so long as he lives** *(presents Paul using the analogy of the marriage bond)*; **but if the husband be dead, she is loosed from the Law of *her* husband** *(meaning that she is free to marry again)*."

"AN ADULTERESS"

"**So then if, while *her* husband lives, she be married to another man, she shall be called an adulteress** *(in effect, the woman now has two husbands, at least in the Eyes of God; following this analogy, the Holy Spirit through Paul will give us a great truth; many Christians are living a life of 'spiritual adultery'; they are married to Christ, but they are, in effect, serving another husband, 'the Law'; it is quite an analogy!)*: **but if her husband be dead** *(the*

Law is dead by virtue of Christ having fulfilled the Law in every respect), **she is free from that Law** *(if the husband dies, the woman is free to marry and serve another; the Law of Moses, being satisfied in Christ, is now dead to the Believer and the Believer is free to serve Christ without the Law having any part or parcel in his life or living)*; **so that she is no adulteress, though she be married to another man** *(presents the Believer as now married to Christ, and no longer under obligation to the Law).*"

"THE BODY OF CHRIST"

"Wherefore, my Brethren, you also are become dead to the Law *(the Law is not dead per se, but we are dead to the Law because we are dead to its effects; this means that we are not to try to live for God by means of 'Law,' whether the Law of Moses, or Laws made up by other men or of ourselves; we are to be dead to all Law)* **by the Body of Christ** *(this refers to the Crucifixion of Christ, which satisfied the demands of the broken Law which we could not satisfy; but Christ did it for us; having fulfilled the Law in every respect, the Christian is not obligated to Law in any fashion, only to Christ and what He did at the Cross)*; **that you should be married to another** *(speaking of Christ),* **even to Him Who is raised from the dead** *(we are raised with Him in Newness of Life, and we should ever understand that Christ has met, does meet, and shall meet our every need; we look to Him exclusively, referring to what He did for us at the Cross)*, **that we should bring forth fruit unto God** *(proper fruit can only be brought forth by the Believer constantly looking to the Cross; in fact, Christ must never be separated from the Work of the Cross; to do so is to produce 'another Jesus' [II Cor. 11:4]).*"

"FLESH" AND THE "LAW"

"For when we were in the flesh *(can refer to the*

unsaved state or to the Believer who is attempting to over-come the powers of sin by his own efforts, i.e., 'the flesh '), **the motions of sins** *(denotes being under the power of the sin nature, and refers to the 'passions of the sin nature ')*, **which were by the Law** *(the effect of the Law is to reveal sin, which Law is designed to do whether it's the Law of God or Laws made up of ourselves; that doesn't mean it's evil, for it isn't; it just means that there is no victory in the Law, only the revelation of sin and its penalty)*, **did work in our members to bring forth fruit unto death** *(when the Believer attempts to live for the Lord by means of Law, which, regrettably, most of the modern church does, the end result is going to be sin and failure; in fact, it can be no other way; let us say it again! if the Believer doesn't understand the Cross, as it refers to Sanctification, then the Believer is going to try to live for God by means of Law; the sadness is that most of the modern church thinks it is under Grace when, in reality, it is living under Law because of not understanding the Cross)*" **(Rom. 7:1-5).**

THE CROSS OF CHRIST

All of this means in brief that we as Believers are mar-ried to Christ. As such, and as stated, He is to meet our every need simply because He Alone can meet our every need. The moment we resort to Law, which refers to placing our Faith in anything else other than the Cross of Christ, this constitutes *"spiritual adultery."* Considering that the modern church knows next to nothing about the Cross of Christ as it refers to our Sanctification, i.e., how we live this life, this means that their Faith is in something other than Christ and the Cross. It doesn't really matter too much what the other thing might be, and granted that the other thing might be something very good in its own right, still, the Lord construes such as *"spiritual adultery."* In fact, this is what deceives Believers.

That in which they have placed their faith is good in its own right, and because it is good, and even Scriptural in its own way, it deceives them into believing that this is the right way to go. But, let us say it again.

Everything we receive from God comes to us by and through Jesus Christ and by the Means of the Cross. He does not give us and, in fact, cannot give us anything other than by and through the Cross. Consequently, our Faith must be registered completely in Christ and what He did for us at the Cross. That being done, the Grace of God, which works exclusively by and through the Cross of Christ, can flow to us in an uninterrupted manner. Otherwise, we cut off the Grace of God, which means we cut off all Blessings. Listen again to Paul. He said:

THE *"YOKE OF BONDAGE"*

"Stand fast therefore in the liberty wherewith Christ has made us free *(we were made free, and refers to freedom to live a Holy Life by evidencing Faith in Christ and the Cross)*, and be not entangled again with the yoke of bondage. *(To abandon the Cross and go under Law of any kind guarantees bondage once again to the sin nature.)*"

"CHRIST SHALL PROFIT YOU NOTHING"

"Behold *('mark my words!')*, I Paul say unto you *(presents the Apostle's authority regarding the Message he brings)*, that if you be circumcised, Christ shall profit you nothing. *(If the Believer goes back into Law, and Law of any kind, what Christ did at the Cross on our behalf will profit us nothing. One cannot have it two ways.)*"

A DEBTOR TO THE LAW

"For I testify again to every man who is circumcised *(some of the Galatian Gentiles were being pressured by false teachers to embrace the Law of Moses, which meant they would have to forsake Christ and the Cross, for it's not possible to wed the two; as well, it's not possible to wed any Law to Grace)*, **that he is a debtor to do the whole Law** *(which, of course, is impossible; and besides, the Law contained no Salvation)*."

"YOU ARE FALLEN FROM GRACE"

"**Christ is become of no effect unto you** *(this is a chilling statement, and refers to anyone who makes anything other than Christ and the Cross the Object of his Faith)*, **whosoever of you are justified by the Law** *(seek to be justified by the Law)*; **you are fallen from Grace** *(fallen from the position of Grace, which means the Believer is trusting in something other than the Cross; it actually means, 'to apostatize')*" **(Gal. 5:1-4).**

"SPIRITUAL ADULTERY," THE GREATEST HINDRANCE

As unfaithfulness in the bond of marriage is so serious that most marriages never survive such, and considering that the Holy Spirit, in essence, refers to unfaithfulness to Christ as *"spiritual adultery,"* we should understand how serious this problem is. In fact, it is meant by the Holy Spirit for us to see the seriousness of such action.

The tragedy is that none of us quite understand that *"spiritual adultery"* is just as bad in the spiritual sense as physical adultery is in the natural sense. Irrespective, however, of what we say or think, the Truth cannot be denied.

Paul tells us that we are married to Christ and, as such, we are to be faithful to Him, and exclusively, which means to place our Faith and trust exclusively in Christ and the Cross, and to keep it exclusively in Christ and the Cross.

MARRIED TO CHRIST

Paul deals with this, as well, in his Second Letter to the

Corinthians. He said:

"Would to God you could bear with me a little in *my* folly: and indeed bear with me. *(In effect, the Apostle is saying, 'indulge me.')*

"For I am jealous over you with godly jealousy *(refers to the 'jealousy of God' [Ex. 20:5; 34:14; Nah. 1:2])*: for I have espoused you to one husband *(not jealous of the Corinthians' affection for himself, but of their affection for Christ)*, that I may present *you as* a chaste virgin to Christ. *(They must not commit 'spiritual adultery,' which refers to trusting in things other than Christ and the Cross.)*"

"THE SIMPLICITY THAT IS IN CHRIST"

"But I fear, lest by any means, as the serpent beguiled Eve through his subtilty *(the strategy of Satan)*, so your minds should be corrupted from the simplicity that is in Christ. *(The Gospel of Christ is simple, but men complicate it by adding to the Message.)*"

"ANOTHER JESUS"

"For if he who comes preaching another Jesus *(a Jesus who is not of the Cross)*, whom we have not preached *(Paul's Message was 'Jesus Christ and Him Crucified'; anything else is 'another Jesus')*, or *if* you receive another spirit *(which is produced by preaching another Jesus)*, which you have not received *(that's not what you received when we preached the True Gospel to you)*, or another gospel, which you have not accepted *(anything other than 'Jesus Christ and Him Crucified' is 'another gospel')*, you might well bear with *him*. *(The Apostle is telling the Corinthians they have, in fact, sinned because they tolerated these false apostles who had come in, bringing 'another gospel' which was something other than Christ and the Cross)*" **(II Cor. 11:1-4).**

In fact, the far greater majority of the modern church is pro-claiming *"another Jesus."*

WHAT DOES *"ANOTHER JESUS"* ACTUALLY MEAN?

"Another Jesus" means that they were proclaiming Jesus, but were ignoring the Cross. In fact, those interlopers then were promoting the Law of Moses, claiming that it must be kept alongside accepting Jesus. And, if the people did not accept the Law of Moses, meaning that the men would be circumcised, etc., they were not Saved, or else, they were not a complete Christian. Today, it's a little different.

It is not so much the Law of Moses that's being promoted presently, but rather, something in the place of the Cross.

The modern church, at least after a fashion, is preaching Jesus, but it is Jesus, the *"good Man,"* or the *"Miracle Worker,"* or the *"great example,"* or the *"great teacher,"* etc. All of this means that they are claiming that man can reach his potential if he will only change a few habits, etc., and, thereby, be more like Jesus. In fact, the modern church is ignoring the real problem of man, which is sin.

SIN

We must ever understand that man is in trouble, and I mean terrible trouble, not so much for what he does, even though that is very, very important, but mostly for what he is. Millions today think they are going to Heaven because they do not commit adultery, do not steal, etc. While it's certainly good that they don't do these things, none of that are the criteria. The criteria is that mankind is a sinner, and that his problem can be addressed only by Jesus Christ, the Saviour, meaning that man must admit what he is, a sinner, and, thereby, accept Christ as his Saviour and Lord (Jn. 3:16; Rev. 22:17).

When it comes to the Believer, we must, as well, admit that our real problem is sin, but this the modern church will not do. As stated, it claims that the real problem of the modern Christian is just that he simply needs to change his habits and become a better person.

While all of us need to be a better person, still, it's Jesus Christ the Saviour from sin that can make us such, and only Jesus. Let me say it again.

The problem with the modern Christian is *"sin."* The only cure for that problem and the only answer for that problem is that we place our Faith in Christ exclusively, and what He did for us at the Cross, understanding that the Cross of Christ is the only answer for sin. When this is done, and I might quickly add, maintained, meaning that our Faith ever remain in Christ and the Cross, then the Holy Spirit, Who Alone can bring about His Fruit within our lives, will begin to do His Work.

If the Believer places his faith in anything else, and I mean anything else, such as the Lord's Supper, fasting, Water Baptism, good works, giving money to the Work of the Lord, performing good deeds, his church, his religious denomination, etc., such a Christian is, in fact, living in a state of *"spiritual adultery."* While the other things mentioned are good things, and in which every true Believer will engage himself, still, the Object of Faith must always be, and without exception, and continue to be, the Cross of Christ (Rom. 6:1-14; 8:1-2, 11; I Cor. 1:17-18, 23; 2:2; Gal., Chpt. 5; 6:14; Eph. 2:13-18; Col. 2:14-15).

HOW SERIOUS IS THIS MATTER OF *"SPIRITUAL ADULTERY"*?

I will answer that by asking another question, *"How serious is unfaithfulness as it regards marriage between a husband and wife?"*

If I remember correctly, it was in late winter of 1992. We were then having two prayer meetings a day, which continued for ten years, and to which I continue to personally subscribe.

That particular morning, as four or five of us gathered for prayer, I began to petition the Lord for particular things in my own personal life, which I felt I needed. In a very short period of time the Spirit of God covered me greatly.

The Lord took me away from my own personal needs, although they were many, to the condition of the church, and I speak of the church world as a whole. He took me to the First Chapter of the great Prophet Isaiah. I will quote both Text and notes from THE EXPOSITOR'S STUDY BIBLE that which the Lord gave me as it regards the church. He said:

"Hear, O heavens, and give ear, O Earth: for the LORD has spoken, I have nourished and brought up children, and they have rebelled against Me. *(In this Verse, all nature is invoked to hear Jehovah make complaint of the ingratitude of His People. The invocation is cast in the same form which is so common in Deuteronomy [Deut. 4:26; 30:19; 31:28; 32:1].*

"To step out of the Song of Solomon into Isaiah is to pass from sunshine to shadow. The love that exults in the one laments in the other.

"Actually, Isaiah is not the One actually speaking here, but rather Jehovah. The Prophet is only His mouthpiece.)

"The ox knows his owner, and the ass his master's crib: but Israel does not know, My People do not consider. *(The meaning of this Verse seems to be, 'My People do not consider Me, do not reflect on My relation to them as Lord and Master.')*"

"THEY ARE GONE AWAY BACKWARD"

"Ah sinful nation, a people laden with iniquity, a seed of evildoers, children who are corrupters: they have forsaken the LORD, they have provoked the Holy One of Israel unto anger, they are gone away backward. *(According to Isaiah, holiness is the most essential element of God's Nature; hence, he would call Him 'the Holy One of Israel.'*

"In their forsaking the Lord, Judah did not renounce His

worship, but actually continued it; however, it was reduced to a mere formality. The people 'honored Him with their lips, while their hearts were far from Him' [Isa. 29:13].)"

"THE WHOLE HEAD IS SICK, AND THE WHOLE HEART FAINT"

"Why should you be stricken anymore? you will revolt more and more: the whole head is sick, and the whole heart faint.

"From the sole of the foot even unto the head there is no soundness in it; but wounds, and bruises, and putrifying sores: they have not been closed, neither bound up, neither mollified with ointment. *(The statement of Verses 5 and 6 not only describes moral character, or rather the lack thereof, but also the severity of future just but unavailing punishment. Israel refused to repent notwithstanding such punishment.*

"The 'head' and 'heart' of Israel respectively represented the intellectual and moral natures. Israel had turned away from God in both her mind and heart.

"The deadly 'bruises' and 'sores' of Israel, while but a spiritual analogy, still, could not be cured by anything except the Lord)" **(Isa. 1:2-6).**

If these Passages described the condition of the church in 1992, and they most definitely did, then how much worse is the situation now? *"Spiritual adultery"* is the problem!

WHAT THE SPIRIT IS SAYING TO THE CHURCHES

Regarding the Messages of Christ to the seven Churches of Asia, which, in fact, typify the Church Age from the Early Church unto the present, in every one of these Messages He closed it by the admonishment, *"He who has an ear, let him hear what the Spirit says unto the Churches"* (Rev. 2:7, 11, 17, 29; 3:6, 13, 22).

The short phrase, *"He who has an ear,"* refers to those who truly want what *"thus saith the Lord."* In other words, they are listening for the Voice of the Holy Spirit.

The modern church is now in the Laodicean Age. In other words, the Message of our Lord to the church at Laodicea describes the time in which we now live. It is the closing Message, meaning that the Dispensation of the Church is almost over. The following is the Message to this church, which, in effect, is the Message to the modern church. Our Lord said:

"And unto the Angel *(Pastor)* of the Church of the Laodiceans write *(this is the 'apostate church'; we do not know when it began, but we do know it has begun; it is the last church addressed by Christ, so that means the Rapture will take place very shortly)*; These things says the Amen, the faithful and true witness *(by contrast to His Church, which is not faithful and true)*, the beginning of the Creation of God *(Jesus is the Creator of all things)*."

"LUKEWARM"

"I know your works, that you are neither cold nor hot *(characterizes that which is prevalent at this present time)*: I would you were cold or hot *(half measures won't do)*.

"So then because you are lukewarm, and neither cold nor hot *(if a person is lukewarm towards something, it means he hasn't rejected it, but at the same time he has by no means accepted it; in the Mind of God, a tepid response is equal to a negative response)*, I will spue you out of My mouth. *(There is no prospect of Repentance here on the part of this church, or Restoration. In fact, there is Divine rejection.)*"

"HAVE NEED OF NOTHING"?

"Because you say, I am rich, and increased with goods,

and have need of nothing *(they equated the increase in material goods with Spiritual Blessings, which they were not)*; **and knowest not that you are wretched, and miserable, and poor, and blind, and naked** *(the tragedy lay in the fact that while this church gloated over material wealth, she was unconscious of her spiritual poverty; again indicative of the modern church!).*"

"GOLD TRIED IN THE FIRE"

"**I counsel you to buy of Me gold tried in the fire, that you may be rich** *(what they needed to 'buy' could not be purchased with money, but only with the Precious Blood of Christ, which price has already been paid; but the modern church is not interested)*; **and white raiment, that you may be clothed, and *that* the shame of your nakedness do not appear** *(refers to Righteousness which is exclusively of Christ and the Cross; this tells us that the Laodicean Church is extremely self-righteous; not having the Righteousness of Christ, they are 'naked' to the Judgment of God)*; **and anoint your eyes with eyesalve, that you may see.** *(The modern church is also spiritually blind.)*"

"REPENT"

"**As many as I love, I rebuke and chasten** *(implies a remnant)*: **be zealous therefore, and repent.** *(The modern church desperately needs to repent for its rebellion against God's Divine Order [Christ and the Cross] and for following cunningly devised fables [II Pet. 1:16].)*"

THE *"VOICE"* OF THE LORD

"**Behold, I stand at the door, and knock** *(presents Christ outside the church)*: **if any man hear My Voice** *(so much religious racket is going on that it is difficult to 'hear*

His Voice'), **and open the door** *(Christ is the True Door, which means the church has erected another door)*, **I will come in to him, and will sup with him, and he with Me.** *(Having been rejected by the church, our Lord now appeals to individuals, and He is still doing so presently.)*"

THE OVERCOMER

"**To him who overcomes will I grant to sit with Me in My Throne** *(the overcomer will gain the prize of the Throne, which can only be done by one ever making the Cross the Object of his Faith)*, **even as I also overcame, and am sat down with My Father in His Throne.** *(This presents Christ as our Substitute, going before us, and doing for us what we could not do for ourselves.)*

"**He who has an ear, let him hear what the Spirit says unto the Churches.** *(In plain language, the Holy Spirit is saying, 'Come back to Christ and the Cross!')*" **(Rev. 3:14-22).**

WHAT IS THE SPIRIT SAYING TO THE CHURCHES?

I firmly believe, and with all of my heart, that the Message of the Cross of Christ is what the Holy Spirit is saying to this modern church. The modern church has a modicum of understanding respecting the Cross of Christ as it regards Salvation; however, it has no understanding at all as it regards how the Cross of Christ refers to our Sanctification, in other words, how we live for God on a daily basis. And yet, ninety-nine percent of the Bible is given over to telling us how to live for God. In fact, ninety-nine percent of everything that Paul wrote in his fourteen Epistles, once again, refers to how we live for God. And, it was to Paul that the meaning of the New Covenant was given.

Most definitely yes, a plethora of information is given regarding Salvation, as should be obvious, but almost all of the Bible, which is for Believers, is given over to telling us how to live for God.

Considering that, it becomes obvious as to how much the church has drifted off course, when the truth is, the modern church simply doesn't know how to live for God. It cannot know until it properly understands the Message of the Cross as it regards Sanctification. Not understanding this Message, it is living in a state of *"spiritual adultery,"* which is dragging it even deeper into a morass of sin and shame.

Modern preachers simply do not know how to tell Believers to live for God. In fact, the modern church has become so inundated with humanistic psychology that, anymore, it little knows the True Word of God. Please understand the following:

One cannot have both humanistic psychology and the Message of the Cross. One or the other must go. Either one cancels out the other. Sadly, and regrettably, the modern church has opted for humanistic psychology, and in doing so, it is destroying itself. This is the reason that in the Eyes of God the modern church is *"wretched, miserable, poor, blind, and naked."* *"Spiritual adultery"* is the problem.

TO SUM UP

If the Believer doesn't understand the Cross of Christ as it refers to Sanctification, in other words, how we live for the Lord on a daily basis, the only other alternative is *"spiritual adultery."* And, to be sure, even as physical adultery destroys a marriage, likewise, *"spiritual adultery"* will destroy the marriage of the Believer with the Lord. It cannot be otherwise!

> *"Beneath the Cross of Jesus,*
> *"I fain would take my stand,*
> *"The shadow of a mighty Rock,*
> *"Within a weary land;*
> *"A home within the wilderness,*
> *"A rest upon the way,*
> *"From the burning of the noontide heat,*
> *"And the burden of the day."*

"Oh, safe and happy shelter!
"Oh, refuge tried and sweet!
"Oh, trysting place where Heaven's love,
"And Heaven's justice meet.
"As to the holy Patriarch,
"That wondrous dream was given,
"So seems my Saviour's Cross to me,
"A ladder up to Heaven."

"There lies beneath a shadow,
"But on the further side,
"The darkness of an awful grave,
"That gapes both deep and wide;
"And there between us stands the Cross,
"Two arms outstretched to save,
"Like a watchman set to guard the way,
"From that eternal grave."

"Upon the Cross of Jesus,
"My eye at times can see,
"The very dying form of One,
"Who suffered there for me;
"And from my smitten heart, with tears,
"Two wonders I confess,
"The wonders of His glorious Love,
"And my own worthlessness."

"I take, O Cross, your shadow,
"For my abiding place;
"I ask no other sunshine than,
"The sunshine of His Face;
"Content to let the world go by,
"To know no gain nor loss,
"My sinful self my only shame,
"My glory all the Cross."

CHAPTER THIRTEEN

What Does It Mean To "Walk After The Spirit"?

QUESTION:

WHAT DOES IT MEAN TO "WALK AFTER THE SPIRIT"?

ANSWER:

The understanding of what it means to *"walk after the flesh,"* and to *"walk after the Spirit,"* constitutes itself as one of the most important questions that any Believer could ask. Failure to understand the answer to these questions is to fail indeed! But, tragically, most Believers do not have the slightest knowledge as to what *"walking after the flesh"* or *"walking after the Spirit"* means. To understand one, both must be understood. Concerning this, Paul said:

> ***"There is** therefore now no condemnation (guilt) to them which are in Christ Jesus (refers back to Rom. 6:3-5 and our being baptized into His Death, which speaks of the Crucifixion),* **who walk not after the flesh** *(depending on one's personal strength and ability or great religious efforts in order to overcome sin),* **but after the Spirit.** *(The Holy Spirit works exclusively within the legal confines of the Finished Work of Christ; our Faith in that Finished Work, i.e., 'the Cross,' guarantees the help of the Holy Spirit, which guarantees Victory)"* **(Rom. 8:1).**

"WALKING AFTER THE FLESH"

Let's first of all address ourselves to *"walking after the flesh"* because Paul addressed this first as well.

What is the flesh, as Paul uses the word?

It was the Holy Spirit Who gave this word to Paul to use in order to explain this most important question.

The word *"flesh"* in the Greek is *"sarx,"* and means, at least as Paul here used the word, *"human nature with its frailties and passions."* In other words, it pertains to that, which is indicative to human beings, namely what we can do as a human being. It refers to one's talents, abilities, intellect, education, motivation, efforts, etc. Within themselves, these things aren't wrong. The Holy Spirit through Paul is simply telling us that what we must be in the Lord, and what we are meant to be in the Lord, which is to overcome the world, the flesh, and the Devil, cannot be done by the means of human ability alone. Regrettably, that's the way that most Christians are trying to live for God. They are trying to do so by the means of the *"flesh."* Paul said the following as it involves this all-important question.

"WEAK THROUGH THE FLESH"

"For what the Law could not do, in that it was weak through the flesh *(those under Law had only their willpower, which is woefully insufficient; so despite how hard they tried, they were unable to keep the Law then, and the same inability persists presently; any person who tries to live for God by a system of laws is doomed to failure, because the Holy Spirit will not function in that capacity)*, God sending His Own Son *(refers to man's helpless condition, unable to save himself and unable to keep even a simple Law and, therefore, in dire need of a Saviour)* in the likeness of sinful flesh *(this means that Christ was really human, conformed in appearance to flesh, which is characterized by sin, but yet sinless)*, and for sin *(to atone for sin, to destroy its power, and to save and Sanctify its victims)*, condemned sin in the flesh *(destroyed the power of sin by giving His Prefect Body as a Sacrifice for sin, which made it possible for sin to be defeated in our flesh; it was all through the Cross)*" (Rom. 8:3).

"THE RIGHTEOUSNESS OF THE LAW"

"That the Righteousness of the Law might be fulfilled in us *(the Law finding its full accomplishment in us can only be done by Faith in Christ, and what Christ has done for us at the Cross)*, **who walk not after the flesh** *(not after our own strength and ability)*, **but after the Spirit** *(the word 'walk' refers to the manner in which we order our life; when we place our Faith in Christ and the Cross, understanding that all things come from God to us by Means of the Cross, ever making it the Object of our Faith, the Holy Spirit can then work mightily within us, bringing about the Fruit of the Spirit; that is what 'walking after the Spirit' actually means!)*" **(Rom. 8:4).**

MINDING THE THINGS OF THE FLESH

"**For they who are after the flesh do mind the things of the flesh** *(refers to Believers trying to live for the Lord by means other than Faith in the Cross of Christ)*; **but they who are after the Spirit the things of the Spirit** *(those who place their Faith in Christ and the Cross, do so exclusively; they are doing what the Spirit desires, which alone can bring Victory)*" **(Rom. 8:5).**

THOSE IN THE FLESH CANNOT PLEASE GOD

"**So then they who are in the flesh cannot please God.** *(Refers to the Believer attempting to live his Christian Life by means other than Faith in Christ and the Cross)*" **(Rom. 8:8).**

THE CHRISTIAN IS NOT TO WALK AFTER THE FLESH

"**But you are not in the flesh** *(in one sense of the word is asking the question, 'Since you are now a Believer and no longer depending on the flesh, why are you resorting to the flesh?')*, **but in the Spirit** *(as a Believer, you now have the privilege of being led and empowered by the Holy Spirit; however, He will do such for us only on the premise of our*

Faith in the Finished Work of Christ), **if so be that the Spirit of God dwell in you** *(if you are truly Saved)*. **Now if any man have not the Spirit of Christ, he is none of His** *(Paul is saying that the work of the Spirit in our lives is made possible by what Christ did at Calvary, and the Resurrection)*" **(Rom. 8:9).**

WE AREN'T DEBTORS TO THE FLESH

The Apostle goes on:

"**Therefore, Brethren** *(means that Paul is addressing Believers)*, **we are debtors** *(refers to what we owe Jesus Christ for what He has done for us on the Cross)*, **not to the flesh** *(we do not owe anything to our own ability, meaning that such cannot save us or give us victory)*, **to live after the flesh** *('living after the flesh' pertains to our works, which God can never accept, and which can never bring us victory, but rather, defeat)*" **(Rom. 8:12).**

"IF YOU LIVE AFTER THE FLESH, YOU SHALL DIE"

"**For if you live after the flesh** *(after your own strength and ability, which is outside of God's Prescribed Order)*, **you shall die** *(you will not be able to live a victorious, Christian life)*: **but if you through the Spirit** *(by the Power of the Holy Spirit)* **do mortify the deeds of the body** *(which the Holy Spirit Alone can do)*, **you shall live** *(shall walk in Victory; but once again, even at the risk of being overly repetitive, we must never forget that the Spirit works totally and completely within the confines of the Cross of Christ; this means that we must ever make the Cross the Object of our Faith, giving Him latitude to work)*" **(Rom. 8:13).**

The word *"walk"* **in the Greek is** *"peripateo,"* **and means, at least as Paul here uses the word,** *"how one comports oneself,* *how one orders one's behavior."* It refers to our everyday living before God and for God.

HOW TO LIVE FOR THE LORD

Regrettably, the modern church little knows how to live for God. The reason for that is simply because the modern church doesn't understand the Cross of Christ as it regards Sanctification and, as well, the modern church little knows how the Holy Spirit works within our hearts and lives. If any thought is given to the Holy Spirit at all, it is simply that whatever He does is something that is automatic. It isn't! The Holy Spirit works exclusively within the parameters of the Finished Work of Christ. In fact, it is the Cross of Christ which gives the Holy Spirit the Means by which He does all things. Understanding very little of this, if any at all, means that most modern Christians simply do not know how to live for God.

The following constitutes some of the statements commonly used, which purports to tell people how to live for the Lord.

YOU'VE GOT TO TRY HARDER ...

If that is the correct answer, *"You've got to try harder,"* just how hard is enough? Once again, this reeks with the flesh. It is trying to do something by human ability that simply cannot be done, yet that's the advice that is given to most Christians when they face problems. They are told to *"try harder."*

HUMANISTIC PSYCHOLOGY

Probably a statement that is used more than anything else at this time is, *"You need professional help."* Of course, they are speaking of humanistic psychology. In this, the statement, *"Christian psychology,"* is bandied about as though it is a different type of psychology. It isn't!

In fact, in true terms, there is no such thing as Christian

psychology, just as there is no such thing as Christian biology, or Christian physics, etc. The term, *"Christian psychology,"* is used often in order to make people believe that there is a special type of psychology for Christians, etc. Again we state, there isn't!

Some Christian psychologists, so-called, are even advocating presently that modern man is facing problems that are not addressed in the Bible. As such, modern man needs both the Bible and psychology, that is, if he is to live a well-ordered life. Now, that's a strange statement!

The very idea that the Holy Spirit, when giving us the Word of God, suddenly became at a loss for words, when it came to modern man, is ridiculous. Listen to what the Holy Spirit did say.

"HAS GIVEN US ALL THINGS THAT PERTAIN UNTO LIFE AND GODLINESS"

"Grace and peace be multiplied unto you through the knowledge of God, and of Jesus our Lord *(this is both sanctifying grace and sanctifying peace, all made available by the Cross)*,

"According as His Divine Power has given unto us all things *(the Lord with large-handed generosity has given us all things)* that *pertain* unto life and godliness *(pertains to the fact that the Lord Jesus has given us everything we need regarding life and living)*, through the knowledge of Him Who has called us to Glory and Virtue *(the 'knowledge' addressed here speaks of what Christ did at the Cross, which alone can provide 'Glory and Virtue')*."

"EXCEEDING GREAT AND PRECIOUS PROMISES"

"Whereby are given unto us exceeding great and Precious Promises *(pertains to the Word of God, which alone holds the answer to every life problem)*: that by these *(Promises)* you might be partakers of the Divine Nature *(the Divine Nature implanted in the inner being of the believing sinner becomes the source of our new life and actions; it comes to everyone at the moment of being 'Born-Again'),* **having escaped the corruption that is in the world through lust.** *(This presents the Salvation experience of the sinner, and the Sanctification experience of the Saint)"* **(II Pet. 1:2-4).**

Now, either the Lord did give us *"all things that pertain unto life and godliness,"* or else Peter didn't tell the truth, and we must turn to other means.

I happen to believe that Simon Peter did tell the truth, did write exactly what the Holy Spirit told him to say, and that it applies to modern man as it has applied to all down through the ages. So, the Believer has a choice.

You can accept what Peter, James, John, and Paul said to us, or you can accept that which is given to us by Freud, Maslow, Rogers, etc. I will say as Joshua of old, *"But as for me and my house, we will serve the LORD"* (Josh. 24:15).

IT IS EITHER THE CROSS OR THE FLESH

If the Believer doesn't have his Faith exclusively in Christ and the Cross, and on a daily basis (Lk. 9:23), then whatever it is he is doing, and no matter how good it may seem in its own right, he will be functioning in the flesh. The end result will be destruction.

WHAT IT MEANS TO *"WALK AFTER THE SPIRIT"*

Let us see what walking after the Spirit isn't!

"Walking after the Spirit," of course, refers to the Holy Spirit and does not refer to doing Spiritual things. While these Spiritual things may be good and very beneficial in their own way, that's not what Paul is talking about.

Before a small group of Believers in a prayer meeting a short time ago, I asked them this very question, *"What does it mean to walk after the Spirit?"*

One said, *"It means being faithful to Church."* Another said, *"It means giving money to the Work of God."* Another said, *"It refers to witnessing to people about the Lord."* Another said, *"It refers to not doing bad things."*

In fact, such a list is almost endless.

None of that, as valuable as it may be in its own right and way, is what Paul was talking about when he spoke of *"walking after the Spirit."*

"Walking after the Spirit" refers to the Believer placing his or her Faith exclusively in Christ and what Christ has done for us at the Cross. The Cross of Christ is what has given the Holy Spirit the legal Means to do all that He does within our lives.

Before the Cross, the Holy Spirit was greatly limited as to what He could do with Believers. It was because the blood of bulls and goats were woefully insufficient to take away sins. While it served as a stopgap measure, so to speak, until Christ would come, it was very limited in its accomplishments. Animal sacrifices served the purpose, but they could by no means do what Jesus did for us at Calvary's Cross.

With the Cross as a historical fact, meaning that it is an accomplished work, which also means that it will never have to be done again, we can now rejoice in its benefits. So, when we speak of the Cross, it must be clearly understood that we are not speaking of a wooden beam. We are speaking of what Jesus did there, the Victory He won there, the price He paid there, and the Sacrifice of Himself. It is that of which we speak.

"THE LAW OF THE SPIRIT OF LIFE IN CHRIST JESUS"

The manner in which the Holy Spirit works is so ironclad that the Holy Spirit Himself referred to it as a *"Law."* This means that this Law will not be broken by the Holy Spirit or abrogated. He said:

"**For the Law** *(that which we are about to give is a Law* *of God, devised by the Godhead in eternity past [I Pet. 1:18-20]; this Law, in fact, is 'God's Prescribed Order of Victory')* **of the Spirit** *(Holy Spirit, i.e., 'the way the Spirit works')* **of Life** *(all life comes from Christ, but through the Holy Spirit [Jn. 16:13-14])* **in Christ Jesus** *(any time Paul uses this term or one of its derivatives, he is, without fail, referring to what Christ did at the Cross, which makes this 'life' possible)* **has made me free** *(given me total Victory)* **from the Law of Sin and Death.** *(These are the two most powerful Laws in the Universe; the 'Law of the Spirit of Life in Christ Jesus' alone is stronger than the 'Law of Sin and Death'; this means that if the Believer attempts to live for God by any manner other than Faith in Christ and the Cross, he is doomed to failure)*" **(Rom. 8:2).**

WHAT THE HOLY SPIRIT ALONE CAN DO

The Apostle now tells us why we cannot serve God, thereby bringing about Victory, by the means of the flesh. He said:

"**And if Christ** *be* **in you** *(He is in you through the Power and Person of the Spirit [Gal. 2:20])*, **the body** *is* **dead because of sin** *(means that the physical body has been rendered helpless because of the Fall; consequently, the Believer trying to overcome by willpower presents a fruitless task)*; **but the Spirit** *is* **life because of Righteousness** *(only the Holy Spirit can make us what we ought to be, which means we cannot do it ourselves; once again, He performs all that He does within the confines of the Finished Work of Christ).*"

TO QUICKEN OUR MORTAL BODIES

"**But if the Spirit** *(Holy Spirit)* **of Him** *(from God)* **Who raised up Jesus from the dead dwell in you** *(and He definitely does)*, **He Who raised up Christ from the dead** shall also quicken your mortal bodies *(give us power in our mortal bodies that we might live a victorious life)* by His Spirit Who dwells in you *(we have the same Power in us, through the Spirit, that raised Christ from the dead, and is available to us only on the premise of the Cross and our Faith in that Sacrifice)*" (Rom. 8:10-11).

THE POWER OF "WALKING AFTER THE SPIRIT"

Let us say it again. *"Walking after the Spirit"* refers to the Believer placing his or her Faith exclusively in Christ and the Cross, and maintaining it exclusively in Christ and the Cross. That's why Paul said:

"For Christ sent me not to baptize *(presents to us a Cardinal Truth)*, but to preach the Gospel *(the manner in which one may be Saved from sin)*: not with wisdom of words *(intellectualism is not the Gospel)*, lest the Cross of Christ should be made of none effect. *(This tells us in no uncertain terms that the Cross of Christ must always be the emphasis of the Message)*" (I Cor. 1:17).

"THE POWER OF GOD"

The Apostle then said:

"For the preaching *(Message)* of the Cross is to them who perish foolishness *(Spiritual things cannot be discerned by unredeemed people, but that doesn't matter; the Cross must be preached just the same, even as we shall see)*; but unto us which are Saved it is the Power of God. *(The Cross is the Power of God simply because it was there that the total sin debt was paid, giving the Holy Spirit, in Whom the Power resides, latitude to work mightily within our lives)*" (I Cor. 1:18).

"CHRIST CRUCIFIED"

"But we preach Christ Crucified *(this is the Foundation of the Word of God and, thereby, of Salvation)*, unto the Jews a stumblingblock *(the Cross was the stumblingblock)*, and unto the Greeks foolishness *(both found it difficult to accept as God a dead Man hanging on a Cross, for such Christ was to them)*" **(I Cor. 1:23).**

The Bible student must understand that Paul is saying here that irrespective of the fact that the Cross of Christ was a stumblingblock to the Jews and foolishness to the Gentiles, for that's what the word *"Greeks"* actually means here, still, the Cross must be preached.

WHY MUST THE CROSS BE PREACHED?

The only thing standing between mankind and eternal Hell is the Cross of Christ.

The only thing standing between the Church and total apostasy is, as well, the Cross of Christ. Unfortunately, the temptation then, as well as now, was to trim one's sails, in other words, to compromise the Message. If the Message of the Cross is compromised, let all understand, there is nothing else to take its place. The only way that man can be Saved is by and through what Jesus Christ did at the Cross, which makes it all possible. The only way, as well, that the Christian can live a Victorious Life is by one's Faith being placed exclusively in Christ and the Cross. So, if the Cross is destroyed, then Salvation and Sanctification are made impossible.

The record is clear. If we *"walk after the flesh,"* spiritual wreckage will ultimately be the result. Conversely, if we *"walk after the Spirit,"* Victory will be ours, and in every respect. Please note carefully the following:

FOCUS: The Lord Jesus Christ (Jn. 1:1-2; 14:6; Col. 2:10).

OBJECT OF FAITH: The Cross of Christ (Rom. 6:3-5;

I Cor. 1:17-18, 21, 23; 2:2; Col. 2:14-15).

POWER SOURCE: The Holy Spirit (Rom. 8:1-2, 10-11).

RESULTS: Victory (Rom. 6:14).

Now let's use the same little formula but change the way that it is being addressed, which is the case as it regards most of the modern church.

Focus: Works

Object of faith: One's performance

Power source: Self

Results: Defeat.

"Jesus, I my Cross have taken,
"All to leave and follow Thee,
"Destitute, despised, forsaken,
"You, from hence, my all shall be."

"Perish every fond ambition;
"All I've sought, or hoped, or known;
"Yet how rich is my condition!
"God and Heaven are still my own."

"Let the world despise and leave me,
"They have left my Saviour, too;
"Human hearts and looks deceive me;
"You are not, like them, untrue;"

"And while You shall smile upon me,
"God of Wisdom, Love, and Might,
"Foes may hate, and friends forsake me;
"Show Your Face, and all is bright."

"Man may trouble and distress me;
"'Twill but drive me to Your Breast;
"Life with trials hard may press me;
"Heaven will bring me sweeter rest."

"Oh, 'tis not in grief to harm me,

"While Your Love is left to me!
"Oh, 'twere not enjoy to charm me,
"Were that joy unmixed with Thee!"

"So, then know your full Salvation;
"Rise o'er sin, and fear, and care,
"Joy to find in every station,
"Something still to do or bear."

"Think what Spirit dwells within thee;
"Think what Father's Smiles are thine;
"Think that Jesus died to win thee:
"Child of Heaven, can you repine?"

"Haste thee on from Grace to Glory,
"Armed by Faith, and winged by prayer;
"Heaven's eternal Day's before Thee;
"God's Own Hand shall guide you there."

"Soon shall close your Earthly mission,
"Soon shall pass your pilgrim days,
"Hope shall change to glad fruition,
"Faith to sight, and prayer to praise."

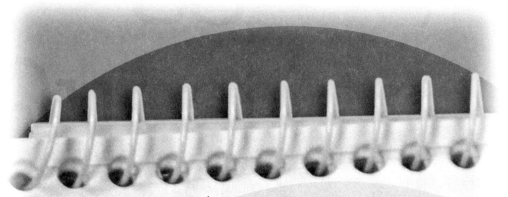

CHAPTER FOURTEEN

Will The Holy Spirit Leave This Earth At The Rapture Of The Church, As Taught By Some?

QUESTION:

WILL THE HOLY SPIRIT LEAVE THIS EARTH AT THE RAPTURE OF THE CHURCH, AS TAUGHT BY SOME?

ANSWER:

No. The Holy Spirit will not be taken from this Earth at the time of the Rapture of the Church, i.e., *"the Resurrection,"* as taught by some!

When I was a kid coming up in Church, even though we had some excellent Preachers come our way, at times I would hear some preachers talking about the Holy Spirit being taken from the Earth when the Rapture of the Church takes place. They would then go on to add that at that time, while people could be Saved, and they were speaking of the Great Tribulation Period, still, they would have to do so, they said, without the convicting Power of the Holy Spirit.

None of that is correct!

In the first place, no one can be Saved unless he is drawn by the Holy Spirit and, as well, experience Regeneration by the Holy Spirit (Jn. 6:44; 3:1-8). Without going into detail, Jesus addressed this when He spoke to Nicodemus about being Born-Again. He actually said that everyone who is Saved is *"born of the Spirit"* (Jn. 3:8).

We know from the Word of God that millions of people in the Great Tribulation, which will be seven years in length, will come to Christ, meaning they will be Saved. Concerning this, the Scripture says:

TRIBULATION SAINTS

"**After this I beheld, and, lo, a great multitude** *(pertains to martyrs who gave their lives for the Lord Jesus Christ in the Great Tribulation)*, **which no man could number** *(represents the many, possibly millions, who will* *be Saved in the Great Tribulation)*, **of all nations, and kindreds, and people, and tongues, stood before the Throne, and before the Lamb** *(by use of the word 'Lamb,' we know and realize that their sin-stained garments have been washed in the Blood of the Lamb)*, **clothed with white robes, and palms in their hands** *(could be paraphrased, 'dressed in richest wedding garments of purest, dazzling white'; these are God's Blood-bought; the palms represent joy [Neh. 8:17])*."

WORSHIP OF THE LORD

"**And cried with a loud voice** *(proclaims great joy)*, **saying, Salvation to our God which sits upon the Throne, and unto the Lamb.** *(Once again, we are told here how God has brought about Salvation. It is through what Jesus did at the Cross, and through that means alone.)*
"**And all the Angels stood round about the Throne, and** *about* **the Elders and the four Beasts, and fell before the Throne on their faces, and worshipped God** *(this tremendous volume of worship and praise has to do with what Jesus did at the Cross, in His Atoning for all sin by the giving of Himself in Sacrifice)*,
"**Saying, Amen** *(is the proclamation that God has provided Salvation to humanity through the Work of the Lamb)*: **Blessing, and Glory, and Wisdom, and Thanksgiving, and Honour, and Power, and Might,** *be* **unto our God forever and ever. Amen.** *(As the praises to God the Father are sevenfold, they are also sevenfold to God the Son [Rev. 5:12]. This shows that both God and the Lamb are regarded in Heaven as entitled to equal praise.)*"

WHO ARE THESE . . .?

"**And one of the Elders answered, saying unto me** *(proclaims one of the twenty-four addressing questions* *that are in John's mind, but have not been asked)*, **What are these which are arrayed in white robes?** *(This would be better translated 'Who are these?')* **and whence came they?** *(Where do they come from?)*

"**And I said unto him, Sir, you know** *(presents reverent regard, but definitely not worship)*. **And he said to me, These are they which came out of great tribulation** *(refers to a specific group)*, **and have washed their robes, and made them white in the Blood of the Lamb.** *(They were Saved by trusting Christ and what He did at the Cross. In the Book of Revelation, the emphasis placed on the Cross is overwhelming.)*"

"THE THRONE OF GOD"

"**Therefore are they before the Throne of God, and serve Him day and night in His Temple** *(all of this particular group came out of the Great Tribulation)*: **and He Who sits on the Throne shall dwell among them.** *(The One Who sits on the Throne will cast His protecting Tabernacle over all the Saints of God, which, in effect, is His Presence.)*"

THE LAMB OF GOD

"**They shall hunger no more, neither thirst anymore; neither shall the sun light on them, nor any heat** *(proclaims a perfect environment)*.

"**For the Lamb which is in the midst of the Throne shall feed them** *(not only did the Lamb save them, but He as well 'shall feed them'; not only does our Salvation come by and through what Jesus did at the Cross, but we 'live' by what Jesus did for us at the Cross as well)*, **and shall lead them unto living fountains of waters** *(symbolic of the Holy Spirit [Jn. 7:37-39])*: **and God shall wipe away all tears from their eyes.** *(All things causing sorrow will be forever gone)*" **(Rev. 7:9-17).**

THE DAY OF PENTECOST

Furthermore, when Peter preached his great message on the Day of Pentecost, he said:

"But this is that which was spoken by the Prophet Joel *(please notice that Peter did not say, 'this fulfills that spoken by the Prophet Joel,' but rather, 'this is that . . .' meaning that it will continue)*;

"And it shall come to pass in the last days, saith God *(proclaims these 'last days' as beginning on the Day of Pentecost, and continuing through the coming Great Tribulation)*, I will pour out of My Spirit upon all flesh *(speaks of all people everywhere and, therefore, not limited to some particular geographical location; as well, it is not limited respecting race, color, or creed)*: and your sons and your daughters shall prophesy *(includes both genders)*, and your young men shall see Visions, and your old men shall dream Dreams *(all given by the Holy Spirit; the Hebrew language insinuates, 'both your young men and old men shall see Visions, and both your old men and young men shall dream Dreams'; it applies to both genders as well)*."

"IN THOSE DAYS OF MY SPIRIT"

"And on My servants and on My handmaidens I will pour out in those days of My Spirit *(is meant purposely to address two classes of people who had been given very little status in the past, slaves and women)*; and they shall prophesy *(pertains to one of the 'Gifts of the Spirit' [I Cor. 12:8-10])*:

"And I will show wonders in Heaven above, and signs in the earth beneath; blood, and fire, and vapour of smoke *(pertains to the fact that these 'days of My Spirit' will cover the entirety of the Church Age, even into the coming Great*

Tribulation; that time limit has now been nearly two thousand years):

"**The sun shall be turned into darkness, and the moon into blood** *(not meant to be literal, but rather, that the moon will look blood red because of atmospheric conditions)*, **before that great and notable Day of the Lord come** *(the Second Coming)*:

"**And it shall come to pass, *that* whosoever shall call on the Name of the Lord shall be Saved** *(Joel 2:30-32; presents one of the most glorious statements ever made; it includes both Jews and Gentiles equally)*" **(Acts 2:16-21).**

These Passages plainly tell us that many will be Saved in the coming Great Tribulation and, as well, that this time is included in *"those days of My Spirit,"* meaning the way the Holy Spirit operates in this Dispensation of Grace, all made possible by the Cross.

Again we say, *"No,"* the Holy Spirit will not be taken out of the world during the coming Great Tribulation.

A MISUNDERSTANDING OF THE TEXT

The Apostle Paul in dealing with the Rapture of the Church and the advent of the Antichrist made this statement:

"**And now you know what withholds** *(speaks of the Church)* **that he might be revealed in his time.** *(This speaks of the Antichrist who will be revealed or made known after the Rapture of the Church.)*

"**For the mystery of iniquity does already work** *(concerns false teaching by false teachers)*: **only he** *(the Church)* **who now lets** *(who now hinders evil)* ***will let*** *(will continue to hinder)*, **until he** *(the Church)* **be taken out of the way.** *(The pronoun 'he' confuses some people. In Verses 4 and 6, the pronoun 'he' refers to the Antichrist, while in Verse 7, 'he' refers to the Church.)*

"**And then** *(after the Rapture of the Church)* **shall that**

Wicked *(the Antichrist)* **be revealed** *(proving conclusively that the Rapture takes place before the Great Tribulation [Mat. 24:21]),* **whom the Lord shall consume with the Spirit of His Mouth** *(should have been translated, 'the Breath of His Mouth' [Isa. 11:4]),* **and shall destroy with the brightness of His Coming** *(both phrases refer to the Second Coming)*" **(II Thess. 2:6-8).**

Some confuse the pronoun *"he,"* as given in Verse 7, as referring to the Holy Spirit. It doesn't! It refers, as stated in the notes, to the Church, which will be taken out of this world at the Rapture.

It is the truly Blood-bought, Spirit-filled Believers who hinder evil in this world. When all Blood-bought Believers are taken out at the Rapture, one can well imagine the evil that will then overtake the world, making possible the advent of the Antichrist.

THE CHURCH REFERRED TO AS A MAN

In a sense, Paul, as guided by the Holy Spirit, referred to the Church as a *"man."* He said:

"**Having abolished in His Flesh** *(speaking of His Death on the Cross, by which He redeemed humanity, which also means He didn't die spiritually, as some claim)* **the enmity** *(the hatred between God and man, caused by sin),* **even the Law of Commandments** *contained* **in Ordinances** *(pertains to the Law of Moses, and more particularly the Ten Commandments)*; **for to make in Himself of twain** *(of Jews and Gentiles)* **one new man,** *so* **making peace** *(which again was accomplished by the Cross)*;

"**And that He** *(Christ)* **might reconcile both** *(Jews and Gentiles)* **unto God in one body** *(the Church)* **by the Cross** *(it is by the Atonement only that men ever become reconciled to God),* **having slain the enmity thereby** *(removed the* *barrier between God and sinful man)*" **(Eph. 2:15-16).**

The Holy Spirit, Who is God, is everywhere. He cannot be confined to one particular place. Even though He is in my heart and my life with my physical body actually being a Temple of the Holy Spirit (I Cor. 3:16), still, He is in the hearts and lives of every single Believer on the face of this Earth. He once dwelt between the Mercy Seat and the Cherubim in the Temple, but now, due to the Cross, which lifted the terrible sin debt, at least for all who will believe, He can now make our physical bodies His Abode, which He does at conversion.

No, the Holy Spirit will not be taken out of this world in the coming Great Tribulation, but will remain here, moving on hearts and lives that they come to Christ. In fact, the Scripture says that a great part of the Work of the Holy Spirit is that He ever gives the great invitation for men to come to Christ. The Scripture says:

"And the Spirit and the Bride say, Come. *(This presents the cry of the Holy Spirit to a hurting, lost, and dying world. What the Holy Spirit says should also be said by all Believers.)* And let him who hears say, Come. *(It means if one can 'hear,' then one can 'come.')* And let him who is athirst come *(speaks of Spiritual Thirst, the cry for God in the soul of man).* And whosoever will, let him take the Water of Life freely *(opens the door to every single individual in the world; Jesus died for all and, therefore, all can be Saved, if they will only come)*" **(Rev. 22:17).**

CHAPTER FIFTEEN

Why In All Of My Writings Do I Refer To The Third Person Of The Godhead As The Holy Spirit Instead Of The Holy Ghost?

QUESTION:

WHY IN ALL OF MY WRITINGS DO I REFER TO THE THIRD PERSON OF THE GODHEAD AS THE HOLY SPIRIT INSTEAD OF THE HOLY GHOST?

ANSWER:

I refer to the Third Person of the Godhead as the Holy Spirit instead of the Holy Ghost because He is not a ghost, but rather, the Spirit.

THE OLD TESTAMENT

Not one time in the Old Testament, and rightfully so, did the King James translators use the word *"ghost,"* as it refers to the Holy Spirit. They always used the word *"Spirit"* (Gen. 1:2; 6:3; Ex. 31:3; 35:31; Judg. 3:10; I Sam. 19:23; II Chron. 15:1, etc.).

The Hebrew word for Spirit is *"Ruwach,"* and means several things, but, as it refers to the Holy Spirit, could probably be described more than all as meaning, *"Life, but only of a rational Being."*

IN THE NEW TESTAMENT

The word *"Spirit"* in the Greek is *"Pneuma,"* and means basically the same as it does in Hebrew, *"Life, but of a rational Being, a vital principal,"* at least as it refers to the Holy Spirit.

WHY DID THE KING JAMES TRANSLATORS IN THE NEW TESTAMENT AT TIMES USE THE WORD *"GHOST,"* INSTEAD OF *"SPIRIT,"* WHEN REFERRING TO THE HOLY SPIRIT?

When the King James translators mentioned the Holy Spirit without the prefix *"Holy,"* they always referred to Him as *"the Spirit."* It was only when they used the prefix *"Holy"* that they used the word *"Ghost."*

The word *"Ghost"* in the sixteen hundreds had a different meaning then than now. Now it refers to a bodily apparition, which does not apply to the Holy Spirit at all. And yet, when Mark spoke of Jesus dying on the Cross, saying, *"He so cried out, and gave up the ghost"* (Mk. 15:39), he uses an entirely different Greek word. The word is *"Ekpneo,"* and means *"to expire, to die."*

We must remember that the King James translation is just that, a translation. I personally think it's the best translation in the world, and it's the translation I always use; however, we must understand that there are some words in the King James which have changed meaning over the years. The word *"ghost"* is one of those words.

The correct name of the Third Person of the Trinity is *"The Holy Spirit."* He is a Person, labeled as such by none other than the Lord Jesus Christ. Our Lord used personal pronouns when speaking of Him, which means He isn't a ghost, but rather, *"the Spirit"* (Jn. 14:16-17).

Incidentally, when the Prophets of the Old Testament spoke, and the Apostles of the New Testament, they did not use Elizabethan English. In other words, they didn't use words like *"Thee,"* or *"Thy,"* or *"Thou,"* or *"Hast,"* etc.

Those words were used in England during the time of the King James translation. They aren't used anymore. In THE EXPOSITOR'S STUDY BIBLE, in some cases, I elected to change those particular words to words which now mean the same identical thing, but are words which we use presently. Some people have the erroneous idea that the King James translation is inspired. It isn't. In fact, no translation is inspired. Only the original Manuscripts were inspired, as should be obvious.

While I personally think the King James translators, overall, did an excellent job, still, we must understand that it is a translation, and that words between then and now at times change. Let me give you another example.

CONVERSATION

Peter said, *"Forasmuch as you know that you were not redeemed with corruptible things, as silver and gold, from your vain conversation received by tradition from your fathers"* (I Pet. 1:18).

The Greek word translated *"conversation,"* in England some five hundred years ago, referred to *"lifestyle."* Now it means converse or talk between two or more parties. So, when we read it in the King James Version, according to our understanding of the word *"conversation"* at present, we are getting a false understanding of this particular Verse. Peter is not speaking of conversation as we think of such, but rather, the manner of one's behavior, or one's lifestyle. So, for the Verse to be translated correctly, it would have to read, *"from your vain lifestyle received by tradition from your fathers."*

Once again, I state that in my opinion the King James translation is the finest in the world, and despite the fact that it has a few words that are now outdated. Holy Ghost is one of them. *"Holy Spirit"* is the correct term and the way it should be translated.

"Shepherd Divine, our wants relieve,
"In this our evil day;
"To all Your tempted Followers give,
"The power to watch and pray."

"Long as our fiery trials last,
"Long as the Cross we bear,
"Oh let our souls on You be cast,
"In never-ceasing prayer!"

"The Spirit of interceding Grace,
"Give us in Faith to claim;
"To wrestle till we see Your Face,
"And know Your hidden Name."

"Till You Your perfect Love impart;

"Till You Yourself bestow;
"Be this the cry of every heart,
"I will not let You go."

"I will not let You go, unless,
"You tell Your Name to me;
"With all Your great Salvation bless,
"And make me all like Thee."

"Then let me on the mountaintop,
"Behold Your open Face;
"Where Faith in sight is swallowed up,
"And prayer in endless praise."

Bibliography

INTRODUCTION
D.R. McConnell, *A Different Gospel*, Hendrickson Publishers, Massachusetts, 1995, pgs. 142-143.

CHAPTER 4
W.E. Vine, *Vine's Expository Dictionary of New Testament Words, Unabridged Edition*, McDonald Publishing Co., McLean, Virginia, pg. 949.

NOTES